Creative
CORRECTION

Extraordinary Ideas for Everyday Discipline

Lisa Whelchel

Tyndale House Publishers, Inc.
Wheaton, Illinois

The author wishes to thank the many parents who have contributed creative correction ideas to this book, both in the original edition and in this revised version. Though these contributors have become too numerous to mention by name, their help is deeply appreciated and gratefully acknowledged.

Editors: Betsy Holt and Larry Weeden
Cover design and interior illustrations: Lovgren Advertising and John Duckworth

*This book is lovingly dedicated to my grandmother
Velma "Nanny" French.*

*"But from everlasting to everlasting
the LORD's love is with those who fear him,
and his righteousness with their children's children—
with those who keep his covenant
and remember to obey his precepts" (Psalm 103:17–18).*

All that is good in our family has been passed down through you.

Contents

$\mathcal{A}$cknowledgments

Steve—God knew me better than I knew myself when He chose you for me. You are everything I wanted, more than I will ever need, and exactly what I desire.

Tucker, Haven, and Clancy—Nothing I have ever done or will do in this lifetime compares with the privilege of being your mommy. Thank you for the joy of watching you grow " . . . in wisdom and stature, and in favor with God and men" (Luke 2:52).

My mother—This is my opportunity to arise and call you blessed (Proverbs 31:28). Thank you for keeping, teaching, and adoring my kids while I wrote this book. I want to be a grandmother just like you when I grow up.

Roy—Thank you for allowing my mom to be a full-time grandmother. I am grateful for your sacrificial love as a grandfather and a stepfather.

My father—You worked hard to provide me with every opportunity for my dreams to come true. Thank you for fond childhood memories.

Pastor Jack Hayford—I am teaching my children what you taught me. Thank you.

Focus on the Family—Thank you for allowing me to partner with you in your ministry and for trusting me with your constituents.

Mark Maddox—You have been a caring touch-point in this delicate balance of business and ministry.

Larry Weeden—Thank you for teaching me to write more from the left side of my brain.

Betsy Holt—I may have baked the cake, but you are responsible for the icing—and that's my favorite part. Thank you.

Doug Knox and all the staff at Tyndale House—It feels like family already.

Gladys Marie Brown—Thank you for coming to my rescue.

Susan Munao—Thank you for your godly example of a Christian businesswoman and for the phone calls that made this all happen.

Bill Jensen—Thank you for believing in me and my big ideas from the beginning.

Ron Smith and Smith Music and Management—It's easy to dream big when you have such great people supporting you.

Morris Proctor and Scott Lindsey—Thank you for providing me with the Logos Library Bible Software System. Otherwise, I would *still* be working on this book.

Cyber prayer partners and faithful friends—Robin Aveni, Curt and Alice Cauble, Tim and Cindy Cauble, Mick and Janice Clark, Shawn Craig, Janet Decker, Deb Goldstone, Shirley Grose (for the "Pinetop" experience), Mari Hanes, Valerie Johnson, Sherilyn Jones, Fred and Anastatia Jove, Bill and Jeanie Lero (for the dinners), Debby Lillenberg, Tom and Denise McDonald, Myrene Morris (for the "Gazebo" times), Terri Mullen, Kevin Odean (for *the* letter), Andrea Rodriguez, Debby Riekeberg, Connie Scheffler (you should start a catering business), Sallie Schnee, Lynn Vakay, and Gloria Wilson. Thank you.

Foreword

It has been my privilege for more than fifteen years to call Lisa Whelchel a close friend, prayer partner, and sister in the Lord. During that time I have seen her develop from a young, successful actress in Hollywood into the wonderful wife, mother, and woman of God she is today. In our countless prayer times together throughout the early years, she regularly asked God to send her the husband He had for her. She had been painfully lonely for the kind of companionship that comes only with a God-ordained, committed marriage.

When Lisa met Steve and they were married, all of us in their circle of friends called it "the Royal Wedding." The beautiful princess and the handsome prince had finally found one another, and we were tremendously relieved.

Within several years, the tiny blessings came one after the other, and Lisa soon had her hands full with three children under three years old. She quickly made the decision not to return to her work on television so that she could pour herself into being the best mother and wife possible. But Lisa was wise enough to know that she couldn't do it well without completely relying on God for guidance. I can testify that she has done just that, and in the process gathered great riches to impart to us all.

Lisa has creative ideas for motivating children to do right, help out, work hard, think clearly, and learn. And she delivers them with clever stories and illustrations that make everything, *including the point,* clear and memorable. I've always known Lisa to be humorous, real, intelligent, caring, compassionate, and deeply devoted to God and family. Each attribute comes forth in this book. The way Lisa and Steve are raising their children works. I know because it is the way I raised mine—with love, discipline, and solid teaching that has eternal significance and lasting power in a child's life.

Lisa once told me that she wanted to be like me when she grew up. I'm so glad she didn't stop there. She has gone beyond me and many other parents with her unique, thoughtful, inspired, ingenious, and often funny methods of child rearing. She gives such innovative, practical suggestions that it almost makes me want to raise my children all over again so I can use some of her ideas. *(Almost!)* I wish I'd had this book twenty years ago when my children were young. I doubt if my three "twenty-somethings" would fall for the "Sad Marble, Happy Marble" trick today. So I guess *I* will have to wait until the grandchildren arrive. However *you,* dear reader, can benefit from it right now.

Stormie Omartian

Disclaimer

Before you begin reading this book, let's make a pact: If we ever run into each other's children on the streets—even if that means literally "on the streets"—let's not judge each other as bad parents. Let's give one another the benefit of the doubt. After all, we're doing the best we can. You've probably seen the bumper sticker "Christians aren't perfect, just forgiven." Well, in light of this parenting pact, I propose a new one: "My children aren't perfect, but neither are yours."

I remember one Sunday after church, my husband, Steve, and I were talking with the teachers from our parenting class. Our then four-year-old son, Tucker, came rushing out of Sunday school, having wriggled free from his grandfather's hand, and ran through the sanctuary, nearly knocking me over. All the while, he was talking loudly, hoping to get the adults to be quiet and listen to him. I shot him the "You're going to get it when you get home" look, but it was to no avail. He began entertaining himself by climbing onto the balcony rails, nearly falling into the lower sanctuary in the process. In less than two minutes, Steve and I had failed three of our parenting courses: "Teaching Your Children Church Etiquette," "No Interrupting," and "Learning Health and Safety."

Embarrassed to even look our parenting teachers in the face, I scrambled for excuses. "Oh, it's time for his nap," I said quickly. "He's probably coming down with something." I should have just been honest and said, "He's not really our son."

Actually, that wouldn't be such a stretch: Tucker, like all of us, is a son of Adam, the first child on earth—so he comes by his sin naturally. In fact, the roots of misbehavior can be traced all the way back to Adam. Sin has less to do with our parenting ability and more to do with the state of our kids' hearts. After all, I would venture to guess that God was a good Father—yet both Adam and his wife, Eve, disobeyed Him. So don't feel guilty if your children aren't perfect. This is not a reflection on you and your parenting skills (or lack thereof!).

My purpose in writing *Creative Correction* is to give you hope, not a guilt complex. I've read a lot of self-help parenting books, and ironically, they often make me feel worse about myself as a parent. I'll pick one up, hoping to find some help—only to finish the book convinced that I'm a terrible mom because I haven't been doing all the things the author suggested. There are a lot of those books out there. Here are just a few I've run across:

- Parenting books that promise to take my children from Billy the Kid to Billy Graham in 10 easy steps.
- Parenting books that declare that their way is the only way, and if I don't follow this way, I'm doing it the wrong way.
- Parenting books that promise that if I do everything right during my children's formative years, they will blossom as adults.
- Parenting books that inform me that I've already passed the formative years and it's too late to make a difference.

- Parenting books that tell me to talk more, listen more, play more, read more, bake more, Rushmore, furthermore.
- Parenting books that tell me to work less, buy less, worry less, nag less, eat less, doubtless, blameless.
- And my personal favorite: parenting books that imply that there is one magic formula, and if I can ever find it and follow it perfectly, my children will turn out okay.

If you bought *Creative Correction* thinking you had finally found *the* book, please close it immediately and return it for a full refund. I'm not about to make false promises. If, on the other hand, you've realized that what works for one child may not necessarily work for another, and that some creativity is in order, *Creative Correction* is the book for you.

You love your children, and I love mine. So let's give each other room to try new things, learn from our failures, and find what works best for each of our kids.

By the way, if you ever find yourself at a red light behind a white minivan with a bumper sticker that reads, "My children aren't perfect, but neither am I," please honk. I'd love to meet you.

Chapter 1

The Facts of My Life

I received an e-mail from the editor of a magazine for which I had recently been interviewed. The note read: "Lisa, I'm reviewing the article and looking at everything you do, and I wonder at one quote. You say, 'Moms must be careful not to attempt to do it all; you have to be willing to let a few things slide.' May I ask, what on earth do you let slide?"

I e-mailed the following response:

> Dear Susan,
>
> There are lots of things that slide. I'm embarrassed at the things that get pushed to the bottom of the priority list. Let me name a few:
>
> @ Healthy meals—tonight the kids had cereal for dinner.
>
> @ The last time I did any "spring cleaning" was the spring of aught 5.
>
> @ I desperately need to exercise, but I figure I log in at least 20 minutes a day on the "Stairmaster," hauling laundry up to and down from the bedrooms.

@ I promised my daughter a year ago that I would teach her to sew.

@ I've made the same New Year's resolution three years in a row—to have each of our neighbors over for dinner.

@ My latest obsession is scrapbooking, but I'm still cropping pictures of my kids from when they were in diapers.

@ I come from a long line of readers and yet even my magazines stack up by the bed, untouched (though they do make an attractive nightstand).

@ Thankfully, I'm not much of a shopper, so I don't lose time there; but then again, my wardrobe reflects that.

@ Wouldn't it be nice if I answered all those wonderful letters people send me?

@ My husband would be in heaven if I did my nails every week, but at this point he's going to have to wait until Jesus comes.

@ When I suggest, "Let's make some homemade cookies," we don't head for the mixer, we reach for the freezer and the sharpest "slice and bake" knife that's not in the dishwasher.

@ I really mean to write to my senators.

@ At the onset of Y2K, I embarked on a "Read through the Bible in a Decade" program. My goal is to reach the book of Habakkuk before my last child enters high school.

AFTER THE FACTS

Sound like anyone at your house? A lot has changed since my days playing "Blair" on *The Facts of Life*. Shortly after the birth of my third baby, an actress friend remarked to me, "After having worked for so many years, it must be nice to be able to relax and not work for a while." I had three children in diapers at the time, and I was tempted to slap her with a wet wipe. Yeah, I'm leading a really "Pamper-ed" lifestyle these days.

Of course, I wouldn't trade it for all the money in Hollywood. I love my life! I will always be grateful for the fun I had while I was on television, but it can't compare with the joy I'm experiencing now.

I don't remember ever making a conscious decision to quit show business and become a stay-at-home mom. In fact, I'd always assumed I would continue working even after I had children. But for some reason, I never got another job I auditioned for. Go figure! It might have had something to do with the fact that I was married during the last season of the show; then, for the first five years of my marriage, I was either pregnant, nursing, or trying to lose baby fat. By the time I was back in fighting shape, I had three adorable preschoolers below the belt—and that is where it would hit me if I had to leave them every day.

I am fortunate to be married to a wonderful man: Steve. He agreed to let me stay home while he continued his job as an associate pastor and director of information technologies at our church. Poor guy! He thought he was marrying a rich, young starlet. We were barely home from the honeymoon when he began saying good-bye each morning to an unemployed mommy with a baby in her arms, spit-up on her shoulders, an extra 10 pounds on her hips, and two tiny toddlers clinging to her legs. (By the way, honey, did I mention that I'm not a natural blonde?)

I don't think I will ever take for granted the privilege of being my children's mother and the opportunity to stay home with them. I consider it a luxury because I understand it is an option many families aren't able to afford. I've also walked with the Lord long enough to have learned that what is right for one family may not be what's best for another. Therefore, you won't find me making any judgments about working mothers. Who knows—I may be called back to work someday, too.

It sure would be hard to obey the Lord if He asked that of me, though. I love to watch my kids each day become more and more their own persons. I've often been told, "Enjoy them while they're young, because they grow up before you know it." I personally have not found that to be the case. It feels as if they've been small forever. But I'm enjoying every minute of their childhood.

HAVE YOU MET MY CHILDREN?

Let me introduce you to my little darlings. Steve has come up with a great way to describe our children: in color groups. Tucker, who is nine years old at the time of this writing, is our firstborn. He is your basic eight-pack of primary colors. Tucker is bold and original. You need fire? He's brimming with red. Could use a little sunshine? He exudes joyful yellow. You want green? He's full of life. I'm sorry, but he's rarely blue. Can I offer you some orange? Tucker is all the colors you really need in one place. No need for any big, fancy box with a built-in sharpener.

Haven, our eight-year-old daughter, is the middle child. She represents the jewel tones: the beautiful, rich, intricate shades. She is as gorgeous as a scarlet rose, as deep as the forest green, and as complicated as the midnight-blue sky. And what a gem she is!

Clancy, our seven-year-old daughter, is the baby. We first considered pastels to describe her, because she's been so calm from the moment she was born. Our only hesitation was that lavender and sea-foam green don't do justice to her sparkling personality. Then Steve thought of fluorescents. Perfect! Crayola introduced the colors "neon carrot," "magic mint," and "razzle-dazzle rose" just in time to describe delightful Clancy.

Every year in our family Christmas letter, I include a quote from each of our children. It is usually a snippet of something they've said during the year that reflects their personalities at their current ages. It helps our friends and family stay in touch as the kids grow. Maybe it will create a quick snapshot for you, too.

In our last holiday letter, I shared this story about our son: The kids and I had just finished our morning prayer when Tucker asked, "So, what catalog does God order out of?"

"What are you talking about?" I asked.

With a smile sneaking out one side of his mouth, he quipped, "Well, you just asked God to order Grandmother's day. So I was wondering, will He simply call to the angels and say, 'I want a Tuesday and a Thursday, and send them over to Genny Coleman right away'?"

As you can tell, Tucker is a real jokester.

Last year was an exciting one for Haven. She finally lost her first tooth. She had been wiggling it for about a year. Actually, she started by fiddling with her two top teeth until I informed her that her bottom teeth would come out first. (Of course, Tucker heard me from across the room and, in typical big brother style, yelled, "Ooooh, yuck! Haven has teeth on her bottom?")

Haven put her "bottom" tooth under her pillow with a note to the tooth fairy. I left the money and kept the tooth and letter to put in her memory box. Then I hid them in my brush drawer under Steve's tray. The next morning, Haven borrowed my brush and found the note and tooth.

She raced down the stairs and, with a look of betrayal, said, "So you're the one who left the money!"

I felt awful. Her first tooth and she had already discovered the secret. She'd never have the thrill of believing in the tooth fairy again. "Yes, honey," I answered gently. "Are you disappointed?"

With folded arms, she replied, "Yes, I am. Now, I'm going to leave it under my pillow again, and this time let the tooth fairy get it!"

I already have Clancy's quote for this year's Christmas letter. Last summer, we took a family vacation and drove up the West Coast, because the girls were going to be in a friend's wedding. On the drive back, we spent two days in San Francisco, where we were given the opportunity to stay in a lovely hotel. The chandeliers hanging in the lobby were bigger than our entire living room at home. The kids received backpacks, compliments of the hotel, filled with maps and literature about San Francisco.

As we were packing up to leave, Clancy came running to me in a panic. "Where are all the coupons that were in my backpack?" she cried.

I told her reassuringly, "I took them out to give them to Grandmother in case she wants to bring Uncle Casey back here later this summer."

"But I need them!" she said.

My eyebrows rose. "Why?"

She crooked her little finger and motioned me down to her

face. Then she whispered in my ear, "Because I'm thinking about coming back here on my honeymoon."

I hope these stories help you to formulate a composite of my little ones. You'll have plenty of opportunities to fill in more of the details as you read along. After all, my children are the reason I've written this book in the first place.

Is He ADHD or Am I Crazy?

From the moment of my first child's conception, I started reading parenting books. Well, okay, maybe not right at that particular moment, but soon thereafter. I determined that if there was a right way to raise children, I was going to find it. Steve and I attended our first parenting classes before we began our Lamaze classes. We certainly didn't want to ruin our child for life by neglecting a crucial ingredient in the first few months of infancy. We found out later that we had already blown it for our baby by not reading aloud Plato and playing classical music while he was in utero.

After Tucker was born, I continued to read books on every subject from colic to college. We also attended classes on high-chair manners and hosted water-baby swimming lessons. By the time Haven and Clancy showed up, Steve and I were parenting experts.

Life was rolling merrily along until the arrival of El Niño. (El Niño is an irregular weather phenomenon that brings massive amounts of rainfall and extreme humidity to usually arid areas, such as the American Southwest.) Tucker became even more irritable and hyperactive and often was uncontrollable. He had been somewhat moody in the past, but we had chalked up his erratic behavior to fatigue and crankiness. With the onset of El Niño, however, Tucker started to *wake up* that way.

We assumed we were not being strict enough, so we buckled down more tightly. But our discipline would only send him screaming to his room, kicking toys along the way and slamming the door behind him. Even more confusing, the next day he would wake up and be the enjoyable, incredible, affectionate boy we had grown to know and love. It was like living with Dr. Jekyll and Mr. Hyde. We explored every possible explanation, visiting over a half-dozen specialists. Tucker went through 15 bottles of vitamins, nine months of allergy shots, six homeopathic remedies, five elders who prayed for healing, three weeks of elimination diets, two air-purification filters, and one natural-light box for seasonal affective disorder. The majority of the doctors diagnosed him with ADHD (attention deficit and hyperactivity disorder) and recommended medication.

But there was one glaring inconsistency. He was an absolute angel during the summer months. This had nothing to do with school, either. Early on we had noticed the pattern in his behavior, so we began home-schooling him during the summer and taking a break in the winter, when Tucker's ability to focus was next to nil. This approach had been relatively successful.

It wasn't until the next year, after El Niño had come and gone—leaving our family as if it had been hit by a tornado as opposed to a deluge of showers—that we realized the common thread: weather changes. Apparently, when the wind, rain, heat, or cold sets in, Tucker's allergies go haywire. Unfortunately, they have yet to make a rainy-day pill.

OUR TRAVELS ALONG THE PARENTING HIGHWAY

Until that stormy year, we had been zipping happily down the parenting highway. Our plan was to continue along the interstate—

but then we ran into the roadblock of Tucker's "weather condition." We had to pull off the road and map out an alternate route. We still knew where we wanted to end up: with happy, healthy kids who love God's ways—we just had to find another way to get there.

Maybe you have run into roadblocks, as Steve and I did with our son. We had to come up with quite a few creative ways to get around the hurdles in order to keep moving forward—such as homeschooling Tucker through the summer to work around his allergy problems. Have you found yourself feeling as if you've tried everything with your child and you're still facing the same obstacles? If so, take heart; this is a book *full of ideas* when you have *no idea* what to do!

Perhaps you've found yourself at a crossroad and don't know which way to turn. You know what you want for your child, but you aren't sure how to achieve those goals. Your desire is for someone to stop telling you where you're supposed to be and to start telling you how to get there. It is my prayer that you find some practical direction in this book.

In fact, whether you're facing a fork in the road, a dead end, or are completely lost, don't give up. It might simply be time to forge a new path ahead or pick up the map and discover where you veered off course. If you feel overwhelmed, let me come alongside and remind you of what you already know to be true but, in the confusion of a "superhighway" lifestyle, lost sight of along the way.

Tools to Create a Work of Art

I have attempted to organize this book with busy parents like you and me in mind so that no matter where you find yourself on this parenting journey, there is help within easy reach. Each chapter is divided into two parts: The first section contains stories about me and my family, illustrating common issues that we as parents most often face. I have found that I learn the most about child-rearing by talking with a fellow mom over a cup of tea as we share our struggles, victories, and ideas. It is from this viewpoint that I offer my insights on such subjects as sibling conflict, respect, spanking, failure, reaching the heart, and discipline.

The second section of each chapter, the "Toolbox," is my favorite part. Over the years, I have gathered a variety of creative yet practical ideas from moms all across the country. I have also come up with many tips of my own in an effort to make my role as a parent both effective and fun. Raising three unique children, including one that exhibits ADHD symptoms nine months out of the year, has required a mixture of approaches. Those ideas make up each chapter's toolbox.

As you well know, the parenting adventure is different with each child—and it's vital to recognize and adapt to your children's various temperaments, strengths, and weaknesses. Think of yourself as a sculptor shaping and molding the lives of your young ones. With each child, you may be working with a different medium. You could be endeavoring to form one youngster who appears to be as hard as marble. As an artist, you might use a chisel, hammers, even water, while sculpting your masterpiece. You may have another child who is more pliable, like clay. Even then, as a potter, you might use fire, a knife, and your bare hands.

It doesn't matter what substance you're working with, be it wood, ice, bronze, wax, sand, steel, or foam. Each raw material requires a distinct combination of tools to strike the balance between respecting its uniqueness and steadfastly pursuing the potential beauty within.

In the "Toolbox" section at the end of each chapter, I will present different tools and creative ways to use them as we allow the Lord to work through us, shaping our children in His image (see Colossians 3:10). Let's take a sneak peek into my "supply closet." I have found *storytelling* to be an enjoyable and effective way to reach the hearts of children, while *rewards* keep hope alive. *Scripture* instills a respect for authority, and teaching children an *eternal perspective* will help keep them on track. Finally, *prayer* is the master tool of the trade, for both parents and kids. As you'll see, there's no reason discipline has to be boring!

HOW TO USE THIS BOOK

Hopefully, once you've finished reading *Creative Correction,* you'll have gleaned a few nuggets of wisdom. To keep those ideas accessible, put a book mark in the "Topical Index." That way, whenever you find yourself in a tough parenting situation, you can easily find a solution.

For instance, perhaps you've caught your little one in a lie. Go to the back of the book, find "Lying" in the index, turn to the page(s) listed, and choose the tool you think would be most effective in your particular situation. It may be a story written in the second half of chapter three that illustrates the importance of honesty. The index may also lead you to related scriptures listed at the end of chapter two. If you're searching for creative methods of discipline—a punishment to fit the "crime"—you might turn to chapter five. Or you could flip to chapter four after determining that your child's lying is slowly becoming a habit and should be broken by setting up an incentive program. Finally, if one of my children has had a problem with a given discipline issue, the page number listed in italic will show you how I chose to handle the situation.

Experiment. If one idea doesn't work, try something else and come at it from another direction. But don't dismiss a failed method altogether; it may work on another child or at another stage of childhood. Believe me, your departure from the ordinary ways of correction will keep your kids on their toes, wondering what you'll next pull out of your bag of tricks. The road is long, but it doesn't have to be dull.

I sincerely wish parenting were simple, but it's not. It is my hope, however, that this book will, in some way, make your journey a little easier. But if I can't help in that area, I'll shoot for "more enjoyable" at least—which reminds me of the time I reprimanded Tucker for fooling around during a kindergarten lesson. Exasperated, I told him, "Tucker, the more you goof around, the longer this is going to take."

"And the funner it's going to be!" he responded with a grin.

When it comes to parenting, I agree with Tucker. Goof around a little. It will make the journey "funner!"

Chapter 2

Learning from the Ultimate Parent

It was a toddler rite-of-passage night in our home. After sleeping for her first year in a cradle in the master bedroom walk-in closet, Clancy was graduating to a real crib. Meanwhile, Tucker was parking his car-shaped bed by the curb in exchange for bunk beds, and Haven was relinquishing the baby bed for the bottom bunk.

Haven was nervous about the switch to a big-girl bed. She crawled, wide-eyed, into her new bottom bunk and lay there stiffly, clutching her "geekie" (blanket), sucking on her "bappy" (pacifier), while cuddling her "Barney" (dinosaur). She fixed her gaze on the bottom of the top bunk, as if she were afraid to even look around the room.

Tucker was anxious, too, but he was also excited. Wired and hopping around the room, he couldn't wait to try out his new bed. When it actually came to crawling up to the top bunk, however, he hesitated. Tucker had suddenly "forgotten" how to climb a ladder. After several minutes of coaxing, we finally got him into bed, but the challenge didn't end there. Within 15 minutes, he had bumped his head on the ceiling, trying to stand up, caught his arm in the rail, trying to lean over and talk to Haven; and gotten his foot stuck between the wall and the bed, trying to turn the light switch on with his toe.

None of us was getting much sleep—and after enduring half an hour of Tucker's noisy mischief, Steve had had enough. He scrambled out of bed and stormed into the children's room.

"If you kids don't settle down," he ordered, "you will sleep in your old beds!" To drive home his point, Steve stood for a moment, gazing at Tucker and Haven. His hands were held up in exasperation, and he was clothed in nothing but his briefs.

Tucker obviously couldn't get past the figure of Steve standing half-clothed in the shadows. "Dad," he commented, "you look like you're about to die on a cross like Jesus!"

Suppressing a chuckle, Steve gave up and went back to bed.

Tucker's comment made us all laugh, but it reveals a nugget of truth: Our children closely identify us with God. We as parents represent Him to our kids. As they observe us each day, they create a picture of Him in their minds and hearts. They may paint an angry tyrant, waiting to pounce on their tiniest mistake, or they may sketch a God so little and far removed as to barely exist. Sadly, some children even draw God to be their own size.

Given that our children learn to relate to God through our example, we must take seriously our job of parenting. God has blessed us with this role; I believe it's our primary purpose as parents. But how can we represent Him to our kids and do it in a healthy way? How can we help them to understand that obeying us—in love—is directly related to loving and obeying their heavenly Father? We'll tackle these issues throughout this chapter, and hopefully by the end, we'll understand that raising God-loving children should be our highest and primary goal. But even the best parents don't always have their priorities right. So first, let's look honestly at some of the other goals well-meaning parents often pursue in raising their kids.

EVALUATING OUR PRIORITIES

When it comes to having misplaced priorities, I'm definitely guilty! Much of the time, my goal in parenting is simply to have well-behaved children—not for some higher, godly purpose, but for my own peace and quiet. My life is so much simpler and more enjoyable when the kiddos obey me without arguing and when they get along with each other. As a result, I'm quick to correct them, sometimes in anger, when my comfort is disturbed, without considering how I'm modeling God to them.

What hidden motives do you sometimes have? Do you ever struggle with pride? I do. It's easy to want other people to admire our little ones and, in effect, praise our parenting skills. When our kids are on their best behavior, it makes us, their parents, look good. And when someone notices, it can feel as though all our hard work is finally paying off.

For some people, being prideful isn't their main stumbling block. But is guilt? Some of us base our parenting priorities on how guilty we feel. We have this false, often unrealistic ideal of how our children should behave; and when they don't cooperate, we blame ourselves, thinking we're doing something wrong. All of these motivations— desire for peace and quiet, pride, and guilt—are understandable. But they are still wrong. If we parent with the wrong motives, we will ultimately crumble when the "growing" gets tough. So it's vital that we step away from the pandemonium of parenting from time to time and remind ourselves of the true goal—to have kids who are drawing an accurate picture of God in their hearts and learning how to relate to Him as their Creator each day.

Modeling God to our kids is a tall order. In fact, I would be the first to admit that my representation of God is imperfect. But that's the nature of a reflection. It's backward in a mirror, upside-down in a spoon, blurry in a window, and always one-dimensional. Though we should strive to be godly, we can never perfectly reflect God. Instead, our goal should be to ensure that our reflection of God draws our children closer to Him—and that it makes them long to touch the real thing.

LEARNING FROM GOD, THE PERFECT PARENT

How can we accomplish such a goal? The best way is to look at how God parents His own children and then imitate what we see. The biblical book of Hebrews offers key insight into God's parenting style. It says, " . . . My son, do not make light of the Lord's discipline, and do not lose heart when he rebukes you, because the Lord disciplines those he loves, and he punishes everyone he accepts as a son" (12:5–6).

God loves us and wants what's best for us. Because He cares so deeply, He disciplines us when we need it. He loves us too much to let us continue down the wrong paths. God allows us to experience difficulties and hardship because, with His help, our problems then grab our attention and help to steer us back on course. Hebrews 12:5–6 perfectly illustrates how God balances the tension between loving us, His children, unconditionally and teaching us the consequences of sin.

This, to me, is creative parenting! Yet it can be a difficult model for us, as earthly parents, to follow. It's tempting after a long day at work for us, and an equally taxing day at school for our children, to "cut them some slack" when we get home. "After all," we rationalize, "we get so little time to be together. I don't want them to feel that all I do is bark at them." We have once again fallen prey to the false assumption that we can demonstrate our love better by giving in to our children rather than by holding a firm line.

Too often we assume that if we exercise our God-given authority as parents to discipline, our children won't love us. We think love means never making them unhappy. In reality, it means doing what's best for them—even when that requires unpleasant consequences. When I have to deny my children something they want, I often remind them and myself, "It's the same love that tells you no that tells you yes."

Many of today's "experts" argue that discipline is controlling and that it prevents kids from fully expressing themselves as individuals. To that I say, "Let's hear a hallelujah!" I've seen my child fully expressing himself, and it's not a pretty sight. Here's an example.

One Monday morning, Steve, the kids, and I were having breakfast with another family at a local restaurant. Before sitting down, we played musical chairs until the adults were at one end of the table and the children were at the other. Even so, breakfast was chaotic. Shrieks, paper napkins, and food flew continuously at us from the kids' side. Of course, our son, Tucker, was right in the middle of the action. Five years old at the time, he was under the table, on top of the table, around the table—everywhere except seated nicely in front of his chocolate chip happy-face pancake. It didn't take long for us to realize that we wouldn't be able to converse for longer than 30 seconds at a time. Finally, Steve and I gave up and went home for a nap. (We made Tucker lie down, too.)

Before going to my own bed and assuming the ostrich pose with my head buried under the pillows, I flopped onto Tucker's bed and stared at my rambunctious son. "What got into you this morning?" I asked, not really expecting an answer.

Tucker shook his head as if he couldn't believe I'd asked him such a crazy question. "Mom," he said, "you know sin *is* pleasurable for a season!" (Before you mistakenly think Tucker is some Bible scholar, consider that there are certain scriptures of which I've had to remind him repeatedly.)

Don't kid yourself about your kid. As my story illustrates, all children are born with foolishness bound up in their hearts. That is why it's so important that we as parents follow God's example and discipline our little ones. That's what our children really want from us, anyway—discipline and rules. They don't test the boundaries hoping to discover the weak spot and be set free. They want to make sure the fortress walls are solid so they can relax and enjoy being a kid. Intuitively, children know that the safest place to be is in the protection of someone bigger and stronger. They wonder if we can really protect them.

So how solid are your fortress walls? I want you to consider granting yourself the permission to be more strict, to erect those boundaries a little closer to home. Your child may put up a fuss; the world may not understand; but you know God's truth. And His Word attests that " . . . the LORD disciplines those he loves, as a father the son he delights in" (Proverbs 3:12).

HOW TO PRESENT THE PICTURE

Discipline, when administered consistently and lovingly, encourages willing obedience. Obedience is based on trust. And at the heart of trust is love. I can obey God, my heavenly Father, because I know He loves me and I can trust that anything He asks of me is ultimately for my own good. In the same way, our children need to be convinced that we love them unconditionally. They need to trust that when we require them to do something—and discipline them when they disobey—we're doing it for their own good.

There are many ways to help our little ones develop conviction and trust in us, and by doing so, present to them an accurate picture of God. Let me describe a couple of practical ways my husband and I have tried to do this. One example is a game Steve and I play with our kids called the "Faith Fall." Steve gets on his knees, and one of the kids stands in front of him, holding on to a chair with her back toward him.

Steve asks her, "Do you trust me?"

"Yes," she answers.

"Do you really trust me?" he queries again.

She answers affirmatively.

Once more, he asks, "Do you trust me with your life?"

"Yes!" she shouts, giddy with anticipation.

"Then let go," Steve directs her, "and I'll catch you."

At this point, she lets herself fall backward, and Steve catches her just before she hits the ground. After the other two kids take their turns, Steve and I explain the exercise.

"Just as you can trust Daddy to catch you," we tell the kids, "you can also trust God—even when something seems scary or doesn't make sense. He cares enough to catch His children, and He's strong enough not to drop us!"

This game, the "Faith Fall," has helped them to understand the principle of trust. Steve and I often refer to it when the kids feel that God has asked them to do something, but they're scared or uncertain about whether He will be there to help them through it.

Another way we have sought to teach them about trust and obedience is by using the umbrella illustration. One day I drew a picture of a large umbrella. Standing underneath were Tucker, Haven, and Clancy. Not being a terribly gifted artist, I had to label the stick figures so the kids would know who was who. Then I marked the umbrella as "Mommy and Daddy." (To be honest, the umbrella looked a little like Mommy on a bad hair day, but I still needed to identify that Daddy was part of the picture.) After that, I explained the drawing.

"When you are being obedient to the things Daddy and I have taught you," I told the children, "you are safely under the umbrella of our protection. The world might 'rain' all sorts of problems and temptations on you, but you are protected.

"God has designed Mommy and Daddy to be an umbrella for your own safety," I continued. "If you choose to disobey and walk out from under our covering, you'll have to deal with the harsh elements of the world."

This illustration has helped the kids to comprehend *why* it's important for them to follow our instruction. It has also been helpful to reference when they feel we're making a bad decision. When that happens, Steve and I explain that even though they might think Mommy and Daddy's choice is wrong, it is still safer to obey us and remain under our "umbrella" than to be vulnerable to the dangers and lies of the world. God, we tell them, will deal with us if our choices are bad.

But presenting a picture of God involves more than just playing games and giving illustrative examples. In modeling Him to our kids, Steve and I have found it vital to demonstrate love and respect toward each other as well. The apostle Paul addressed family relationships, saying, " . . . Each one of you also must love his wife as he loves himself, and the wife must respect her husband" (Ephesians 5:33). His next words are to the children: "Honor your father and mother" (6:2).

I'm convinced that the placement of those verses together is no coincidence. Children will be motivated to respond to us, their parents, as they should when Mom and Dad love each other as *they* should. With your spouse, think seriously about the way you relate to each other. What kind of message are you sending to your children? Modeling respect and love in marriage is essential when presenting a healthy picture of God. If we respect our spouses, our children will respond more positively when we demand respect from them. And when our kids respect us, their earthly parents, they will learn to respect God, their heavenly Parent.

There are a number of ways to train children to respect authority. I grew up in the South, where I was taught to reply, "Yes, sir" or "Yes, ma'am" when following instruction. In addition to this custom, I have taught my children to address their best friend's mother as, for example, "Mrs. Cleaver," as opposed to "June." You can teach these lessons on the same day your kids learn to say "Please" and "Thank you" and call it Manners 101.

To further encourage an attitude of respect, require your children to give you their full attention when you're speaking to them. How many conversations have you had with your child, his eyes fixed on the TV screen as a little Italian man jumps over rolling turtles? If he's anything like Tucker, he doesn't even need a video game to be distracted. So when I talk to Tucker, I expect him to stop what he's doing, be still, and look me in the eye. I sometimes ask him, "If I were to offer you $100, would you listen to me?" This captures his attention long enough to remind him that King Solomon, who was the wisest man who ever lived, said that it is better to get wisdom (which, of course, comes from Mom and Dad) than silver or gold (Proverbs 16:16).

SUBTLE FORMS OF DISRESPECT

By training our kids to respect authority, we're teaching them how to relate to God. They can't obey Him if they haven't learned to listen to Him; they won't listen to Him if they don't respect Him; and if they don't respect Him, they won't submit to Him. Let's evaluate the level of submission our children currently exhibit with us and look at how this might transfer to their relationships with God.

When giving your child an instruction, does he often argue with you or ask, "Why?" What kind of attitude does he have? Do his actions say, "I will obey just enough to get by," or "I will obey you, but I will do what I want first"? Do you have any young lawyers in your family? You know, the little negotiator who always has a better idea about how to do something than the way you've instructed her. Moses, in the book of Exodus, decided to do things his own way and, as a result, didn't get to lead the children of Israel into the Promised Land after putting up with them in the wilderness for 40 years.

The Bible tells us that as the people of Israel were trekking through the wilderness, they got thirsty. So the Lord told Moses to gather the people, speak to a specific rock, and water would gush out. Instead of speaking to it, however, Moses hit it twice with his staff. Water flowed from the rock—but the Lord punished Moses for his disobedience, prohibiting him from leading the Israelites into the Promised Land (Numbers 20:6–12). Moses' story is extreme, but it shows the importance of doing things God's way. Which of God's promises might our children miss out on because they wanted to do things their way?

Disobedience comes in many forms, including whining. It can be a little harder to recognize, but once I realized that whining was just manipulation in a cute dress, I was more inclined to put my foot down about it. This became such an issue in our house that my kids thought it was one of the Ten Commandments. Here's an example.

When our house was being built, I penciled scriptures on the walls before they were painted. One day, Tucker zoomed in from the backyard (he only knows one speed), grabbed a pencil, and ran up the stairs to what would eventually become his room. My curiosity was piqued, so I followed him and caught him marking on the walls.

"Don't worry, Mom," he said quickly. "I'm writing scriptures, too."

I leaned forward, interested to see what his scribbles actually said. After all, Tucker had only recently learned to read!

Pointing to the first set of hieroglyphics, he said proudly, "See? It says, 'Thou shalt not whine.'"

I'm comforted to know that my children aren't the only ones who whine—the children of Israel were notorious for it! Once, when they were complaining about not having enough meat, God got angry and said to them, "Fine! You want meat? I'll give you so much that it will pour out of your nostrils!" (See Numbers 11.) Let's train our children to be content with our instruction so that they don't have to learn the hard way what whining will get them. Remember, it's possible to develop not only a loving relationship with your kid, but also one that requires them to submit to you. Your interaction with them will provide the foundation for their relationships with God.

THE BIBLE AS THE FINAL WORD

Teaching our children to obey us and our words is primarily to teach them to obey God and His Word. In her book *For Instruction in Righteousness*, Pam Forster writes:

> Our child needs to understand that the authority that we, as parents, exercise over him is delegated to us by God. When we discipline a child for wrongdoing, we do so because God says his action is wrong, not because of some arbitrary standard we have fabricated. Our children are much more open to correction when God's standard, not ours, is held up before them. If the Bible is our authority, our children will grow to understand that "right" and "wrong" are based on God's standards, not our own personal standards.[1]

I love that! Because the rules I'm instilling are God's, I no longer have to respond with "Because I'm the mom. That's why!" I can recite an appropriate scripture and then calmly tell my kids, "Honey, I didn't make up these rules, God did. And this is what He says makes life work. And because I believe Him and I love you, I'm going to enforce what He says."

How can we teach our children God's standards for discipline? We could spout off Bible verses for each infraction and transform ourselves, right before our children's eyes, into caricatures of every "fire and brimstone" evangelist we've ever seen on television. Though the Bible is referred to as the "sword of the Spirit," I don't think it was meant to be used as a weapon to threaten our kids. While that approach may scare our children into obeying us, it won't necessarily encourage our children to love Scripture. And we need that balance of love and obedience in presenting a true picture of God.

Our children will respond best to the Bible when they have learned to love it. But first they need to see that *we* love God's law. I was recently interviewed for a Mother's Day television special. The host asked me, "How would you most want your children to remember you?" After tossing out *Sports Illustrated* swimsuit model and Martha Stewart, I settled on this one image and replied, "I would like my children to remember waking up every morning and peeking through the banisters to see me reading my Bible in my special chair, having a cup of coffee with Jesus and listening to what He wanted to tell me through His Word that day."

I hope that picture stays in their minds, and that my kids will eventually love God's Word so much that reading it will be as much a part of their daily routine as brushing their teeth. And that should be the goal: for our kids to cherish God's law. Listen to a stanza from a beautiful poem in the Bible: "Because I love your commands more than gold, more than pure gold" (Psalm 119:127). I would love to know that, like the author of these verses, my children had also come to understand God's goodness and the happiness that comes from obeying His Word.

In the following "Toolbox" section, I have listed common childhood infractions, along with some corresponding scriptures. It is encouraging to realize that God doesn't often deal in generalities. He has some very specific things to say about His children's behavior. These would be wonderful scriptures for your children to know and memorize, but they are primarily for you, the parent. As you read over the following verses and are reminded of God's instructions, I pray you will gain a fresh resolve to teach God's Word to your kids and train them according to His ways.

Learning from the Ultimate Parent

Toolbox

"All Scripture is God-breathed and is useful for teaching, rebuking, correcting and training in righteousness, so that the man of God may be thoroughly equipped for every good work."
(2 Timothy 3:16–17)

Aggravating/Stirring Up Strife

Proverbs 15:18—"A hot-tempered man stirs up dissension, but a patient man calms a quarrel."

Proverbs 10:12—"Hatred stirs up strife, but love covers all sins" (NKJV).

Proverbs 26:21—"As charcoal to embers and as wood to fire, so is a quarrelsome man for kindling strife."

Anger

Proverbs 29:11—"A fool gives full vent to his anger, but a wise man keeps himself under control."

James 1:19–20—"My dear brothers, take note of this: Everyone should be quick to listen, slow to speak and slow to become angry, for man's anger does not bring about the righteous life that God desires."

Ephesians 4:26–27—"'In your anger do not sin': Do not let the sun go down while you are still angry, and do not give the devil a foothold."

Arguing

Proverbs 18:2—"A fool finds no pleasure in understanding but delights in airing his own opinions."

Proverbs 13:10—"Pride only breeds quarrels, but wisdom is found in those who take advice."

2 Timothy 2:23–24—"Don't have anything to do with foolish and stupid arguments, because you know they produce quarrels.

And the Lord's servant must not quarrel; instead he must be kind to everyone, able to teach, not resentful."

Attentiveness

Proverbs 12:11—"He who works his land will have abundant food, but he who chases fantasies lacks judgment."

Proverbs 4:20—"My son, pay attention to what I say; listen closely to my words."

Attitude

Proverbs 15:15—"All the days of the oppressed are wretched, but the cheerful heart has a continual feast."

Proverbs 17:22—"A cheerful heart is good medicine, but a crushed spirit dries up the bones."

Bad or Perverse Language

Ephesians 4:29—"Do not let any unwholesome talk come out of your mouths, but only what is helpful for building others up according to their needs, that it may benefit those who listen."

Proverbs 4:24—"Put away perversity from your mouth; keep corrupt talk far from your lips."

Bragging/Boasting/Being Prideful

Proverbs 27:2—"Let another praise you, and not your own mouth; someone else, and not your own lips."

Proverbs 12:23—"A prudent man keeps his knowledge to himself, but the heart of fools blurts out folly."

1 Peter 5:6—"Humble yourselves, therefore, under God's mighty hand, that he may lift you up in due time. Cast all your anxiety on him because he cares for you."

Cheating

Proverbs 15:3—"The eyes of the LORD are everywhere, keeping watch on the wicked and the good."

Luke 16:10—"Whoever can be trusted with very little can also be trusted with much, and whoever is dishonest with very little will also be dishonest with much."

Complaining

Philippians 2:14–15—"Do everything without complaining or arguing, so that you may become blameless and pure, children of God without fault in a crooked and depraved generation, in which you shine like stars in the universe."

Numbers 11:1—"Now the people complained about their hardships in the hearing of the LORD, and when he heard them his anger was aroused."

1 Thessalonians 5:18—"Give thanks in all circumstances, for this is God's will for you in Christ Jesus."

Confessing

Proverbs 28:13—"He who conceals his sins does not prosper, but whoever confesses and renounces them finds mercy."

James 5:16—"Therefore confess your sins to each other and pray for each other so that you may be healed. The prayer of a righteous man is powerful and effective."

1 John 1:9—"If we confess our sins, he is faithful and just and will forgive us our sins and purify us from all unrighteousness."

Controlling the Tongue

James 1:26—"If anyone considers himself religious and yet does not keep a tight rein on his tongue, he deceives himself and his religion is worthless."

Proverbs 29:20—"Do you see a man who speaks in haste? There is more hope for a fool than for him."

Proverbs 13:3—"He who guards his lips guards his life, but he who speaks rashly will come to ruin."

Proverbs 18:7—"A fool's mouth is his undoing, and his lips are a snare to his soul."

Deceiving

2 Corinthians 4:2—"We have renounced secret and shameful ways; we do not use deception, nor do we distort the word of God. On the contrary, by setting forth the truth plainly we commend ourselves to every man's conscience in the sight of God."

Mark 4:22—"For whatever is hidden is meant to be disclosed, and whatever is concealed is meant to be brought out into the open."

Defying/Rebelling

Psalm 106:43—"Many times he delivered them, but they were bent on rebellion and they wasted away in their sin."

James 4:17—"Anyone, then, who knows the good he ought to do and doesn't do it, sins."

Ecclesiastes 8:11—"Because the sentence against an evil work is not executed speedily, therefore the heart of the sons of men is fully set in them to do evil" (NKJV).

Delighting in Correction

Proverbs 12:1—"Whoever loves discipline loves knowledge, but he who hates correction is stupid."

Proverbs 19:20—"Listen to advice and accept instruction, and in the end you will be wise."

Hebrews 12:5–6—" . . . 'My son, do not make light of the

Lord's discipline, and do not lose heart when he rebukes you, because the Lord disciplines those he loves, and he punishes everyone he accepts as a son.'"

Hebrews 12:11—"No discipline seems pleasant at the time, but painful. Later on, however, it produces a harvest of righteousness and peace for those who have been trained by it."

Diligence

Proverbs 22:29—"Do you see a man skilled in his work? He will serve before kings; he will not serve before obscure men."

1 Corinthians 9:27—"But I discipline my body and bring it into subjection, lest, when I have preached to others, I myself should become disqualified" (NKJV).

1 Timothy 4:15—"Be diligent in these matters; give yourself wholly to them, so that everyone may see your progress."

Discernment

Proverbs 15:21—"Folly delights a man who lacks judgment, but a man of understanding keeps a straight course."

Proverbs 4:25–27—"Let your eyes look straight ahead, fix your gaze directly before you. Make level paths for your feet and take only ways that are firm. Do not swerve to the right or the left; keep your foot from evil."

Doing Good

Philippians 4:8—"Finally, brothers, whatever is true, whatever is noble, whatever is right, whatever is pure, whatever is lovely, whatever is admirable—if anything is excellent or praiseworthy—think about such things."

Colossians 3:2–3—"Set your minds on things above, not on earthly things. For you died, and your life is now hidden with Christ in God."

1 John 2:15—"Do not love the world or anything in the world. If anyone loves the world, the love of the Father is not in him."

3 John 1:11—"Dear friend, do not imitate what is evil but what is good. Anyone who does what is good is from God. Anyone who does what is evil has not seen God."

Fearfulness

Proverbs 3:24–26—"When you lie down, you will not be afraid; when you lie down, your sleep will be sweet. Have no fear of sudden disaster or of the ruin that overtakes the wicked, for the LORD will be your confidence and will keep your foot from being snared."

Psalm 56:3–4—"When I am afraid, I will trust in you. In God, whose word I praise, in God I trust; I will not be afraid. What can mortal man do to me?"

Friendships

Proverbs 13:20—"He who walks with the wise grows wise, but a companion of fools suffers harm."

Proverbs 1:10,15—"My son, if sinners entice you, do not give in to them. . . . [M]y son, do not go along with them, do not set foot on their paths."

Proverbs 12:26—"A righteous man is cautious in friendship, but the way of the wicked leads them astray."

1 Corinthians 15:33—"Do not be misled: 'Bad company corrupts good character.'"

Generosity

Proverbs 11:24—"One man gives freely, yet gains even more; another withholds unduly, but comes to poverty."

Luke 6:30–31—"Give to everyone who asks you, and if anyone takes what belongs to you, do not demand it back. Do to others as you would have them do to you."

Luke 6:38—"Give, and it will be given to you. A good measure, pressed down, shaken together and running over, will be poured into your lap. For with the measure you use, it will be measured to you."

Acts 20:35—" . . . It is more blessed to give than to receive."

2 Corinthians 9:7b—" . . . God loves a cheerful giver."

Gossip

Proverbs 16:28—"A perverse man stirs up dissension, and a gossip separates close friends."

Proverbs 20:19—"A gossip betrays a confidence; so avoid a man who talks too much."

Proverbs 11:13—"A gossip betrays a confidence, but a trustworthy man keeps a secret."

Greed

Proverbs 28:25—"A greedy man stirs up dissension, but he who trusts in the LORD will prosper."

Luke 12:15—"Then he [Jesus] said, 'Watch out! Be on your guard against all kinds of greed; a man's life does not consist in the abundance of his possessions.'"

Jealousy

Galatians 5:26—"Let us not become conceited, provoking and envying each other."

James 3:16—"For where you have envy and selfish ambition, there you find disorder and every evil practice."

Judgment

Matthew 7:1–2—"Do not judge, or you too will be judged. For in the same way you judge others, you will be judged, and with the measure you use, it will be measured to you."

John 8:15—"You judge by human standards; I pass judgment on no one."

1 Corinthians 4:5a—"Therefore judge nothing before the appointed time; wait till the Lord comes. He will bring to light what is hidden in darkness and will expose the motives of men's hearts."

Matthew 7:3—"Why do you look at the speck of sawdust in your brother's eye and pay no attention to the plank in your own eye?"

Kindness

Proverbs 11:17—"A kind man benefits himself, but a cruel man brings trouble on himself."

Ephesians 4:32—"Be kind and compassionate to one another, forgiving each other, just as in Christ God forgave you."

Laziness

Proverbs 10:4—"Lazy hands make a man poor, but diligent hands bring wealth."

Proverbs 12:24—"Diligent hands will rule, but laziness ends in slave labor."

Ephesians 6:6—"Obey them [your masters] not only to win their favor when their eye is on you, but like slaves of Christ, doing the will of God from your heart."

Listening

Proverbs 12:15—"The way of a fool seems right to him, but a wise man listens to advice."

Proverbs 13:1—"A wise son heeds his father's instruction, but a mocker does not listen to rebuke."

Lying

Proverbs 12:19—"Truthful lips endure forever, but a lying tongue lasts only a moment."

Proverbs 12:22—"The LORD detests lying lips, but he delights in men who are truthful."

Proverbs 21:6—"A fortune made by a lying tongue is a fleeting vapor and a deadly snare."

Leviticus 19:11—"Do not steal. Do not lie. Do not deceive one another."

Psalm 34:13—"Keep your tongue from evil and your lips from speaking lies."

Manners

1 Corinthians 10:31—"So whether you eat or drink or whatever you do, do it all for the glory of God."

Modesty

Proverbs 11:22—"Like a gold ring in a pig's snout is a beautiful woman who shows no discretion."

Proverbs 31:30—"Charm is deceptive, and beauty is fleeting; but a woman who fears the LORD is to be praised."

1 Corinthians 12:23b—"And the parts that are unpresentable are treated with special modesty."

Money

Proverbs 21:20—"In the house of the wise are stores of choice food and oil, but a foolish man devours all he has."

Proverbs 22:7—"The rich rule over the poor, and the borrower is servant to the lender."

Obedience

Psalm 119:129—"Your statutes are wonderful; therefore I obey them."

Luke 11:28—"Blessed rather are those who hear the word of God and obey it."

John 14:15—"If you love me, you will obey what I command."

Colossians 3:20—"Children, obey your parents in everything, for this pleases the Lord."

Psalm 119:60—"I will hasten and not delay to obey your commands."

Patience

Romans 8:25—"But if we hope for what we do not yet have, we wait for it patiently."

Romans 12:12—"Be joyful in hope, patient in affliction, faithful in prayer."

Ephesians 4:2—"Be completely humble and gentle; be patient, bearing with one another in love."

Peacemaker

Proverbs 20:3—"It is to a man's honor to avoid strife, but every fool is quick to quarrel."

Proverbs 19:11—"A man's wisdom gives him patience; it is to his glory to overlook an offense."

James 3:18—"Peacemakers who sow in peace raise a harvest of righteousness."

Matthew 5:9—"Blessed are the peacemakers, for they will be called sons of God."

Peer Pressure

Proverbs 29:25—"Fear of man will prove to be a snare, but whoever trusts in the LORD is kept safe."

Proverbs 4:14–15—"Do not set foot on the path of the

wicked or walk in the way of evil men. Avoid it, do not travel on it; turn from it and go on your way."

Titus 2:12—"It teaches us to say 'No' to ungodliness and worldly passions, and to live self-controlled, upright and godly lives in this present age."

Acts 5:29—"Peter and the other apostles replied: 'We must obey God rather than men!'"

1 Timothy 4:12—"Don't let anyone look down on you because you are young, but set an example for the believers in speech, in life, in love, in faith and in purity."

Respect for Authority

Romans 13:1—"Everyone must submit himself to the governing authorities, for there is no authority except that which God has established. The authorities that exist have been established by God."

Hebrews 13:17—"Obey your leaders and submit to their authority. They keep watch over you as men who must give an account. Obey them so that their work will be a joy, not a burden, for that would be of no advantage to you."

Respect for Parents

Proverbs 20:20—"If a man curses his father or mother, his lamp will be snuffed out in pitch darkness."

Proverbs 30:17—"The eye that mocks his father, and scorns obedience to his mother, the ravens of the valley will pick it out, and the young eagles will eat it" (NKJV).

Ephesians 6:2–3—"'Honor your father and mother'—which is the first commandment with a promise—'that it may go well with you and that you may enjoy long life on the earth.'"

Responsibility

Proverbs 12:10—"A righteous man cares for the needs of his animal, but the kindest acts of the wicked are cruel."

Revenge

Proverbs 20:22—"Do not say, 'I'll pay you back for this wrong!' Wait for the LORD, and he will deliver you."

Leviticus 19:18—"Do not seek revenge or bear a grudge against one of your people, but love your neighbor as yourself. I am the LORD."

Self-Centeredness

Psalm 119:36—"Turn my heart toward your statutes and not toward selfish gain."

Philippians 2:3–4—"Do nothing out of selfish ambition

or vain conceit, but in humility consider others better than yourselves. Each of you should look not only to your own interests, but also to the interest of others."

James 3:16—"For where you have envy and selfish ambition, there you find disorder and every evil practice."

Self-Control

Proverbs 25:28—"Like a city whose walls are broken down is a man who lacks self-control."

Proverbs 16:32—"Better a patient man than a warrior, a man who controls his temper than one who takes a city."

Proverbs 5:23—"He will die for lack of discipline, led astray by his own great folly."

2 Timothy 1:7—"For God did not give us a spirit of timidity, but a spirit of power, of love and of self-discipline."

Sharing

1 Timothy 6:18—"Command them to do good, to be rich in good deeds, and to be generous and willing to share."

Hebrews 13:16—"And do not forget to do good and to share with others, for with such sacrifices God is pleased."

Acts 4:32—"All the believers were one in heart and mind. No one claimed that any of his possessions was his own, but they shared everything they had."

Sibling Rivalry

Proverbs 17:14—"Starting a quarrel is like breaching a dam; so drop the matter before a dispute breaks out."

Proverbs 25:21–22—"If your enemy is hungry, give him food to eat; if he is thirsty, give him water to drink. In doing this, you will heap burning coals on his head, and the LORD will reward you."

Romans 12:10—"Be devoted to one another in brotherly love. Honor one another above yourselves."

Romans 12:18—"If it is possible, as far as it depends on you, live at peace with everyone."

Romans 12:21—"Do not be overcome by evil, but overcome evil with good."

John 15:13—"Greater love has no one than this, that he lay down his life for his friends."

Romans 12:15–16a—"Rejoice with those who rejoice; mourn with those who mourn. Live in harmony with one another."

1 Peter 3:8–9—"Finally, all of you, live in harmony with one another; be sympathetic, love as brothers, be compassionate and humble. Do not repay evil with evil or insult with insult, but with blessing, because to this you were called so that you may inherit a blessing."

1 John 2:9–10—"Anyone who claims to be in the light but hates his brother is still in the darkness. Whoever loves his brother lives in the light, and there is nothing in him to make him stumble."

Speaking Unkindly

Proverbs 15:4—"The tongue that brings healing is a tree of life, but a deceitful tongue crushes the spirit."

Proverbs 12:18—"Reckless words pierce like a sword, but the tongue of the wise brings healing."

Proverbs 15:1—"A gentle answer turns away wrath, but a harsh word stirs up anger."

Proverbs 18:21—"The tongue has the power of life and death, and those who love it will eat its fruit."

Stealing

Leviticus 19:11—"Do not steal. Do not lie. Do not deceive one another."

Ephesians 4:28—"He who has been stealing must steal no longer, but must work, doing something useful with his own hands, that he may have something to share with those in need."

Proverbs 10:2—"Ill-gotten treasures are of no value, but righteousness delivers from death."

Talking Too Much

Proverbs 10:19—"When words are many, sin is not absent, but he who holds his tongue is wise."

Proverbs 17:28—"Even a fool is thought wise if he keeps silent, and discerning if he holds his tongue."

Proverbs 21:23—"He who guards his mouth and his tongue keeps himself from calamity."

Teasing

Proverbs 26:18–19—"Like a madman shooting firebrands or deadly arrows is a man who deceives his neighbor and says, 'I was only joking!'"

James 3:5—"The tongue is a small part of the body, but it makes great boasts. Consider what a great forest is set on fire by a small spark."

Ungratefulness

Colossians 2:6–7—"Just as you received Christ Jesus as Lord, continue to live in him, rooted and built up in him, strengthened in the faith as you were taught, and overflowing with thankfulness."

Colossians 3:15—"Let the peace of Christ rule in your hearts, since as members of one body you were called to peace. And be thankful."

Colossians 4:2—"Devote yourselves to prayer, being watchful and thankful."

Miscellaneous Scriptures

1 Corinthians 13:4–7—"Love is patient, love is kind. It does not envy, it does not boast, it is not proud. It is not rude, it is not self-seeking, it is not easily angered, it keeps no record of wrongs. Love does not delight in evil but rejoices with the truth. It always protects, always trusts, always hopes, always perseveres."

Galatians 5:22–23—"But the fruit of the Spirit is love, joy, peace, patience, kindness, goodness, faithfulness, gentleness and self-control. Against such things there is no law."

John 3:16—"For God so loved the world that he gave his one and only Son, that whoever believes in him shall not perish but have eternal life."

Romans 8:28—"And we know that in all things God works for the good of those who love him, who have been called according to his purpose."

Galatians 6:7–9—"Do not be deceived: God cannot be mocked. A man reaps what he sows. The one who sows to please his sinful nature, from that nature will reap destruction; the one who sows to please the Spirit, from the Spirit will reap eternal life. Let us not become weary in doing good, for at the proper time we will reap a harvest if we do not give up. Therefore, as we have opportunity, let us do good to all people, especially to those who belong to the family of believers."

Ephesians 6:13–17—"Therefore put on the full armor of God, so that when the day of evil comes, you may be able to stand your ground, and after you have done everything, to stand. Stand firm then, with the belt of truth buckled around your waist, with the breastplate of righteousness in place, and with your feet fitted with the readiness that comes from the gospel of peace. In addition to all this, take up the shield of faith, with which you can extinguish all the flaming arrows of the evil one. Take the helmet of salvation and the sword of the Spirit, which is the word of God."

Romans 8:38–39—"For I am convinced that neither death nor life, neither angels nor demons, neither the present nor the future, nor any powers, neither height nor depth, nor anything else in all creation, will be able to separate us from the love of God that is in Christ Jesus our Lord."

Chapter 3

The Heart of Obedience

I was busily working at the computer when I heard the sound that strikes terror into every mother's heart: silence. My two-year-old daughter, Haven, was supposed to be playing in her room—and usually didn't play so quietly. Still a bit green around the edges as a mother, I immediately discounted the obvious— "She's up to no good"—and naively assumed she had fallen asleep. I left my work, walked down the hall, and peeked into her room. Smiling, I saw that she'd crawled into bed and was now taking an early nap.

This is great, I thought. *Now I have a few extra minutes of peace to get some work done.*

As I turned to redeem this precious gift of time, I noticed Haven had fallen asleep with the covers pulled over her head. It didn't look as though she could breathe, so I tiptoed to her bed and gently adjusted the blanket. Instead of finding a sleeping child, I was greeted with a mischievous smile that peeked out from behind a pacifier. I lifted the blanket higher and found the source of this guilty glee: Haven was clutching the Holy Grail of toddler booty: the remote control! As any parent of an "ankle-biter" knows, the remote control ranks up there with VCR buttons and the telephone receiver as a big no-no.

That episode with Haven certainly wasn't the first—or the last—time one of my kids has tried to cover up his or her crime. As this story illustrates, until our children learn to obey by their own free choice, they will continue to think the objective is to see how much they can get away with without getting caught. That's why it's critical, especially as our children get older, for us to take a two-step approach to parenting: We must teach the heart as well as discipline the flesh. While it's important that our kids learn to follow our instruction, they must also understand the reasons behind our restrictions and standards so that they may choose, by an act of the will, to obey. This is the real heart of obedience.

Children who grow up in legalistic, strict environments in which the parents never explain the purpose of discipline will often obey just as long as Mom and Dad are watching, then act up the second their parents turn their heads. On the other hand, kids who grow up in homes that lack rules and standards, where the parents are buddies rather than authority figures, often know the right thing to do but don't have the willpower to carry it out.

It takes time and energy to teach our kids *why* they're being corrected, rather than to simply dole out the punishment. For example, if Clancy interrupts me while I'm talking on the phone, the most convenient thing for me to do is to send her to her room. This stops her negative behavior and allows me to continue my conversation with only a brief pause in my personal agenda. But it's not the best approach, because all Clancy has learned is that this time she got caught. The next time she has a burning question, she'll probably interrupt me again.

I'm not saying we shouldn't send children to their rooms. But discipline alone isn't enough; we must follow up. So after I send Clancy to her room, I should cut my conversation a little short and then join her upstairs. That way I can explain to her why interrupting is inconsiderate—both to me and to the other person on the line. I can relay that when she interrupts me, she is communicating a selfish message: that what she has to say is more important than what I or anyone else has to say. This gives me the opportunity to talk to Clancy about putting others first.

Of course, we as parents should be sensitive to our kids, too. Often the question *is* important! So at our house, we use a wonderful technique, called the "Interrupt Rule," that we learned in a parenting class. Using this technique, our kids will gently rest a hand on my side when they need to get my attention. I'll lay my hand on theirs, acknowledging the request to speak, and then at a logical break in my conversation, I'll excuse myself and briefly turn my attention to my child.

It takes time to follow up our discipline by explaining the rules and then describing what to do in the future. But it's worth it! We'll be raising children who do the right things for the right reasons.

PARENTING FROM THE INSIDE OUT

Our objective as parents should be to gradually progress from motivating our children externally—correcting the flesh, or their actions—to motivating them internally, inspiring their hearts. The process is a little like baking bread from scratch. First, you add the basic ingredients and work them in thoroughly. Then you add the yeast mixture and knead the dough for at least 10 minutes. (This is hard work, but it can strengthen those flabby arms!) Next, you cover the dough with a wet cloth and let it rise until it doubles in size. After that, you take it out of the bowl and push, pull, and press some more. You set it aside to rise a second time (double-rising improves the flavor and consistency of the bread). Then, after another kneading cycle, you can finally shape the dough, put it in a greased pan, and bake it. Oh, there's nothing like the smell of freshly baked bread!

You're probably wondering what baking bread has to do with raising a child. My answer? A lot! When our children are young, we spend much of our time stirring in the basic ingredients—giving them the care they need each day, such as feeding, changing, rocking. As they get older, we add the yeast mixture and knead the dough—instructing, disciplining, and praising them as they incorporate God's values into their lives. This stage takes a lot of time and energy, but it's amazing how much we as parents are strengthened in the process, especially in our flabbiest areas.

There comes a point, after we've mixed and kneaded, pausing to let our words sink in from time to time, that we must simply wait—and pray. At this stage, most of the "raising" of our children will need to come from the inside, from their hearts. If our instruction, or yeast, is not doing its job, our kids will "fall" and turn out flat and hard after they've faced any heat. But if our guidance and wisdom have remained with them, they'll continue to grow and bring joy and fulfillment to others. And there is nothing like the inviting fragrance of a house filled with godly children!

The transition from correcting our children's behavior to motivating their hearts is vital. If our kids don't learn to own their decisions, to understand why they should make good choices, they will suffer for it. We can't always keep them from making bad decisions; eventually they must make their own choices. That's what God intended when He gave us free will. He wants our hearts to be in the right place when we make a decision. He says, "If you love me, you will obey what I command" (John 14:15). Our attitudes are more important to Him than our actions—so much so that He doesn't want us to do the right things for the wrong reasons. In fact, God condemned the religious leaders of His day for obeying out of fear, pride, and habit instead of love (see Matthew 23:26).

As a parent, I think I understand why God wants this. Love and obedience that are coerced aren't nearly as wonderful as when they're given freely. For example, as much as I love the kisses I steal from my sleeping children, they're not nearly as sweet as the ones they give me when they wake up in the morning, run down the stairs, and climb onto my lap. With God, the principle is the same. I envision Him sitting on His heavenly throne, anxiously waiting for His children to wake up and pour out their love on Him.

God has given our children the free will to choose or reject Him, so we, their parents, must give them good reasons to follow His ways. The goal is for our kids to make obedient choices because they know it's the right thing to do, because it pleases God—not because they want to avoid correction. If our children are motivated to obey only out of fear, they'll miss the whole point of obedience.

I must confess that if I'd been able to force my children to obey me out of fear while they were young, I would have parented that way. It's so much easier—but it's the wrong approach. In hindsight, I'm glad I was unsuccessful at using fear tactics. It would have made life simpler while my kids were young, but I'd rather see them obey me—and God—wholeheartedly, out of love.

KEEPING IT BALANCED

Of course, there's always the temptation to let the pendulum swing too far to the other side and neglect to discipline the flesh. That approach is dangerous, though, for our kids need correction. It isn't enough to give only information and unconditional love in the hope that they will eventually make the right choices.

I have to confess again that I have given this technique my best shot, too. I've been known to give my children an overdose of information when a little bit of correction would have been more effective. In fact, I did it as recently as last week. I had just delivered lecture number 286, addressing an aspect of Tucker's behavior that needed improving, when he made a comment that made me cringe.

"You know, Mom," Tucker said seriously after listening to me drone on, "you should put all these sermons on a tape so I can play them when I go to bed. That way, they'd get into my heart all night—and if I'm having trouble settling down, they can help put me to sleep!" (Tucker didn't mean any disrespect—I really *am* that verbose sometimes. Please pray for me.)

As you can see, we can talk our children to death. If we do not discipline them when they're young, they will have a difficult time disciplining themselves when they're older. We have all seen lives cut short because of self-indulgence. One of the reasons parents often pamper and indulge their kids is that they want to have a wonderful relationship with them. I want that, too—but placing too much emphasis on friendship is risky. When we try to be best buddies with our children too soon—giving them lots of pep talks without any corrective discipline—we put ourselves on their level, and they lose the security of knowing someone bigger and wiser is looking out for them. What our children really need when they're young is a parent, not a best friend.

One of the greatest rewards of parenting is friendship with our children; but if we get the prize before we finish the race, the ones who end up being penalized are our children. Our friendship with them will evolve later, as they mature.

Practical Ways to Address the Heart

How can we specifically address our children's hearts, giving them a healthy balance of discipline and instruction, love and correction? Let me share a few ways I've tried to teach my kids that obedience comes from the heart.

As I mentioned in chapter two, one good way to begin any correction is to let your kids know what the Bible says about their wrongdoing. God's Word does more than dole out commands; it often explains the reasons behind them. One day when Tucker was about five years old, he kept arguing with me. I corrected him, but then I shared this Bible verse: "Do everything without complaining or arguing, so that you may become blameless and pure, children of God without fault in a crooked and depraved generation, in which you shine like stars in the universe" (Philippians 2:14–15).

I sat him down and explained, "Tucker, you are a child of God and you shine like a star—but when you argue, your light begins to fade. I want you to always shine brightly, so please think about your attitude."

The words sank in. Later he started to complain and argue, but then he caught himself. "Mommy," he asked, cupping his hand over his mouth, "am I still shining?"

I smiled at him. "You are now."

In addition to using Scripture, we also can reach our children's hearts by allowing their wrongdoings to be an opportunity for teaching, not just a cause for reprimand. Before I pronounce a sentence, I'll ask my kids, "Why are you receiving this correction?" It's important that they admit their mistake, acknowledging that they deserve to be disciplined. Then I will follow up by questioning, "How could you have handled it differently, in a way that would have been more pleasing to Jesus?" Answering this helps them to articulate what they should have done, and it encourages them to do the right thing next time.

Teaching goes beyond addressing their actions, though. When our kids slip up, we have the opportunity to focus on their motives as well. With our help, they can learn at a fairly early age to examine the true reasons for their behavior. We can help them to identify wrongful motives and then lead them in prayer as they ask the Lord to change their hearts.

When getting to the heart of obedience, we also need to instruct our children to be mindful of how their words and actions affect others. Matthew 12:34 reads, " . . . Out of the overflow of the heart the mouth speaks." I learned firsthand the importance of instilling this concept when Tucker was three years old. One evening, I was serving hot dogs with chili and sauerkraut for dinner.

"I can't eat this. It's yucky!" Tucker announced, sticking out his tongue at the steaming vegetable on his plate.

After a long day of chasing toddlers, I didn't appreciate his views on my choice of food. "You should never say food is 'yucky,'" I told him with a frown. "I'd like you to politely eat at least some of it."

Tucker forced a few bites, and I assumed the issue was over.

A week later, we were having dinner at a friend's house. During the meal, Tucker turned to the hostess and ever-so-politely remarked, "This food is very yucky, but I'm eating it anyway."

I almost choked on my dinner. Unfortunately, I'd forgotten to teach Tucker that the reason we don't say food is "yucky" is that it could hurt the feelings of the person who had prepared it—another reason it is essential for us to address the heart, not simply subdue the flesh.

THE POWER OF STORIES

Employing Scripture and allowing our kids' mess-ups to turn into teachable moments are great ways to focus on the heart of obedience. Yet I've found the most effective way to get through to my children is by using word-pictures, object lessons, and stories. They tend to remain in our children's hearts, shaping them from the inside when we aren't around to shape them from the outside.

Please bear with me while I share a personal story with you. I promise that eventually it will help to make my point.

"Daddy, tell us about when we were in Mommy's tummy." Thus began a seemingly innocent conversation while we were making our weekly family pilgrimage to the neighborhood grocery warehouse.

Seeing Tucker strapped beyond arm's reach in his booster seat, Haven taunted her brother. "Tucker, you can't have a baby 'cuz you're a boy. Only girls can have babies!"

Not to be one-upped, he snapped back: "Yeah, well, get ready, Haven, because they're going to get a knife and cut your belly open to get it out!"

In an attempt to head off toddler trauma, Steve cut in. "Not necessarily. Not all babies have to be cut out."

I shot him a quick "Oh, no, don't go there!" look, but it was too late.

"Then how do they get out?" came Clancy's tiny voice.

Steve, realizing he was beyond the point of no return, tried to sound nonchalant. "From Mommy's private area."

"Ohh, yuck!" the kids chorused.

"I'm sure glad I didn't come out that way!" Tucker said.

Tucker might have been relieved that he wasn't born naturally, but back then, I sure wasn't. When my doctor informed me at my thirty-ninth week appointment that Tucker was not in the right position in my womb, and that if he didn't turn around in 48 hours I would have to have a cesarean section, I was sorely disappointed. We had just finished our Lamaze classes, and I was ready to go for the gold! Instead, I didn't even qualify for the finals. True to the doctor's word, Tucker was born by C-section.

Less than a year later, when the little stick turned blue, indicating my second pregnancy, I was determined to have a traditional birth. When the big day finally arrived, Steve and I rushed to the hospital, where I slipped into something a little more comfortable: my hospital lingerie with the easy-open back. My contractions were doing their job, so the nurse untied the little string at the back of my gown, and I felt the pain to end all pain—the blessed epidural.

My doctor arrived and checked my progress. He assured me everything was fine and that soon it would be time to push. I had just begun to relax, however, when pandemonium broke out. The doctor checked my monitor, and after spouting orders to the nurse, he nervously informed me that the baby's heartbeat was erratic. He was going to have to perform an emergency C-section.

I was crushed. I couldn't believe that after I'd made it through the hardest part of labor, my dream of experiencing a traditional childbirth wasn't going to come true. As they wheeled me down to the operating room, I fought back bitter tears.

Suddenly I felt the Lord tell me, *Rejoice in all things.*

Biting my lip, I conceded. *Okay, Lord,* I prayed. *Thank You for this C-section. I will praise You in all things, and I will rejoice in You.*

Minutes later, I found out why God had allowed the C-section. As the doctor made the incision, his eyes widened, and he motioned for Steve to take a picture of my stomach. There was a gaping hole just beneath the first layer of skin. My previous C-section scar had ruptured six of the seven sewn layers, exposing a small window. In an instant, I realized that if I had delivered Haven the way I'd wanted to, we wouldn't have known about the rupture until later, after much internal bleeding. But that's not the primary miracle in this story.

Haven was born with a potentially fatal blood disease called group B strep. The mother harbors it in the birth canal, and the baby ingests the infection when she passes through during delivery. Haven, however, had contracted the disease in the womb; somehow the bacteria had made its way in. If she had been born naturally—passing through the birth canal—she would have ingested more of the bacteria and surely would have died. Because the Lord sometimes says no to our dreams in order to produce something better in our lives, we were able to catch Haven's illness in time for it to be completely eradicated. The doctors were never sure how she contracted the disease, but it's no mystery why she survived. Again I say, "Rejoice!"

Recently, I tried to help Haven understand why God sometimes says no to our requests. I told her the story of her birth and reminded her that God sees the big picture, that He is working all things together for our good.

Stories are powerful! (Maybe that's why Jesus told so many of them.) They can help our children more easily understand God's ways and commands, effectively teaching them the heart of obedience. For example, we can encourage our children to not give up by having them memorize Philippians 4:13—"I can do everything through him who gives me strength"—until they can recite it in their sleep. But as powerful as that verse is, if we also reach their hearts with such stories as "David and Goliath," we will watch them overcome the giants in their world.

It's possible that if your child is getting in trouble for the same thing over and over again, he doesn't really comprehend what he's doing wrong. Assuming he is old enough to understand, see if you can come up with a story that helps him grasp the reason for your instruction. If you've had trouble finding appropriate stories, feel free to browse through the following stories, word-pictures, and object lessons. There might just be something that will work for you.

The Heart of Obedience

Toolbox

Anger

"Likewise the tongue is a small part of the body, but it makes great boasts. Consider what a great forest is set on fire by a small spark" (James 3:5).

Prepare to build a fire for your children. Gather some twigs and sticks, a match, lighter fluid, and a bucket of water. (Be careful with this object lesson, however. If you don't have a fireplace, wait until you're on a camping trip.) As you stack the firewood, explain to your children that the wood represents our words. Just as wood can be used to build things or burn things, so can our words—they can build people and relationships up or they can burn them down.

Next, strike the match. The match represents our anger—and when our words (the wood) and anger (the match) mix, the outcome can be deadly.

Once our anger has flashed, we have a choice: We can fuel the fire by adding more wood (angry words) or even by adding lighter fluid (physical outbursts), or we can decide to put the fire out.

If it's a small fire, we might simply cover the flame with a damp dishcloth. We can put out our anger by overlooking the offense. And it works! As the Bible attests, "Love covers over all wrongs" (Proverbs 10:12b). Of course, the quickest and most effective way to extinguish a fire is to douse it with water—or forgiveness. When we forgive someone and then choose to forget the incident, we quench our desire for revenge.

Arguing

Here's a fun and easy object lesson that will teach your children how to end an argument. Grab a ball and head outside to play catch. Point out to your child that you are able to play the game because both of you are participating. Then drop the ball suddenly and walk away. Your child will probably be a little upset and want to continue to play, but no matter how badly she may want to, she won't be able to by herself. Explain to her that an argument is a lot like playing catch. As soon as one person chooses to drop the ball, or argument, and walk away, the quarrel is over.

The next time you overhear a squabble between siblings, ask this question: "Who's going to drop the ball?"

(By the way, you may want to finish that little game of catch before you head back inside.)

Attentiveness

Hide an old-fashioned alarm clock (the kind that ticks loudly) somewhere in a room and tell your child to find it. Don't help her, though—remind her to listen for the ticking it makes. Once she finds the clock, reward her with 30 extra minutes of playtime. Then explain the lesson.

Tell your child that she found the clock because she was listening carefully—and because of that, she was rewarded. Remind her that we often "lose" time when we don't pay attention or listen. But the reward of attentiveness is often more time to play later.

Bad or Perverse Language

With your child watching, fill two measuring cups—one with water from the faucet, and the other with water from the toilet bowl. Empty the water from both glasses into the sink; then, without washing them out, refill the glasses with Kool-Aid or some other tasty drink. Ask your child which cup would he most like to drink from. (If he's not being a smart aleck, he'll choose the one that was filled with water from the faucet.)

Now explain the lesson: Our language must be clean if we want others to listen to our testimonies about God. If our mouths have previously been full of "potty talk," our words of witness, no matter how sweet, will probably be rejected. If we want to be effective witnesses for God, we must keep our talk clean, or we'll be polluting the pure truth of the gospel.

Bragging/Boasting/Being Prideful

Imagine that you are at a symphony and a world-premier flautist has taken center stage. People have traveled from all over to hear him bring his flute to life. That evening, the audience is not disappointed. When the final note is played, the crowd jumps to its feet in a standing ovation.

Then something strange happens. The flute jumps out of the man's hands and begins bowing and blowing kisses to the audience. "Thank you! Thank you!" it chimes.

The audience laughs uproariously at this spectacle. They know the truth: A flute is just the instrument. It is the person breathing life into it who deserves the credit.

We can explain to our children that it is just as silly to brag when we do something great. It is God who has given us the abilities and gifts to succeed. We should enjoy them, but give God the praise.

Cheating

Ananias sold some property for a lot of money. He gave only part of the money to the apostles; but, wanting to look generous, he claimed it was the full amount. His wife, Sapphira, had agreed to this deception.

Peter, one of the apostles, knew the truth. "Ananias," he said, "the money from the property was yours to spend however you wanted. But you lied and kept some of the money for yourself. Why would you do that? You weren't lying to us—you were lying to God."

As soon as Ananias heard these words, he fell to the floor and died.

A few hours later, Sapphira arrived, not knowing what had happened.

"Was this the price you and your husband received for your land?" Peter asked her.

"Yes," she replied, "that was the price."

"How could the two of you even think of conspiring together to test the Spirit of the Lord?" Peter demanded. "Just outside that door are the young men who buried your husband. They will carry your body out, too."

Sapphira instantly fell to the floor and died. (See Acts 5:1–11.)

Our children probably won't die from cheating or lying. Yet this story emphasizes an important truth: When we cheat or lie, we're really trying to con God. (Of course, this is silly to do because He knows everything!) And even though we won't die sudden deaths from cheating, we will still experience the deadly results of lying. It will squelch our trustworthiness, honor, and reputations.

Complaining

Once upon a time there lived twin boys who, aside from looking identical, were opposite in every way. One was an eternal optimist, always able to look on the bright side of life, while the other was a pessimist, who complained about everything. One year for their birthday, their father conducted an experiment. He loaded the pessimist's room with every imaginable toy and game; but the optimist's room, he filled with horse manure.

That night the father went to the pessimist's room, where he found the boy crying bitterly amid his new gifts.

"I have to read all these instructions before I can do anything with this stuff," complained the boy, frowning. "And I need a ton of batteries, too."

After trying to comfort his son, the father left the miserable boy and walked down the hallway to his brother's room. Amazingly, this little boy was smiling and dancing around the piles of manure.

"What are you so happy about?" the father asked.

The boy grinned. "With all this manure, there's got to be a pony in here somewhere!"

The next time your child starts to complain, remind him to look for the "pony."

Controlling the Tongue

James 3:3 reads, "When we put bits into the mouths of horses to make them obey us, we can turn the whole animal." James then goes on to apply this analogy to our tongues, saying that our words can direct our entire person. This is where we get the phrase "bridling the tongue."

If you don't have access to a horse, show your children a picture of a horse with a bit in its mouth. Point out how small the bit is compared with the size of the horse. Demonstrate how the bit is connected to the bridle, which is held in the rider's hands. Explain that a wild horse must first be "broken" and then trained to interpret the rider's cues. If the rider tugs on the right side of the bridle, the horse turns to the right, and vice versa. The bridle controls the horse. Similarly, if we can bridle, or control our tongues, we can often determine the direction our lives will take.

A friend sent this next idea to me via e-mail. Every time Tucker said something unkind or sharp to his sisters, he had to go out to our dog fence and hammer a nail into the post. It was fun the first few times, but then he grew tired of it. I continued to make him do this for a week. I wouldn't tell him why I was making him do it. The next week, every time he said something unkind or harsh, I first made him apologize to his sisters, then had him go out to the post and remove one nail. By this time the old ones were rusting because of the sprinklers and rain. When all the nails were out, I went outside with him.

I explained, "Every time your words wound your sisters, it's like a nail piercing their hearts. If you just leave it there without apologizing, it gets infected and can cause bitterness. Even after you ask their forgiveness, and remove the nail, the hole is still there. Be careful. You can take back the words, but you can't undo the damage they have caused."

You can also illustrate this principle by sticking nails into an orange. After a while, the orange starts to putrefy in reaction to the iron in the nails. When you take the nails out, the damage is evident.

Deceitfulness

Isaac had twin sons, Esau and Jacob. One day, when Isaac was old, almost blind, and near death, he called to his firstborn, Esau.

"Esau," he said, "it's time for me to grant you the blessing of the firstborn son. But before I do, take your bow and arrow and kill some game. Then prepare it for me."

Isaac's cunning wife Rebekah overheard this conversation and concocted a plan of her own. She pulled aside Jacob, the younger twin and her favorite, and said, "Go kill two young goats so I can prepare your father's favorite meal for him. Then take the food to him, and he will bless you instead of your older brother."

There was one problem, though: Esau was big and covered with hair, whereas Jacob was slim and smooth-skinned. So Rebekah dressed Jacob in Esau's clothes and draped a young goat's skin over his hands and chest to give the illusion of hair.

When Jacob entered his father's room with the meal, his father asked, "Who's there?"

"It's Esau," Jacob fibbed. "Sit up, Father, and enjoy this wild game I've killed and prepared for you so that you may give me your blessing."

Isaac may have been old and blind, but he wasn't stupid. "Come here, boy," he said. "I want to feel your skin."

Jacob held out his goat-skinned arm.

His father grunted. "You sound like Jacob, but you feel like Esau. Are you really my firstborn son?"

"Of course," Jacob lied.

It was enough; Isaac was convinced, and he pronounced his blessing upon Jacob. Soon after, Esau returned home. When he discovered Jacob's treachery, he was furious and wanted to kill his younger brother.

Rebekah caught wind of Esau's murderous plot and helped her beloved Jacob leave the country and flee to her brother's house, where he would stay until Esau's anger subsided. (See Genesis 25:19–34, Genesis 27.)

On the surface, this story appears to suggest that deception works and is good if it gets you what you want. But later in the Bible we learn that Jacob's deception had a price. He had no relationship with his twin brother for more than 20 years, and he never saw his mother, Rebekah, again, because she died before he returned home. Jacob himself was deceived later, when his father-in-law promised to give his youngest daughter, Rachel, to him in marriage if Jacob would work for him for seven years. But on the night of the wedding, he switched the daughters—and Jacob ended up marrying the eldest, Leah. He then had to work another seven years before he could marry Rachel, the one he loved.

I tell my children that deception is "lying with your actions instead of your words." And just like lying, we may think we get away with it, but God sees everything—and ultimately He loves us too much to let us go unpunished.

Disobedience

Bradley wanted to become a professional hockey player. So every day after school during the winter, he would head straight for frozen William Hill pond, where he would skate and daydream until dinnertime. One morning his mother told him to come straight home from school because spring was approaching and the ice on the pond would start to melt.

That afternoon after school, Bradley had every intention of obeying his mother, but as he passed the pond, he couldn't resist taking one last lap on the ice. He pulled his skates from his backpack, and after putting them on, he tiptoed onto the ice and slowly made his way to the middle of the pond. *This pond is just fine. Mom wouldn't mind my being here if she knew how thick the ice still is,* he rationalized.

Bradley continued to skate after school for the rest of the week. But then one day, just as he was telling himself that his mother didn't know as much about skating on ponds as he did, the ice began to crack. Petrified, he raced for the edge. But he was too far from the shore. His foot broke through, and icy water filled his skate. Stumbling forward, Bradley fell headfirst onto a sheet of ice and was struck unconscious.

Fortunately, Mr. Hill, the owner of the property, was watching him from inside his house. When he saw the ice break under Bradley, he raced outside and pulled the boy to safety.

Later, Bradley woke up in front of Mr. Hill's fireplace. He had a large knot on his forehead and a numb foot—other than that, he was okay. Bradley was lucky. Not only did he survive almost certain death, but he also learned a valuable lesson about obedience: You may be able to get away with something for a while, but you can be sure that your sins will find you out (see Numbers 32:23).

Focusing

Imagine walking down a gold-paved path toward a majestic castle. It's a lovely day—the birds are singing, the breeze is gently blowing, the sky is blue, and the flowers are blooming. The day is so beautiful that you're tempted to leave the path and turn cartwheels in the meadow. But your goal is to visit the castle, so you stick to the path.

Just when you've decided to stay the course, however, a yellow-and-black butterfly flits right in front of your nose and lands on a flower just ahead of you. You love butterflies, and quietly you sneak toward it. Just as you reach it, the butterfly sails into the air and lands on another flower. Again, you tiptoe up to it, wanting desperately to catch it. This continues for minutes, then hours—and before you know it, you've wandered too far from the path to reach the castle that day. Frustrated, you flop onto the grass. The day is gone, and you have nothing to show for it.

How often do we start chasing "butterflies" when we should be sticking to our path? This story helps illustrate to our children how easily we can get distracted from our goal—and why it's important to stay focused.

Greed

Tucker told me this joke, and I think it perfectly illustrates where our true treasures are: in heaven.

A billionaire was lying on his deathbed. "Lord," he called out, "may I please bring a million dollars with me to heaven?"

The Lord answered, "No."

The man continued to argue with God. "May I at least bring a briefcase full of my wealth?" he petitioned.

Finally, the Lord consented.

Soon after, the man died. As he requested, he was buried with his briefcase. But when the billionaire arrived at the pearly gates, he was stopped.

"I'm sorry, sir," the gatekeeper said, "but you can't bring that into heaven."

The gentleman was quick to explain. "You don't understand! I got permission from the Lord to bring this with me."

"Well, what do you have in there?" asked the gatekeeper, intrigued.

The man unlatched his briefcase and proudly displayed 50 gold bars.

The gatekeeper scratched his brow. "You brought *pavement?*"

Impatience

Gardening is a wonderful way to teach patience to our kids. Buy some strawberry seeds, potting soil, and a pot. With your child, plant the seeds and tend them together. When the first green strawberry appears, let your child eat one. Then make her wait until the fruit is completely ripe before she can have another. Then talk with her about how much better the strawberry tasted when she waited until it was ripe. This is true of many things. If we are patient, things will be much sweeter.

If gardening is too time-consuming or isn't practical for you, you can also teach this object lesson by purchasing ripe and unripe fruit from the grocery store. Then, the next time your child is acting impatient, ask her if she really wants "the bitter fruit of impatience," or if she would rather wait for "the sweetness that comes from being patient."

Jealousy

A wealthy and powerful man with two sons died. In his will, he gave the family business to the older son. To his younger son, he gave his favorite book of short stories. The younger son was jealous of his brother's good fortune and cut off all contact with him. Tossing his father's well-worn book aside, he ran off to live a life of bitterness and rebellion.

Years later, the older brother began another successful company and called his brother, asking him to come home and run their father's business. The young man was thrilled. Finally he would get to experience the life of power he had so desperately wanted.

When he arrived home, he took over the company—but he hated it. The younger son was artistic and creative; he wasn't made for the business world. Under his leadership, the company had to file for bankruptcy. The son lost everything.

As he was packing to leave home, he ran across the book his father had left him. He sat down on the bed and, for the first time, opened it. Out fell three pieces of paper. The first document was the deed to his grandmother's cabin in New England. The second piece of paper was a check for $100,000. And the third was a letter from his father. It read, "Son, you have the talent to write many great stories like the ones in my favorite book. While your brother runs the business, I want you to take a year, live in your grandmother's cabin, and write your first novel. I believe you have the potential to inspire many people with your words. I love you. Dad."

This story is meant to encourage our children to be content with the gifts their Father in heaven gives them. God knows what will ultimately bring us the most happiness. What He has given us may appear small in comparison with what other people have, but as we mature, we'll realize that God knew exactly what He was doing when He made us the way He did.

Laziness

Proverbs 6:6–11 reads: "Go to the ant, you sluggard; consider its ways and be wise! It has no commander, no overseer or ruler, yet it stores its provisions in summer and gather its food at harvest.

"How long will you lie there, you sluggard? When will you get up from your sleep? A little sleep, a little slumber, a little folding of the hands to rest—and poverty will come on you like a bandit and scarcity like an armed man."

These scriptures can encourage our kids to be diligent. Solomon, the writer of Proverbs, uses the ant as an example of hard work because it takes the initiative to forage for food, defend the colony, and take care of its young. But he also points out the dangers of laziness; he reminds us that the best opportunity for a burglar to break into a house is when the owner is asleep. Similarly, when we choose to glide by instead of working hard, Satan, the king of thieves, can rob us of God's blessings.

Listening

Set up an obstacle course in your living room or backyard. This can be as simple as placing some chairs, small tables, shoes, phone books, and perhaps a large bowl of water (assuming you're outside) around for your kids to avoid. Blindfold your child and have him begin the course. In order to miss the obstacles, he must listen carefully to his parent's directions. To make it even more challenging, have siblings yell opposing instructions to trip him up. The only way to successfully finish the course is to be able to tune out all voices but Mom's or Dad's.

We too must listen carefully to our heavenly Father's "gentle whisper" (see 1 Kings 19:12) to navigate the obstacles of life.

Lying

Aesop's fable "The Boy Who Cried Wolf" powerfully illustrates the importance of telling the truth and maintaining trust.

A young shepherd boy was given responsibility for watching

over and caring for his master's sheep. The days were long and uneventful. One especially boring day, the boy decided to have some fun. The sheep were grazing peacefully at the edge of the forest when he yelled at the top of his lungs, "Wolf! Help! Wolf!" The villagers of the nearby town heard his cries and ran to the pasture to rescue the boy and his sheep. But when they arrived, they found only a small boy doubled over in laughter.

A few days later, the boy again shouted, "Wolf! Help! Wolf!" The villagers raced to the rescue for the second time, but were again met by a laughing boy.

One evening, a wolf did appear and began attacking the sheep. The boy screamed in terror, "Wolf! Help! Wolf!" But this time the villagers refused to be fooled; they continued with their tasks, ignoring his cries for help. As the boy stood by, helpless, the wolf killed many of his sheep. The moral of the story is: No one believes a liar—even when he's telling the truth.

Obedience

Naaman, a famous commander of the Syrian army, had an incurable skin disease called leprosy. He had lived with it for years, but one day he heard news that gave him hope: There was a prophet in Samaria who could cure him.

With the king's permission and loaded down with gifts, Naaman went to visit this prophet, Elisha. Before he arrived at the prophet's house, however, he was met by Elisha's messenger, who told him to dunk himself seven times in the Jordan River. If he did, he would be healed.

Naaman was furious. Was this prophet too haughty to deliver the information personally? And how could a bath help, anyway? The Jordan River didn't look any more special than the rivers at home in Syria.

Naaman was about to storm off in anger when his servant stopped him. "Sir," he began nervously, "if the prophet had told you to do something grand, you would have. What will you lose by following this simple instruction?"

Naaman could see his servant had a point. So he swallowed his pride, stopped his arguing, and obeyed Elisha, dunking himself in the river seven times. And he was completely healed. (See 2 Kings 5.)

This story is full of truths about obedience: To learn obedience, you should obey in the small things without arguing, even when you don't understand or agree.

Perseverance

One day while I was sitting beneath a tree at the base of a large hill, something caught my eye. A young girl was traveling with a man I assumed was her father. As they hiked the steep path together, the man stooped down, picked up a rock, and put it in her empty backpack. He repeated this every few feet. Despite this, the girl pressed on, but before reaching the top, she fell from the weight of her burden.

That load is too heavy for such a small child! I thought angrily.

Unable to watch any longer, I raced to her defense. When I reached the top, I saw that she was resting in her father's arms. He had picked her up and carried her the rest of the way.

After catching my breath, I grilled the man. "What kind of father are you?" I demanded. "Why would you purposely make your daughter stumble by increasing her burden?"

He pointed to a distant summit. Beyond many larger hills and deep valleys stood a beautiful castle. He explained: "My daughter is a princess and that is her home. There are challenging roads ahead of her that you cannot see from the foot of the hill. She must be strengthened for the journey ahead. There will come a time when I will remove the stones she is carrying one by one. In the meantime, I will walk beside her, and she will learn to lean on me."

Pestering

When I was a little girl, my family would spend one Sunday afternoon each year with all my aunts, uncles, and cousins. Each spring, we would bring large utility boxes and a yummy picnic lunch and head to the park, where we'd slide down the grassy hills on pieces of cardboard.

That was only half the fun! Afterward, we'd set up the picnic tables with our family favorites: Aunt Betty's pea salad, Aunt Pauline's fruit salad, and my mom's broccoli and cheese casserole. Unfortunately, the flies also loved these special dishes. As soon as we removed the lids from the containers, we'd all start waving our arms around like a bunch of hula dancers to shoo the pests away.

It was aggravating! As soon as we shooed one off of Uncle Leo's potato salad, another would land on Uncle James' baked beans. We'd usually scarf down our food, pack up, and be forced to leave the park early.

Kids can also be pests—especially when siblings are involved. So, kiddos, the next time you start "bugging" someone, remember that all it takes is a little bit of pestering to ruin the whole picnic.

Prioritizing

Gather a mason jar, a cup of uncooked rice, and some walnuts still in their shells. (If you don't have these ingredients, you can use sand and large rocks.) Instruct your child to fill the jar with the rice and then count how many walnuts she can fit inside. Then have her empty out the rice and try the exercise again. Ask her if she can think of a way to fit more walnuts into the jar. This time have her drop the walnuts into the jar first and then pour the rice in. Now have her count the walnuts. (She should have been able to put more in.)

Afterward, explain the exercise: If we take care of our top priorities (represented by the walnuts) first, the other, less essential activities (symbolized by the rice) will always find their place. For example, if we take the time every morning to read our Bibles and pray before we "take on the day," we can usually find the time to accomplish what's necessary.

This exercise also helps to illustrate the importance of doing chores or homework before, for instance, watching cartoons. And it can teach the importance of saving money: If we spend our allowance only on "rice" (such things as candy and trinkets), we'll never have enough left for what we really want.

Use your imagination with this one.

Self-Control

I knew a man who made his living as a truck driver. Every week for 15 years, he drove the same route through the Rocky Mountains. Because the drive was so familiar, he soon became too confident: He stopped testing his brakes before beginning the descent into a small town for deliveries. He even ignored the highway warning signs, designed to prompt truck drivers pulling heavy loads to check their brakes before making the steep descent.

One day, as he was driving along, his left arm hanging out the window, panic seized him. His brake pedal was pressed down to the floor, and the truck wasn't slowing down. His mind raced as he wondered where the next pullout—the emergency gravel incline that stops trucks—was on the road.

Up ahead, he saw one. It was his only hope for survival. With trembling hands and every ounce of strength within him, he steered the speeding truck off its path and up onto the pullout. As his truck stopped midway up the incline, he thanked God. He had driven this route hundreds of times, and he knew that it was the last pullout nearby. If he had driven one more mile, it would have been too late.

I made up this story to help Tucker recognize the warning signs of losing self-control and to have a plan of escape prepared if that happened. I drew this truck driver's route on a piece of paper, and he still has it hanging on his bulletin board. It serves as a reminder to find the nearest "pullout" and regain self-control before his anger becomes destructive and hurts him and probably others as well.

Trusting in Parents

In Corrie tenBoom's *The Hiding Place,* she asked her father what the word "sexism" meant. This is how Corrie remembered the moment: "He turned to look at me, as he always did when answering a question, but to my surprise he said nothing. At last he stood up, lifted his traveling case from the rack over our heads, and set it on the floor.

"'Will you carry it off the train, Corrie?' he said.

"I stood up and tugged at it. It was crammed with the watches and spare parts he had purchased that morning.

"'It's too heavy,' I said.

"'Yes,' he said. 'And it would be a pretty poor father who would ask his little girl to carry such a load. It's the same way, Corrie, with knowledge. Some knowledge is too heavy for children. When you are older and stronger you can bear it. For now you must trust me to carry it for you.'

"And I was satisfied. More than satisfied—wonderfully at peace. There were answers to this and all my hard questions—for now I was content to leave them in my father's keeping."[1]

This passage has been a Godsend to me whenever one of my children walks into the room while Steve is watching the news and hears words like "rape," "incest," or "homosexuality." I don't shun open, honest communication, but I won't discuss something heavy until my child is ready. I don't want the world to burden my kids when they are too young.

Trusting in God

The only survivor of a shipwreck had been washed up on a small, uninhabited island. He prayed feverishly for God to rescue him, and every day he scanned the horizon for help, but none seemed forthcoming. Exhausted, he managed to build a little hut out of driftwood to protect him from the elements and to store his few possessions. But one day, after scavenging for goods, he arrived home to find his little hut in flames, the smoke rolling up to the sky. The worst had happened; everything was lost. He was stunned with grief and anger.

"God, how could You do this to me?" he cried.

There was no answer, and the man fell asleep, exhausted and broken.

Early the next day, however, he was awakened to the sight of a ship approaching the island. Amazingly, it had come to rescue him.

"How did you know I was here?" the man asked, astonished.

"We saw your smoke signal," the captain replied.

This story reminds our kids that while it's easy to get discouraged when things go wrong, they shouldn't lose heart. God is at work in their lives, even in the midst of pain and suffering. A burning hut may simply be a smoke signal summoning God's grace!

Wisdom

A wealthy man was interviewing potential limousine drivers. The first applicant assured him, "I'm the greatest race car driver around. See the cliff over there? I'll begin 200 yards back, reach speeds up to 100 miles per hour, and then brake to a full stop inches from the edge. You'll be safe with me!"

Sure enough, he accomplished exactly that. He was taken aback, however, when the man declared, "You're a fine driver, but not what I'm looking for in a chauffeur."

The next candidate was a professional stuntman. He, too, performed a death-defying maneuver with the car as he sped along as close as he could to the edge of the canyon without driving over. But the rich man didn't want to hire him, either.

By this time, the gentleman was getting worried and wondered out loud whether he would ever find the right person for the job. Just then, a young man who'd been watching the interviews approached him.

"Pardon me, sir," he said tentatively, "but did I hear that you have a position for hire?"

The gentleman looked doubtfully at the boy. "Yes, son, but I'm looking for a chauffeur, and you are much too young."

"I know I'm young," the boy persisted, "but I'm very mature— and I just got my license. May I at least show you my driving skills?"

The gentleman spoke brusquely. "Fine, but you must use your own car."

The boy thanked the man and reassured him that he would not be sorry. He then hopped into his old jalopy and drove toward the canyon. He had not traveled more than a few yards when, recognizing the danger that lay ahead, he slowed down and turned the car around.

Pulling alongside the gentleman, the boy said, "If it's all the same to you, sir, I'd like to demonstrate my skills somewhere less dangerous."

The gentleman breathed a sigh of relief. "That won't be necessary. I've lived long enough to have learned that fulfillment comes not from living life on the edge at full speed, but from living wisely, at a safe distance from danger. You're hired."

Don't see how close you can get to sin without falling. True wisdom means seeing how far away you can get.

Chapter 4

Seeing the Big Picture

$\mathscr{A}$fter *The Facts of Life* had been on the air for a few years, the producers of the show determined that it was time for my character, "Blair," to lose her virginity. In their minds, this was a normal part of growing up and the show needed to address the subject. I expressed my commitment not to be a part of perpetuating that lie, and they graciously did not press the issue.

During the last season, the producers, knowing my convictions, instead chose the character "Natalie" to participate in the traditional "facts of life." Before writing the script, they once again approached me—this time, offering to have "Blair" advocate abstinence within the episode.

In response, I asked to be written completely out of the script. And once again, the producers generously granted my request. Looking back, I sometimes wonder if I made the right decision. It was an ideal opportunity to offer girls a worthy alternative. But at the time, I felt strongly convicted to not even *appear* on an episode that dealt positively with premarital sex. My most immediate reason was that one of my young fans might be channel-surfing and, upon seeing me, stop to watch the episode. As a result, she could be sucked into the propaganda being sold that having sex before marriage is okay.

I made this choice assuming I wouldn't be paid for the episode, because I wasn't going to be a part of it. This was a costly decision, but it wasn't a difficult one. I believed Jesus completely when He said, "Everyone who has left houses or brothers or sisters or father or mother or children or fields for my sake will receive a hundred times as much and will inherit eternal life" (Matthew 19:29).

I realized very early in life that this earthly existence is merely the pregame show, a prelude to the endless glory of heaven. Having this mind-set as a young girl helped me to make godly choices that positively influenced my entire life. That's why, as a mom, I want to train my children to also look past today, to eternity. I'm convinced it's one of the most valuable lessons I can possibly teach them.

There are many ways to focus our children's eyes on eternity, and I've outlined some of those principles throughout this chapter. But as we set out to shape our kids, we must first remember that our ability as parents to instill a long-term perspective in our children is directly tied to our own commitment to maintain one. Like so much of parenting, it begins with us.

LOOKING DOWN THE ROAD

When our children are young, it's easy to become myopic, or shortsighted, in our vision. We zoom around, putting out the fires in front of us, always keeping a fire extinguisher handy, but never taking the time to think about installing a water-sprinkler system for the future. It's important, however, that we stop every so often in the midst of firefighting to look down the road. Are we still guiding our children in the right direction?

You know what happens if you stare at your feet while walking. You begin to lose your balance and don't even realize you've veered off course until it's too late. We need to pause in our journey and take a good, long, loving look at our little ones. We need to take the time to assess their strengths and weaknesses and evaluate what those same character traits will look like down the road in a teenager and, eventually, in an adult.

Sneaking a cookie from the jar when Mom isn't looking is easily punishable with a slap on the hand. Sneaking a pair of earrings from the local mall may also be handled by a slap on the wrist—with handcuffs. Cheating at a board game may result in being sent back to "Start." Cheating on a test in high school will also send you home—possibly in expulsion. Getting angry and hitting a parent would warrant a time-out. Getting angry and hitting a teacher could warrant another form of "time-out"—behind bars.

Don't misunderstand. I'm not saying that if little Susie steals a cookie, she's going to end up in jail someday. What I *am* saying is this: Ignoring moral issues when the implications are toddler-size can reap perilous, teenager-size repercussions. We can't avoid our children's peccadilloes forever—but when would you rather deal with these moral and character issues? When your child is five years old or 15?

JESUS MUSCLES

Let's look at one specific area: self-control. This is a good trait to study, because we can begin helping our children master their impulses early in life. As a toddler, Haven tended to "lose it" whenever her every wish was not granted. When she had a tantrum, we calmly picked her up and placed her in the playpen until she regained self-control and settled down. Tucker, on the other hand, hit his sisters with the nearest toy whenever he didn't get his way. Steve and I dealt with him by first taking away the toy, which usually resulted in much screaming and dispute. Then we sent him to the end of the hall (much less fun than his room) until he could sincerely apologize and give his wounded sister a hug. Oh, the high cost of losing self-control!

As our children have gotten older, we have tried even harder to instill godly character traits like self-control. In some sense, Steve and I have become like "personal trainers" who daily oversee our kids' spiritual "workouts" in an attempt to strengthen their spiritual resolve and willpower.

Now that they are in grade school, we're focusing on specific problem areas. Tucker, at age nine, spends the majority of his time learning to bridle his tongue. He uses every chance to make someone laugh, even if it's inappropriate or hurtful humor. It takes all his resolve to restrain himself. But he's working on his "Jesus muscles" —strengthening his spirit—and they get stronger each day. Tucker is learning the true meaning of the scripture "A man who lacks judgment derides his neighbor, but a man of understanding holds his tongue" (Proverbs 11:12).

Clancy's need for self-control is in a much different area. If given the chance, she will cry when things don't go her way. While she is sensitive by nature, she has also learned that a few well-placed tears work wonders for getting what she wants. She gains godly discipline every time we require her to calm down and relay her latest trauma in a normal rather than whiny tone of voice.

I'm grateful for the opportunity to train my children now, within the safety of the family, while they are small and the consequences are smaller. By teaching them daily to flex their spiritual muscles, it is Steve's and my most fervent prayer that our children will develop the strength of character to face whatever challenges might lie ahead and to make wise choices. But a teen or an adult who has never been taught the value of discipline could wind up deeply in debt, perennially unemployed, promiscuous, or addicted to drugs, alcohol, or food, among other things.

To have the grit to continually instill these godly qualities into our kids' lives, we must keep our focus on the big picture. Remember— whatever we deny our children now is for their good later.

PLANTING POSITIVE SEEDS

Developing a big-picture approach to parenting is more than simply pruning our children's negative traits. We must also help our kids to develop positive qualities, qualities that will constitute their strengths when they are teenagers. Encourage your little ones to pray out loud at the dinner table *before* they start the teenage mumble. Or let them read their Bibles when they go to bed. Young children may see it as a good excuse to stay up longer, but you'll know that even doing these small things can help to engrain godly habits early.

Most positive habits and character traits can and should be taught and encouraged from the earliest possible age. This concept was driven home to me when I had to deal with modesty issues and boy-girl relationships with four-year-old Haven when she developed her first crush on her 12-year-old Uncle Casey's best friend, Brandon. I knew it was serious when she came in one day and announced, "I've decided I don't want to be a boy anymore!"

Until this declaration, she had wanted only to wear jeans. And the only dresses she would wear to church had to be made out of denim.

I tried to conceal my delight at her statement by casually asking, "Really? Why don't you want to be a boy anymore?"

"Because I've found my 'marrying man'!" proclaimed Haven.

My joy was short-lived. A few days later, she sauntered downstairs, dressed in shorts and a midriff-cut jacket, which was intended to go over one of her Sunday dresses.

"Haven," I told her, "you'll need to go put on the little dress that goes with that jacket."

"I want to wear it like this because I think Brandon will like it," she announced.

My eyes widened, but I merely said, "No. It's not modest, and you will need to change."

"Well, when I grow up and have my own family, I can wear it!" Haven fought back.

"Yes, but I trust you will have the wisdom to dress modestly when you grow up," I concluded.

And I believe she will. But now, while she's still young, I intend to help her understand what the Bible means when it says that a godly woman dresses "modestly, with decency and propriety, not with braided hair or gold or pearls or expensive clothes, but with good deeds, appropriate for women who profess to worship God" (1 Timothy 2:9).

My struggles with Haven didn't end there, however. The next thing I knew, she was asking if she could call Brandon to see whether he was back from vacation. I explained that in our family, girls would not call boys. She asked if boys could call boys.

Upon my affirmation, she quickly implored, "Then can Tucker call to see if Brandon is back?"

Yikes! This is happening too early! I understand that a little polka-dot bikini on a six-year-old does not have the same effect it would if worn by a 16-year-old, and puppy love can't be compared to high school dating rituals. But I don't want to explain to my teenager in 10 years why I'm suddenly moving boundary markers. I know it will be much easier to establish safe moral limits sooner rather than later.

AN ETERNAL PERSPECTIVE

As much as we parents need to focus on the big picture of our children's choices, we also need to help them see an even bigger picture: eternity. By embracing this perspective ourselves, and teaching our children to focus on the reality of heaven and the promises waiting for them there, we can greatly influence the choices they make here on earth.

It's important to explain to our children that we are only visitors here on earth and that our real home is in heaven with God (see 1 Peter 2:11). I tell my kids, "The amount of time we will spend here, in contrast to our heavenly home, is like going to a friend's house to play after school compared with the total amount of time you'll live at home until you grow up." I'm aware that my analogy is flawed, but it seems to help my kiddos.

Having this eternal mind-set can make a dramatic difference in a child's life. Haven has struggled with insecurity as long as I can remember. Perhaps it's because she is the middle child, or maybe she simply inherited some of her daddy's melancholy temperament. But around the age of four she heard the Old Testament story of the orphan Esther, who becomes queen and ultimately is used by God to save the Jewish people. Haven somehow identified with the destiny so apparent in Esther's life. No matter how unlike a queen Haven may feel, she believes that God has also put her on earth "for such a time as this" (Esther 4:14).

This sense of an eternal purpose has been a lifeline for Haven. And knowing that the God of the universe has a plan and an eternal home for *your* children should create a lifeline for them, too, helping them to make sound decisions each day.

INVESTMENT COUNSELING

Jesus cautions us to store up our treasures in heaven rather than on earth, where they can be stolen or destroyed or simply wear out over time (see Matthew 6:19). So let's look at how we are teaching our children to view their resources of time, talent, and money in light of eternity.

Most families I know (mine included) spend much of their time running around at a frantic pace. Soccer, basketball, baseball, and football seasons crowd into one another. After tossing in swim meets, band camps, ballet recitals, and karate tournaments, we soon find ourselves painfully overdrawn. Our children don't have to seize every opportunity, take every lesson, and play every sport by the time they are 10 years old in order to be well-rounded. Once again, it's a matter of perspective.

In our family, we try not to be involved in more than one sport or activity at a time—for the whole family. This means Clancy may have to sit it out during baseball season, but then Tucker has to take a break when gymnastics starts again. Steve and I know that as our kids get older, they'll have to pass up many "good" opportunities if we stick to our rule. But paring down on activities has allowed us to slow down and focus on God's "best," for our children individually and for our family as a whole.

Hey, moms and dads! Let's try to keep the bigger picture in mind the next time the sign-up sheets are passed around. What will be more eternally significant in your child's life: a shelf full of trophies or the simple rewards that come from gathering together as a family around the dinner table? Going and doing need to be examined periodically in light of what God considers valuable. Another way to become better stewards of your family's time is by discovering your children's God-given abilities. Doing so will give you the insight you need to teach them how to invest their time *and* talents according to God's plan for their futures.

Once you have found a particular strength the Lord has placed in your child, focus on that area and pursue excellence. Think deep instead of wide. Also, be careful not to overlook giftedness that can seem commonplace, such as service, hospitality, or compassion. You may have to create your own venues for these talents to be exercised, and you will probably need to test the waters to discover your children's gifts, but the effort will reap long-lasting benefits in their lives and in the lives of those they touch.

As our children begin to discern what their God-given talents are, they may be tempted to view their abilities by the world's measuring stick. It's easy to believe society's definition of success, as opposed to how God characterizes achievement. At the time of this writing, Haven wants to be an actress. While I want to encourage her natural inclinations, I also want to protect her from the false weights and measures of the world, which are especially prevalent in the entertainment industry. In 99 percent of the situations I've observed, children who are thrust into show business suffer a "lose/lose" proposition. If they become successful as a child, when they are not mature enough to handle it, they will have no place to go but down when their 15 minutes of fame are up. The majority— those who don't find successful roles—are faced with rejection daily and told after every audition that they are "too short, too fat, too plain, or just not good enough."

Because this constant rejection can be heartbreaking, Steve and I have chosen to provide Haven with opportunities through church and school to expand her natural talents as an actress without introducing her to "the business." Of course, these venues won't make her any money, but we believe withdrawing the lure of money makes it infinitely easier to find God's will, no matter what the situation.

Be sure to teach your little ones that the reason for their natural, God-given talents is not so shortsighted as to simply get a college scholarship, make a lot of money, or become famous. God intends for gifts to be shared and given away to others to strengthen His kingdom. If your children love gardening, remind them that flowers could cheer their elderly neighbors or grandparents. Perhaps your child is a young Rembrandt. Wouldn't a bright Crayola masterpiece brighten the hospital room of a sick friend? This may not bring your kids much money or recognition, but teaching them to honor God with their talents will reap greater, longer-lasting rewards.

GOD'S ECONOMY

Besides instructing our children to be good stewards of their God-given gifts, we also have a clear responsibility to influence their perspective on money. Did you know that God talks about money so often in Scripture that, as a subject, it is second only to love? God gives us the ability and direction to care for our needs through hard work, but He makes it equally clear that, while we must do our part, it is ultimately His responsibility to provide for us. I believe the Bible teaches that the primary reason monetary blessing exists is so that we can give money away (see Luke 6:38). We should encourage our children to give at every opportunity. And as always, the best way to encourage them is through our own example. We want to instill God's money management ideals in their hearts.

One way I train my children to be prudent with their money is by using home bank accounts, which I've set up for each of them. Whenever they receive money, they bring it to me, and I record it in their various accounts. We started out putting 10 percent into their tithe account, 10 percent into their savings account, and 80 percent into their spending account. But I didn't like the message I was sending by equating the value of saving with the privilege of tithing. So we resolved this by putting five percent into savings and opening up a "missionary" account to deposit the other five percent to support a missionary from our church. This also gave them an opportunity to look outward at the world.

God's economy is much more than about tithing money, though. It's about cultivating an overall spirit of giving as well. Even in the most everyday activities, we can teach our kids to see heaven from earth. For instance, I've developed a creative game to address the conflict that occurs between siblings whenever, for example, there is a leftover or odd number of cookies. Suppose I tell Haven and Clancy that they can share the rest of a bag of Oreos. Usually a fight will ensue after several minutes, because they both want the extra cookie. But rather than breaking it in two and hearing the inevitable "She got the bigger half," I ask them, "Who wants the blessing now, and who wants it in heaven?"

My kids know enough about God's economy to realize that their reward in heaven will be much more than a measly cookie. It usually doesn't take long for one of them to give up the treat. (And when they both want the blessing in heaven, I figure *I'll* just have to eat the extra cookie!)

Aside from teaching them about heavenly versus earthly blessings, this approach also teaches our children delayed gratification. But even better, it makes them more like Jesus, who was willing to sacrifice His life for us because of the joy that was set before Him (see Hebrews 12:2).

BONUSES, INCENTIVES, AND REWARDS

If you find it difficult to teach these long-term values to your kids, you might try setting a little joy before them, in the form of incentives. I don't think there is anything wrong with using incentives to help our children make good choices. Even God told the children of Israel, "See, I am setting before you today a blessing and a curse—the blessing if you obey the commands of the LORD your God that I am giving you today" (Deuteronomy 11:26–27). If He's not above giving rewards for obedience to His children, then neither am I! God seems to know that children respond well to them. Why, the first commandment with a promise is "Honor your father and your mother, so that you may live long in the land the LORD your God is giving you" (Exodus 20:12). I believe that in a subtle way, an occasional reward actually helps our children develop an eternal perspective. As they learn to deny themselves now, they can anticipate greater rewards in heaven.

While in the midst of writing this book, I have had to require my children to do their schoolwork more independently. This has been an especially arduous task for Tucker, who sometimes takes until 6:00 P.M. to finish all his work. (To give you some perspective, Haven is doing the same work and is outside playing with the dog by noon.) To help Tucker, I set up an incentive plan. I bought him a packet of baseball cards and told him if he finished his work by 12:00, I would give him five cards. If he finished by 1:00, I would give him four, and so on. It was amazing. Tucker raced through his schoolwork and was putting all five of his new baseball cards in his trading card album by 11:30. Needless to say, we hopped in the car to go buy another packet of cards for the next day.

On the way, Haven got wise to this plan and piped up, "What do I get if I finish all my work quickly?"

Silly me, I asked, "Do you feel that you need extra motivation to get your work done?"

Haven already had an idea brewing. "Yes," she said. "I think you could fill my bubble gum machine with gumballs, and if I finish by 12:00, you could give me five pennies."

I thought that was only fair—not really necessary, but fair. I waited a moment for Clancy to speak up. When she didn't, I inquired, "Clancy, do you feel that it would help you to have a little incentive?"

"No. Just knowing I'm pleasing the Lord is enough for me," she answered sweetly and sincerely.

Clancy's response floored me! But don't give Steve and me too much credit for unbelievable parenting skills. Our system of incentives doesn't always work *that* well. For example, one winter when his allergy/behavioral problems were at their height, seven-year-old Tucker was over the edge, and I was headed there fast. Seeing that I was on the verge of losing it, Steve offered to take time off and keep the kids so I could go a day early to our church's women's retreat and rejuvenate.

The night before I left, Steve told Tucker, "Now, son, tomorrow we're going to have 'boot camp.'"

Tucker perked up. "You mean we're going to exercise?"

Steve was quick to nip that idea in the bud. "No," he said sternly, "we're going to work from 'son' up to 'son' down and learn to make the right choices, even when it's hard."

Tucker, having played character-building, incentive games like this before, nodded. "Oh, I get it," he said, a wide smile on his face. "You promise me a toy and then if I do the right thing all day long, you give it to me!"

Steve sighed. "Well, yes."

Obviously, Tucker had participated in these types of exercises so much that the true meaning of the game—making good choices to develop a big-picture perspective—had lost some of its effect.

As we've found, it's important to maintain a balance in doling out rewards. If you read on in Deuteronomy 11, you'll discover that God didn't just set a blessing before the children of Israel; He also set forth a curse. (I prefer to call it a "correction.") He knew the value of using both rewards *and* corrections to shape the behavior of His children.

We'll explore the topic of administering correction in the next chapter. In the meantime, I've gathered a list of my favorite bonuses, incentives, and rewards to inspire our little ones to look at the big picture.

Seeing the Big Picture

Toolbox

Motivational Rewards

Charts and Calendars

- One of my favorite reward systems is the age-old sticker chart. I purchase little chart pads at a teachers' supply or stationery store, along with tiny stickers. Every time one of my children is kind, obeys without arguing, reads a book, and so on, I'll instruct her to put a sticker on her personal chart. When it is filled with stickers (there are typically around 20 squares), she can go to the "treasure chest." In our home, this chest is a little shelf filled with videos, dime-store toys, or other items I want them to have but don't want to hand out for no reason. If you don't want to keep stocking a treasure chest, you might set forth a specific prize that can be obtained once the chart is completed.

- Get an unused check register, and give it to your child. Each positive behavior is worth a set amount of points (recorded in the "deposits" column). Each negative behavior costs a set amount of points (recorded as a "debit"). The behaviors and their reward or consequence amount are written in the front of the register. Also written is a list of privileges and what each privilege costs in points. For example, 30 minutes of television or video game time cost 30 points. Since taking out the trash without being told is also worth 30 points and he recorded that earlier, you child has enough to buy the privilege. He simply deducts the points in the debit column. The child can also save up for larger privileges like a sleepover that costs 200 points. If he doesn't earn the points or if he loses the points by poor behavior, he isn't allowed the privilege he can't afford.

Chips or Tokens

- At the beginning of the week, I get a bag of Chuck E. Cheese tokens and set up three paper cups with my children's names written on them; we also mark a date on the calendar as "Family Pizza Parlor" night. Then, every day that the kids practice the piano without being told, they get to put a token in their cup. By the end of the week, Steve and I let them spend the tokens they earned on games and rides. (This sure beats doling out expensive tokens like candy!)

- Head out to your nearest teachers' supply store and purchase a small bag of colored chips or tiddledywinks and assign your own value system to them. One idea would be to reward good grades on school papers. For each A, your child earns a blue chip equaling 20 minutes playing video games, watching TV, or playing with a friend. B's earn a yellow chip equaling 10 minutes of fun time. Keep the green chip for an extra five minutes of bonus time, earned by neatness or shown improvement.

- My favorite chips are the chocolate kind! These chips can be given to encourage children to take the initiative to reach out and be sweet to others. Perhaps a handful of chips could be given for calling Grandma just to tell her about their day. Another might be earned for writing a letter or sending an e-mail to a relative who lives out of state. Drawing a picture or playing checkers with an elderly neighbor may warrant a whole sheet of cookies full of chips (to share, of course).

- I love games, so this reward was as fun for me as it was for the kids. Sibling conflict had reached a fevered pitch over a period of several days. I had tried everything I could think of to make these kids get along, but they seemed to thrive on aggravating each other. So I declared "Buddy Bingo" day. I had an old cardboard bingo game out in the garage, with a bag full of tokens and a small bingo-ball cage. We set the cage up in the kitchen, and I handed out a card to each child. For every 30 minutes they could survive without arguing or fighting, I would turn the bingo cage and read the letter/number on the ball. We played this all day long, reading off a new ball on the hour and the half hour if there had been peace for the previous 30 minutes. The first person to get a bingo got a prize, and then we kept on playing until bedtime. Whoever had the most spaces covered at the end of the night got to stay up an hour later with Mom and Dad.

Food

- I have a friend who offered her daughter one ingredient to her favorite cookie recipe every time she had her backpack ready by the door the night before school. By the end of the week, she'd earned all the ingredients, and they baked the cookies and enjoyed them together.
- I realize we are supposed to be serving our children healthy snacks, but it's fun to occasionally surprise them with junk-food treats in their lunch boxes. You might add a pastry or a bag of potato chips with a little note that says, "I noticed how nicely your bed was made this morning." The key is to recognize and reward good behavior.
- When Tucker was ready to enter kindergarten, he had to get the standard barrage of immunization shots. Haven and Clancy accompanied us to the doctor's office, and when they

saw what Tucker had to endure before going to kindergarten, they were petrified for themselves. Kicking myself for bringing the girls along and trying to comfort Tucker, I announced, "Okay, for every needle prick, you get a scoop of ice cream. That means Tucker gets a triple scoop today!" I allowed the girls to get a single scoop, but from that moment on, they again looked forward to entering kindergarten.

- Galatians 5:22–23 reads, "The fruit of the Spirit is love, joy, peace, patience, kindness, goodness, faithfulness, gentleness and self-control." Have your children create some "fruit bucks." Cut out nine slips of paper with a different fruit of the Spirit written on each one. Give your kids the opportunity to earn each of the fruit bucks by demonstrating that particular character trait. When all nine bucks have been earned, give them a fruity-tasting surprise. This could be anything from a box of fruity cereal, to making a fruit salad with Mommy, to having a piece of cherry pie or a scoop of strawberry ice cream.

- If you can get your hands on an old gumball machine, it sure makes a cheap, fun reward for only a penny a pop. (Just don't tell your dentist I recommended this!)

- Any tiny candies, such as Skittles, M&M's, candy corn, or Runts, work well to reinforce a certain behavior all day long.

Money
- Of course, money works just about every time when you want to provide incentive. And you can teach your children to tithe the reward money—motivating and teaching in one lesson!

- Think about putting your child's allowance in loose coins in a jar at the beginning of the week. Then every time you hear a disrespectful tone of voice, for example, remove a coin. At the end of the week, whatever is left is theirs to keep.

- My kids dislike running errands. I usually hear complaining throughout the grocery store, dry cleaners, and department store. In order to make them aware of how often they say something negative, I give them each a dollar in nickels before our afternoon errand crusade. Then I inform them that the last errand will be to the drugstore, and whatever change they have left in the bag, they can spend on candy. In the meantime, they must give me a nickel for every negative word spoken while running errands.

- Some children are constantly asking me to help them with things they are capable of doing for themselves. (I'm not naming any names, but I have one of these children living under my roof.) So I respond, "Fine, but it's gonna cost ya." Fill up a jar of dimes. Then when your child asks for help doing something that he can easily accomplish by himself, ask for a dime. (I will even withdraw a dime myself if his plate is left on the table after a meal, his socks are left on the bathroom floor, or I have to put the milk back in the refrigerator.) At the end of the week, if there are any dimes left, he gets to keep them.

- If your children are too young to keep up with real money, try using "play money" bought at the toy store or taken from an old board game. Let them earn some of this money and then take them shopping at "Mommy's store," a supply of items you keep hidden somewhere for occasions like this. Let them purchase from you items like fancy socks, hair bows, a new football, Silly String, and other fun things.

- You're going to need to buy your children some new clothes when the season changes, right? So, how about tying it to good grades? With the exact amounts depending on your budget, it could look like this: Upon receiving the first report card, they could earn $20 for every A toward buying winter clothes, $10 for each B, and $5 per C. Same thing for the next report card when it comes time to buying a few new spring clothes, and again at the end of the school year for a summer wardrobe.

- A wonderful alternative to a regular cash allowance is to put earned money on a Wal-Mart gift card (or wherever you shop most regularly). This leaves the discretionary spending completely between your child and the store. When the card is empty, she can either argue with the store manager or learn how to make it last longer the next time. It also cuts down on the "Can I haves . . ." in the checkout line. You simply answer, "Sure, whip out your card." It makes her think a lot longer about what she really wants.

Rewarding with Time

- It's not too hard to make your own "time card" to punch, and it's a lot of fun. Take a 3x5 index card and list the chores to be completed each day for a week. Then put a string around a hole-punch and tie it up in a convenient place. Have your children punch their cards after they've completed each chore. At the end of the day or week, have them turn the cards in and receive their payment (whatever you've determined ahead of time). But here's the clincher: They can be docked for chores left undone on a specified day. For example, they aren't allowed to sweep the floor twice on Friday to make up for forgetting on Wednesday and Thursday.

- Haven is under the impression that the purpose in life is to see how fast you can accomplish something. Everything she does is at twice the normal speed. Her piano practices last 10 minutes—and sound like an Alvin and the Chipmunks recital. Her homework is often sporadic and sloppy, and with her chores she's less than meticulous. We've had to find ways to reward her for taking longer to complete a task. Believe it or not, she's not allowed to finish a homework assignment in less than 10 minutes, piano practice in less than 30 minutes, or a chore in less than five minutes. If she completes the task carefully and to our satisfaction in the allotted amount of time, she can shave off one minute the next time. If at any time she begins to rush through slip-shod, she must not only do the work again, but I also reset the time to the maximum allowed.

- Another way we've tried to encourage Haven to slow down and do her work more carefully is by rewarding her with TV-watching minutes. For example, if she has a math test of 30 questions, she can earn one minute of TV time for each correct answer and be docked one minute for each incorrect answer. If she misses five problems, she earns 20 minutes of television viewing. If she's 100 percent correct, she earns double the TV time—for example, an hour of viewing. (Hey, that's enough time to watch two episodes of *The Facts of Life* reruns!)

- Often, the best time to have family devotions is right before bed. For starters, everyone is fed, clean, and in comfy pajamas. Even better, it becomes a reward, since the kids get to stay up later. If they are well behaved and listen attentively, they can stay up longer. If they are inattentive or disruptive, they must go to bed early. Some kids dread having to sit around with the family and talk about the Bible, but even those kids would usually prefer joining in rather than going to bed. It also helps to keep these family times fun. A good family Bible study can be the *Family Night Tool Chest* books.

Rewarding Extra-Good Behavior

- I once ordered a bunch of pencils out of a catalog and had "Caught you doing good!" inscribed on them. I hid them in a drawer and whipped one out whenever I saw one of my kids making a right choice, even when they thought no one would notice.
- Get an old pickle jar, clean it out, and call it the "Pickle a Privilege" jar. Fill it up with little slips of paper with a variety of fun, extra-special privileges written on them. This "Pickle a Privilege" jar is for those times when our children catch us off guard and make one of those extraordinary "just because I want to please God" kinds of choices. When it's time for them to pick a privilege from the jar, have them close their eyes; it's more of a surprise then. Here are just a few privilege ideas: having soda pop with dinner, sleeping

with Mom and Dad for one night, going to a Saturday matinee, choosing the next pizza topping, having a pillow fight, going to work with Dad, eating dessert first, or receiving a "get out of jail free" (correction) card.

- Next Easter time, buy an extra bag of colorful plastic eggs. Keep them handy, along with the Easter basket, for later in the year when your children need an extra nudge of motivation. Fill each egg with a piece of candy or a quarter, a coupon for extra TV time, a slip of paper with a special privilege written on it, and so on. Then every time a child makes a choice that "defeats Satan" as Jesus did when He rose from the dead on Easter Sunday, he or she gets to choose an egg from the basket.

- We've all been asked to donate money to a favorite charity and in exchange had our name put in a raffle box for a chance to win the grand prize. Try this variation at home. Designate a prize at the beginning of the week, or buy a toy and set it beside the "Acts of Charity" box. Throughout the week, whenever one of your children does something from a loving heart, like obeying, peacemaking, or serving a family member, that child gets to put his or her name on a ticket and into the box. At the end of the week, you pull out a raffle ticket and declare the grand prize winner. The more acts of charity, the more chances to win.

- Have you seen those red dinner plates that read "You Are Special Today" around the edges? They're usually used for birthdays and such, but I'm sure you can find occasions to bring one out much more often. Award the use of the special plate any time your child does something that day to deserve special recognition, and then make a big deal about it around the dinner table that night.

Rewarding Gratitude
- To instill the importance of gratitude, postpone a child's privilege to play with a gift until the thank-you note is written. This only prolongs the pleasure five or 10 minutes, but it says a lot about the importance of being thankful.
- Consider starting a new tradition by putting new "Thank You" note stationery in your children's Christmas stockings, or by wrapping cute note cards as an extra gift for their birthday party. That will make it easier for them to write thank-you notes—and the more quickly they do that, the more quickly they can play with their gifts.
- Our church hosts a Harvest Festival each year on October 31. This is a wonderful opportunity for our children to dress up in costumes and get candy without "celebrating" Halloween. The first year, my kids got to keep only half of the candy they received. They kept forgetting to say, "Thank you," when candy was passed out at the various game booths. Our family rule is that if you forget to be grateful, you must give the candy to Mom and Dad.

Miscellaneous Rewards

- Getting children out of bed and ready for school in the morning can often leave everyone either crying or screaming as they head out the door. If you're fortunate, there will be a great cartoon on television 30 minutes before it's time to leave the house. If there isn't, then tape one of your kids' favorite shows and let them watch the show before school *if* they are completely ready to leave. This encourages everyone to get the morning routine finished early, and the day will start much more peacefully.

- Kids seem to have so much homework these days that it's hard for them not to become overwhelmed sometimes. In Tucker's case, if the load is too heavy, he often gives up. I help motivate him by breaking his schoolwork into smaller, "bite-size" chunks. I make a list for him that reads something like this: "Do math, then go shoot 50 hoops. Study spelling words, then go feed Checkers. Read three chapters of assigned book, then take a shower." It may appear to prolong the schoolwork, but it reduces the time he spends complaining and daydreaming. In the end, things get finished more quickly.

- Sometimes young kids have a hard time sitting still at the table. Fortunately, they are able to find pleasure in even the smallest things. Buy a couple of candles to light at the dinner table; then tell your child that if she can sit quietly in her chair throughout the meal, she'll be allowed to blow them out.

- Tucker loves LEGOs, but they are very expensive. To get around this problem, Steve and I bought a LEGO pirate ship kit and told Tucker he could earn only one piece at a time from it. We did allow him to open the box and put the first 10 pieces together according to the instruction booklet. But after that, if he wanted another piece, he had to show initiative, such as picking up a toy from the floor instead of stepping over it, or cleaning the toothpaste off the sink after brushing, or even putting his sister's shoes away for her. Eventually, Tucker finished that LEGO ship, and given the changes we saw in him, it was worth every penny we spent on it.

- I come from a long line of readers, and it breaks my heart to confess that my children would much rather watch a video than read a book. In response, we've implemented a plan that makes us all happy. For every 100 pages my kids read, they may rent a family video of their choice. Once their total reaches 1,000 pages, they may *purchase* a family video of their choice.

- I don't know about you, but there are seasons in my children's lives when I feel as if I'm "on" them all the time. I want them to know how much I love—and like—them, but I can't just let some of their behavior and attitudes slide. If you find yourself in this same position, try purchasing a small journal and placing it on your child's nightstand. After he's gone to sleep and before you retire for the evening, write something encouraging in his journal. It could be noticing an area where you see that he's trying, even if he's not quite there yet. It can be calling out a strength that you see buried deep within him. It could even be a moment you especially enjoyed sharing with him during the day. This will not only be an encouragement first thing in the morning, but it will also be a written record of your love and approval that he can turn to when he's stuck in his room for yet another time-out.

- Create an "Honesty Under Pressure" award and frame it. Then whenever you have a child who tells the truth when it would be a lot easier and advantageous to lie, he gets to display the special award in his room all day. When Daddy returns home at the end of the day, he may turn it in to him in exchange for a trip to the ice cream store.

Bible Verses as Models for Good Behavior

- Proverbs 24:3–4—"By wisdom a house is built, and through understanding it is established; through knowledge its rooms are filled with rare and beautiful treasures."

  When your child gets good grades, reward him by allowing him to buy a decoration for his bedroom.

- Proverbs 1:8–9—"Listen my son [daughter] to your father's instruction and do not forsake your mother's teaching. They will be a garland to grace your head and a chain to adorn your neck."

  Buy a necklace for your child and hide it. Then, when your daughter chooses to obey you rather than go her own way, reward her with the necklace.

- Proverbs 25:12—"Like an earring of gold or an ornament of fine gold is a wise man's rebuke to a listening ear."

  Buy gold earrings to give to your daughter the next time she accepts your correction without being defensive or making excuses.

- Proverbs 2:7—"He [God] holds victory in store for the upright, he is a shield to those whose walk is blameless."

  Boys love shields. Buy a toy one and set it up as a reward your son will receive at bedtime if he can go a day with his walk blameless of a particularly vexing behavior.
- Proverbs 10:4—"Lazy hands make a man poor, but diligent hands bring wealth."

  I don't give an allowance to my children for doing chores, but I do pay (reward) them for chores they do diligently and without being reminded.
- Proverbs 4:9—"She [Wisdom] will set a garland of grace on your head and present you with a crown of splendor."

  Buy a fake crown from a party or costume store. Whenever you catch your child choosing wisdom—for example, listening to you attentively, obeying you immediately, or reading her Bible without being told—place the crown on her head and declare her "Queen of the Hour."

Chapter 5

Creative
Correction

I love to play board games—but Steve can't stand them! He says there's already enough competition in his life. To him, it doesn't make sense to create an artificial setting in the comfort of his own home where he must succeed or fail.

Since Steve refused to indulge my cravings for board games, I took matters into my own hands and started a game group. It's a blast! Every Friday, seven or so of us homemakers from various seasons of life get together to play games, eat, and laugh. We originally called ourselves the "Good Medicine Club," based on Proverbs 17:22, which says, "A joyful heart is good medicine" (NASB). Now we go by MomTime because we discovered that we weren't the only mothers who needed time with other moms. What started in my little kitchen has grown into a full-time ministry made up of small groups of moms meeting for food, faith, friends, and fun all over the U.S.

My original handful of friends began meeting many years ago, when our children were small enough to put down for naps while we engaged in our friendly feuds. Our tots have now grown into raucous non-nappers, so they've been relegated to the backyard, where they play outside while we play inside. Once we've locked the back door, they aren't allowed to interrupt us unless there is bleeding involved. (Let me assure you that our game table sits in front of a large window, where we can keep an eye on the children.)

We are all best friends, both the moms and the kids. Our children have grown up together, and we moms have grown *out* together. (Did I mention that we meet over lunch?) I want to introduce you to a few of these wonderful families. As you become acquainted with these ladies and their children, be sure to notice the crazy mix of parenting styles, strengths, and especially weaknesses.

MEET THE GANG

My Best Friend

Let me first introduce you to my dearest woman friend: my mom. I think my mother is the best mom who ever lived. (Mother Theresa doesn't count!) When we were growing up, she lavished my brother Cody and me with encouragement, affection, and adoration. She was very strict with us and always set high standards, but I strove to exceed her expectations, because I loved and wanted to please her.

Mom probably thought she was done with child-rearing when Cody and I were grown. But some time after, when I was 20 years old—surprise!—my brother Casey was born.

At this writing, Casey is in every sense a 16-year-old. He's a handful, and has always been, even *before* he was born—which is undoubtedly why God put him in my mom's capable hands. When she found out she was pregnant, my mom, because she was over 40, had an amniocentesis test performed. The doctor began the sonogram, but was unable to put the amnio needle into Mom's belly because Casey was turning flips, end over end. He would not stay still long enough for the doctor to safely insert the needle. That should have given my mother some indication of what lay ahead for her. Casey learned to walk at nine months; he learned to run at nine months, two days. And believe me, this mover and shaker hasn't stopped since.

My mom is the perfect mother for Casey because she gives him the freedom and space to express himself creatively. The house is strewn with his elaborate video productions and art projects, and Mom has never complained once.

But my mother also knows when to draw the line. Even though Casey is 16, he's not allowed to see PG-13 movies unless my mom has previewed them; he has never been on a date, and he has to talk on the phone in the family room. (Nothing gets past my mom!) Of course, Casey repeatedly pushes these boundaries as he tries to talk his way into having more freedom. But, being as strong-willed as her teenage son, my mother is more than up to the task of going head-to-head with him.

Sometimes my mother worries that the house is too messy or that she's too domineering when it comes to enforcing the rules with Casey. But I believe God uses even our weaknesses to accomplish His will. I see in her a strong, caring woman who knows when to stand firm and when to relax. Casey is growing up to be a bright, creative, godly young man—and my mom is helping him become everything that God has called him to be.

Denise

I have another friend, Denise, who is also dealing with teenage trials. Denise's son Michael has had a rainbow of hair colors, a loud garage band, and a gold stud in his left ear. Recently, he decided he wants to get his tongue pierced.

Though Denise nixed the pierced tongue idea, she does allow Michael a lot of freedom in altering his appearance. She feels that if she tightens the reins too much, her young stallion might bolt. It hasn't been easy. Many times she has called me, wondering if she could have done something differently to make the "straight and narrow" path more appealing to her son. When I tell her, "I don't think so," I'm not just trying to make her feel better. You see, she has another son who is obedient, well-behaved, and doesn't pierce or dye anything—probably the closest thing to what Jesus was like as a 10-year-old. And she's raised both boys the same way.

Denise is a pastor's wife, and I know she sometimes worries that other mothers may judge her because she has chosen to parent a little leniently. But only she, her husband, and God know what's best for their son. I think it says a lot that she still has Michael's love and confidence. And God still has his heart! Though he may struggle sometimes, Michael felt the call early in his life to become a youth pastor. And I wouldn't mind having Tucker in his youth group someday. There's a lot to be said for the compassion and understanding that is gained when we've experienced God's grace firsthand as a teenager.

Janice

I've known Janice since we taught Sunday school together when I was still single. I used to secretly refer to her and her husband as "Barbie and Ken" because they seemed so perfect. After all these years, my opinion hasn't changed.

Even her kids seem perfect. Our kids are the same ages, but that's where the similarity ends. Janice homeschooled her children in their early elementary school years. Her children were learning Greek when mine were still learning the alphabet; they were wading through algebraic discoveries when mine were merely discovering algae in the wading pool; and they were playing Chopin when my kids were pounding out "Chopsticks."

Janice wishes she had relaxed more, as a parent, teacher, and disciplinarian. But I don't know whether God would have wanted it that way. He gave her children great intelligence, and Janice has challenged her kids to use it. I have a hunch that her strictness and high expectations will allow them to accomplish the purposes God has planned for them.

Shawn

Then there is Shawn. Each one of us thinks she is Shawn's best friend, because Shawn is so warm, encouraging, and devoted. She can rattle off all our birthdays by heart. And her monthly phone bills must be high, because she always knows what's going on in everyone's life—not because she's a busybody, but because she's sincerely interested. She has a heart as big as heaven.

Her youngest son is a late bloomer, but he doesn't know it because Shawn is so patient and gentle with him. Even so, Shawn often gets frustrated. Though she is careful not to place undue pressure on her children, she is not as generous with herself. Shawn feels that she is not getting much accomplished in her roles as wife, mother, and teacher. For instance, she homeschools her boys, but she just had a baby, and these days, they're learning more about diapering than deciphering. I think that on God's SAT exam, Shawn's boys are scoring in the ninetieth percentile. They are going to make incredible husbands and fathers, because they're learning firsthand from their mom what it means to love and serve others.

FREE TO BE YOURSELF

Now that I've given you a thumbnail sketch of these incredible moms, I hope you've realized that there is no right or wrong parenting style. The only real qualification that parents need is a sincere and diligent desire to follow God's ways. God knew your strengths and weaknesses when you signed up to be a parent, and He still hired you. So if He doesn't regret giving you the job of raising His children, then you have nothing to feel guilty about. You are free to be yourself. You know your kids and what they need, so trust the insight God has given you. He assures us in 2 Corinthians 12:9–10 that He will be strong where we are weak. All we have to do is depend on Him.

Raising children is a long, arduous process—especially when you feel as though you're constantly correcting them. But remember, God is not finished with our kids. He will always be our children's heavenly Father, and He will continue to parent our little ones, even after they've grown up. Our senior pastor, Dr. Scott Bauer, has said, "God specializes in the impossible; the possible He leaves up to us." These days it may seem impossible to raise godly children, but God can step in and make the impossible a divine reality.

As a matter of fact, God stepped directly into my life when I was a 10-year-old girl in Texas. Although I was raised in a Christian home, my family wasn't attending church regularly. One Sunday morning, my best friend and I wanted an excuse to wear dresses. It just so happened there was a church across the street and two houses down. Perfect! We put on our dresses, hopped on our bicycles, and went to Sunday school.

The best part of that morning was the orange juice and dough-nuts they served during class. The next weekend, I got a hankering for another doughnuts and returned to church. Soon I was attending for a bigger reason than the yummy breakfast. The more I learned about Jesus' love for me, the more I knew I wanted to spend my life serving Him. Within weeks, my whole family started going to church with me, and shortly thereafter, I made my relationship with God official by walking to the altar in the sanctuary and asking Jesus to forgive my sins and live in my heart.

The reason I'm sharing my testimony is to show you what God can do in the life of a child. Even if we as parents do nothing in the way of guidance or correction, God will still be able to accomplish His purposes in our children. Imagine all He can do *with* our help!

TOOLS FOR THE JOB

In the last chapter, we focused on using rewards, incentives, and bonuses to help mold our children. Now we're going to look at utilizing correction.

As I've illustrated in describing my various friends, we all take different approaches to parenting. Just as there isn't one perfect way to parent, there also isn't one "right" method of correction. Ask anyone who does repair work—you've got to have the right tool for the right job. For example, a screwdriver is great for tightening and loosening screws. And though it can be used to pound in a nail, a hammer gets the job done more quickly and effectively. In the same way, we need to use various tools of correction to bring specific results. We may have to try several different tools before we find the one that works best on each child.

With Tucker, the "screwdriver" approach works wel

end up going around and around on an issue, but if I stay in close contact and continue applying pressure, my point eventually sinks in.

This approach doesn't work with Haven, however. She can be a little harder to budge, and I eventually lose my leverage if I just keep pushing. With her, the "hammer"—specifically, the forked end (the side that removes nails)—is usually most effective. When Haven starts heading in the wrong direction, I often have to back her up and redirect her. Sometimes I have to pry things out of her or straighten her up a bit. But we keep trying until she can hold it all together.

With Clancy, we usually need a few scraps of sandpaper. Steve and I are mostly smoothing out the rough edges with our youngest, but every once in a while, we run into a bump that needs some extra sanding.

CALLING IN THE EXPERT

Effective correction involves more than simply using the right tools. You may own a shiny, new Sears Master Craftsman Deluxe triple-decker toolbox filled with the finest Snap-On tools, but there will still be times you need to call in a professional. In other words, even though you may know the best correction methods in the world, sometimes you'll need the guidance of an expert. Well, have I got an expert for you: Jesus!

Fortunately, His Assistant, the Holy Spirit, is on call 24 hours a day (see John 14:26). Many times when I'm experiencing a crisis with one of my kids and don't know what tool to use, I ask the Holy Spirit. Usually within minutes, He gives me an idea. What's so ironic is that often the solution was right in front of me, but I wasn't sure whether I really had the expertise to fix the problem.

In addition to providing the Holy Spirit, God has also given us an owner's manual—the Bible—to help us with our parenting dilemmas. Let me show you a few verses addressing correction that I've highlighted in my Bible: Ecclesiastes 8:11—"When the sentence for a crime is not quickly carried out, the hearts of the people are filled with schemes to do wrong." I found this to be especially true when my children were very young. Back then, it was essential for me to stop whatever I was doing and take care of the correction right away. Most of the time it was inconvenient, but it helped them to more easily associate the correction with their wrongdoing.

It's amazing how the hearts of our children are "filled with schemes to do wrong" when we are either busy or in a public place. Our little ones figure out quickly when and where we won't quickly carry out the "sentence for a crime." Next time they act up in public, shock them by leaving your half-full shopping cart and taking them directly to the car for correction.

Here's another verse from a well-worn page in my Manual: James 1:20—"The anger of man does not achieve the righteousness of God" (NASB). It's easy for me to get busy with things other than my children, like scrapbooking, responding to e-mail, and, well, writing parenting books. When this happens, I tend to yell at my kids rather than actually get up and parent them. My favorite phrases to yell go something like this: "I've told you over and over again to . . . ," or, "If I have to tell you one more time to . . . ," or, "What's it going to take to get you to . . . !" Sound familiar?

But shouting at our children to cooperate is about as effective as trying to steer a car with the horn. When I finally got it through my thick skull that anger doesn't work, I was able to curb it a bit. Think about it this way: We wouldn't yell at a tomato plant to make it produce. That would be ridiculous! All we can do is give the plant support to help it grow in the right direction, clip off the dead leaves, fertilize and water it, and give it plenty of sunshine. In the end, the fruit it produces comes from God—certainly not as a result of our ranting and raving.

What makes this a sad analogy is that tomatoes don't get bruised by our words as our children do. And yelling at our kids does *not* bring them any closer to godliness. Anger may accomplish our immediate goal, but it won't achieve for them the "righteousness of God," which should be our ultimate goal. Rather than scream and yell, we need to develop and enforce in our children a habit of obedience the first time. It may take some cracking down in the beginning; but if our children defy us, we're eventually going to need to correct them. Wouldn't you rather do it after the first transgression, when you're not so frustrated, than after the twentieth, when you've completely lost control?

These are just two of countless verses in the Bible that address the raising of children. I've included more at the end of this chapter, with accompanying practical applications. By giving us His Word, God has provided a wealth of wisdom for parents. Don't be afraid to use His invaluable Manual!

MORE KEYS TO CORRECTION

Here's another principle I've learned: Don't waste your time on threats. I haven't found that exact wording in my Bible, but I think the spirit of it—"Say what you mean, and do what you say"—is there. Threats will only teach kids the art of gambling. They ask themselves, *Will Mom really follow through this time?* Children know when the odds are in their favor, when it's worth the risk to push the limits. So don't say you're going to do anything you can't carry out. If you've established boundaries ahead of time and consequences for crossing them, be prepared to follow through.

There have been many times the follow-through has been harder on me than on my kids. One summer, I grounded Tucker for a week, forgetting about his friend's upcoming laser tag party. I felt awful, but I knew that giving up a party was a small price to pay for the lesson we were trying to teach him. Fortunately, if we exact punishments that leave a strong impression, we'll usually only have to use them once. The key is to know your child. What's really important to her? Playing in the cul-de-sac, at video games, or with friends? Eating special snacks? Watching a favorite television program?

One effective correction is to rescind the privilege of playing with friends. Unfortunately, this punishes the friends, too, but if your child's actions warrant a stiff penalty, use it. It's a great way to teach him that sin not only affects us, but also ripples out and hurts others. For example, last month, Tucker lost the privilege of playing with his friend Josiah after school because he told the baby-sitter no when she ordered him to his room. This upset Josiah terribly, because he had been waiting all week for this day. Tucker needed to call and ask Josiah to forgive him for the disappointment his sin had caused.

When deciding what punishment to use, be careful with your child's feelings. It's a delicate balance between reaching the heart and bruising it. I found this out the hard way. One night my kids were dawdling at bedtime, so I announced, "If all of you are not in bed in 10 minutes, you will have to put yourselves to bed." They scurried about, but Tucker and Haven didn't make it in time; they were having too much fun in the bathroom.

Tucker was upset, but he just put on his *Adventures in Odyssey* tape, turned out his lamp, and went to bed. Haven was unusually quiet, though. Ten minutes later, I felt prompted to check on her. She was in her bed, crying. As I knelt beside her, she whimpered, "I can't go to sleep unless we say our prayers. I feel secure when you pray with me at night."

I had no idea how important it was to Haven that I put her to bed every night. In trying to reach her heart, I had pierced it. I'll be more sensitive next time.

THE IMPORTANCE OF HAVING FUN

Fortunately, correction doesn't always have to involve tears. Believe it or not, you can have fun teaching your children the principles of correction. My kids and I have had a great time "practicing" obedience. When they were little, for instance, I would send them to three different parts of the house with a toy or two. After a few minutes, I'd call, "Clancy, come here."

"Yes, ma'am," she would respond and immediately come running.

Then I'd say, "Haven, it's time to pick up your toys and go home now." She would quickly put her things in the toy box and come find me by the door.

With Tucker, we practiced "arguing" respectfully. "Tucker, I need you," I'd call to him.

"May I please finish my game first?" he would ask.

"No, son," I replied. "We have to pick up Daddy at work."

"Yes, ma'am. I'll be right there," he'd yell as he put away the game.

This correction was great fun, and it prepared my kids for times when the voice of temptation was louder than Mommy's summons.

As they've gotten older, we've relocated our game to the mall. We call it "Mall Madness." As we walk along together, shopping, I will suddenly give them silly commands that they must obey without arguing, such as "Walk backward," or "Stop and touch your toes," or "Give me a kiss." Occasionally I'll throw in a real command, like "Don't touch that," or "No, you may not have an Icee." My favorite curve, however, is to say no to some reasonable request, like "May I go to the bathroom?"

Even in this lighthearted setting, I'm teaching them that as they grow up, there will be times when they'll need to obey commands from us that don't make sense to them or that might even seem unreasonable. But they will be blessed if they trust and obey.

Teaching them about the blessings that follow obedience is the most fun aspect of playing "Mall Madness." I do this by saying in my most authoritarian voice such things as "Go try on that dress, and if it fits, I'll buy it!" or "You have 60 seconds to pick out any action figure on this row. See if you can obey me."

Parenting can be fun. Granted, administering real correction—punishing a child when she has disobeyed—has to hurt a little to be effective, but that doesn't mean it has to be boring. As I mentioned in the first chapter, I've been forced to come up with a variety of ways to get my point across. Many I've made up, some I've borrowed from friends, and others were submitted through the Focus on the Family Web site. It is my pleasure to pass on these creative corrections to you.

Creative Correction

Toolbox

Problem Areas

Bedroom

- If you repeatedly open the door to your child's room only to catch him in an act of disobedience, take your child's bedroom door off the hinges. It sounds harder to do than it actually is. And it works wonders!

- Here's a solution for a perpetually messy bedroom: Explain to your child, "I cannot bear to look at this room anymore—it's too messy! I'm going to turn off the circuit breaker so I can't see it. When it's clean enough for me to tolerate, let me know and I'll turn your power back on."

- Does your daughter love to change clothes, sometimes two or three times a day? This certainly adds to bedroom cleanup and laundry time. Teach her how to fold her clothes and then require her to take all her clothes out of the drawers, refold them, and put them back in the drawers. Explain to her that you have to do twice as much work when she changes clothes more than once a day without permission.

- We often adjust bedtimes according to our children's behavior that day. For each infraction, they must go to bed five minutes earlier, but if they've been extra good, they can earn the right to stay up an extra five minutes.

- Having a struggle at bedtime? Try this: Next time you're dealing with the usual bathroom trips, cups of water, giggling, and talking, call off bedtime. Declare, "Nobody has to go to bed tonight!" Inform them that they may stay up as long as they like—the operative words being *stay up*. Then have each child stand still in the middle of a separate room of the house. Their warm, comfy beds will look awfully good after just a few minutes of standing alone.

- About an hour before bedtime, call for a "Whole House Sweep." Set the timer for 10–15 minutes. During that time, everyone must put things away that are out of place. When the timer buzzes, check the house. Then move bedtime up five minutes for each item left lying around or out of order.

- Because I so desperately need some down time with my husband in the evenings, I have been known to put the kids to bed very early compared to their friends' bedtimes. For instance, I may put Haven to bed at eight, but she's allowed to stay up and read until nine. She's notorious for leaving her clothes on the floor, however, so I tried this idea sent to me on my Web site: For every piece of clothing lying on the floor when I came to put her to bed, her reading time was reduced by 10 minutes. It worked. After her evening bath, she scurried around like a little mouse, cleaning up her room before I came to tuck her in.

- If you have trouble enforcing the "lights out" rule in your house, make it easy on yourself with this rule. If you put your children to bed, only to look down the hall and see the light shining under the door, simply unscrew the light bulb until they can learn to appreciate the privilege of responsibility.

Car
- Charge a quarter any time someone is caught without a seat belt. Whoever catches the guilty one receives the quarter. Kids can catch parents, too!

- An especially tough but effective correction for teenagers who forget to wear their seat belts is to add an additional day past their sixteenth birthday before they can take their driver's test. Hey, it's important!

Dining Room

- Does your child tend to act up during dinner? Try sending him, along with his plate of food, into the other room to eat alone at the dining room table until he can settle down.
- Haven seems to believe that the dining room chairs have been designed to stand on one or maybe two legs at the most. This has become an unconscious habit, but we're trying to help her break it (before she breaks her own legs or the chair's). Now whenever she tilts back her chair, she is required to remove it from the table and finish her meal or schoolwork standing.
- If you have dawdlers, try this: Whoever is last to the table at dinnertime becomes the server. But there's a catch. Even if you're first, your hands must be clean, or you'll end up serving the food, pouring the drinks, and fetching the condiments (after washing your hands, of course!).
- At our house, eating in the living room is a special occasion. Inevitably, our children push to see if they can turn this exception into a rule. To curb this impulse, we've tied a price to the privilege. Our kids may eat in front of the television if they vacuum the floor when they are finished. This helps them to appreciate the privilege—and keeps them from asking for it every night.
- I heard of a single father who served five plain brussels sprouts to his picky eaters. They had 10 minutes to eat them

or they would get the remaining eight in the pot. This made such an impact on them that he only needed to refer to the "brussels sprout" punishment when the children were tempted to complain about their meals again.

• When our kids don't want to eat what I've cooked for dinner, Steve and I won't make it an issue. They don't have to eat it as long as they've tried at least one bite. If they refuse to do even that, however, they just go hungry. I refuse to be a short-order cook. (They won't starve until the next meal, even though they may feel "starved.") If they eat all their vegetables and protein, though, they are allowed to eat the bread and dessert.

• A neighbor boy complained when his mother burned his toast, so she decided he could do without her cooking for the rest of the day. He got pretty tired of cereal and peanut-butter-and-jelly sandwiches by the end of the day.

School
• If your child misbehaves at school, have him write a 100-word essay on "Why I shouldn't (you fill in the blank) . . . "
• Schoolteachers of the past had a good idea when they made their students write a particular sentence 100 times.
• Dr. James Dobson once mentioned on the Focus on the Family broadcast that his mother threatened to come to his school and sit with him if he continued to make trouble. It's a great idea! (But don't forget, you must be willing to follow through.)
• If your children are constantly turning in sloppy school-work, get a few photocopied pages of printing or cursive

exercises. (These can be found at any teachers' supply store.) Then ask your haphazard child this: "What takes longer: a report done neatly in 15 minutes or one you've sped through in 10 that must be redone and warrants a page of handwriting practice?"

• Whichever toy, TV show, or video game causes your child to be distracted from finishing schoolwork is forfeited until the next opportunity when homework can be finished without dawdling, interruption, complaining, or nagging.

Problem Traits

Controlling the Tongue

• You've heard the reprimand "Hold your tongue!" Make your child do it—literally. Have her stick out her tongue and hold it between two fingers. This is an especially effective correction for public outbursts.

• My kids often lose the privilege of talking. I explain that being able to express yourself is a gift. If they abuse that privilege, either by hurting someone's feelings, speaking inappropriately, or just making needless noise, they cannot speak for a predetermined amount of time. This is especially painful if during that time they have something important to say. It underscores the privilege of speaking and makes them think more carefully about their words.

• My friend Becki tried a variation on this idea in the car. If things got too raucous or there was too much fussing between siblings, she would cry, "Noses on knees!" Her children then had to immediately touch their noses to their knees until she determined that they had learned their lesson.

- The Bible says our tongues are to bring life to others. One day Tucker was in a sour mood and giving us all "attitude." So I made him drink a cup of bitter-tasting health food juice I had stored in the refrigerator, and I told him that his mouth needed to speak a little more health to those around him. I kept the remainder in the fridge long enough for it to be a constant reminder to him of making sure his mouth poured forth life.

- If your older child is arguing that a punishment is unfair, be willing to back down. But explain, "I will rescind the correction *if* you can show me in the Bible where what I required of you was out of line." This usually cuts off any more argument, and even better, it yields a little Bible study.

- Thank goodness for "do-overs"! If someone has the grumpies, he is allowed one "do-over." He can take a deep breath, leave the area, re-enter, re-try, re-ask, or respond differently from the first time, and we can all pretend that the first one never happened.

- Do your children ever call for you from the other room and try to carry on a conversation through the walls? Mine do. I've finally learned to stop answering them. Not only that, but every time they yell from the other room, I count how many times it takes them to realize I'm not talking back before they finally come looking for me and engage in a face-to-face conversation in a normal tone of voice. Then, for each time they yelled, they must wait five minutes before they can ask me the question they were so impatient to ask from the other room.

- Purchase one of those small, plastic garbage cans that are about a foot tall, and set it on your kitchen counter. Fill it with slips of paper on which you've written the dirtiest jobs you can think of, like taking out the garbage, cleaning the garbage cans, vacuuming out the car, scrubbing the toilets, and washing the inside of the refrigerator. Then whenever one of your children starts "trash talking" a sibling or you as a parent, send him to the garbage can for a dirty duty.

- Haven has recently started this shrill, squealing thing. I'm sure she does it for dramatic effect, to emphasize some wrongdoing Tucker has committed. But Steve reached his caterwaul limit one day. Thankfully I had just received an e-mail from a mom who was having the same problem with her young daughter. She came up with a clever way to teach her daughter the importance of being considerate of other people's ears—she made her daughter wear her husband's earplugs during her favorite TV show. I think I'll try that!

- Our children need the freedom to express their feelings, but there's often a fine line between open communication and disrespect. As your kids get older and you perceive their need to tell you how they're feeling, give them the chance to do it respectfully, while you listen without interrupting. If they're too angry or frustrated to speak respectfully, tell them to write you a letter and say whatever is on their heart. The only requirement is that they reread the letter before giving it to you. The majority of the time, this exercise will help them vent their feelings, but they won't end up giving you the letter because they don't feel that strongly anymore.

- I've heard of parents who prescribe "rude medicine" for children who talk back. They give their kids one teaspoon of cider vinegar to heal them of this malady.

Forgetfulness

- As our children get older, it is critical that they learn to be self-reliant. After all, the goal of discipline is self-discipline. Life can teach them this lesson without our help. If they forget their lunches or backpacks or homework or lunch money, don't run up to the school with it every time. Letting them feel the loss will cost them much less than never learning this important life lesson.
- Logical consequences like the one described above provide the best opportunity for correction. But we can also set up artificial logical consequences as correction. If a bike is left in the driveway, it could be run over and destroyed. So take the bike away for two weeks. Was a baseball glove left out in the rain? It's the same principle.
- If you have a child who continually forgets to turn off the lights, make her go a day without using anything that requires electricity. She'll soon get the point.
- Tucker constantly forgot to put his rubber bands back on his braces after meals. We explained that Daddy was paying every month that he wore his braces. If he had to wear them even one month longer because he hadn't been diligent about replacing his rubber bands, that would cost about

$100. We told him that he could pay us three dollars a day for every day he forgot to wear the bands. He only had to pay the price once.

- Does anyone around your house forget to brush her teeth? Put a timer in the bathroom and have her set it for two minutes while she brushes. If she has to be reminded to do it, set the timer for *four* minutes.

- This correction works well if you have a child who is constantly leaving his jacket, backpack, or any other personal belonging behind. Require him to baby-sit the item for three days. It must be carried to school and during mealtime, playtime, bath time, and bedtime. If your child is caught without it at any time, an additional day is added to the original three days.

- Throughout the week, whenever you have to tell your children twice to do something, add 10 minutes to their Saturday work schedules. At the end of the week, before they have free time, their "sentence" must be worked off by "hard labor."

- If you have a child who "forgets" to practice the piano or any other instrument, try adding time to his practice session on the days you have to remind him.

Lying
- For lying or other offenses of the tongue, I "spank" my kids' tongues. I put a tiny drop of hot sauce on the end of my finger and dab it onto my child's tongue. It stings for a while, but it abates. (It's the memory that lingers!) I've also heard of parents using lemon juice or apple-cider vinegar.

- Draw up a contract with your child. After everyone agrees that lying, for example, is a cause for correction, establish and transcribe a reasonable punishment. Have you and your child sign and date the document. Then, whenever a situation comes up that would invite lying, gently remind him about the contract. Knowing that you will follow through on the penalty may be the extra incentive your child needs to choose to tell the truth.
- Last week we ran into a few "heart" issues with Haven. It all came to a head when we caught her lying. Her correction has been to listen to the New Testament on tape. She usually gets to listen to an *Adventures in Odyssey* tape, but for the next 20 nights she will be filling her heart with the Truth.
- If you catch your young child shoplifting, secretly alert a store clerk to summon the manager or, better yet, a uniformed security officer to give your child a little talk. The impact—far greater than hearing a lecture from Mom—could thwart a bigger problem down the road.

Messiness
- Tidying up the house can be a full-time job when you have little ones. Part of my children's morning chore list includes "Pick up personal belongings." They know I mean business—if anything is still left at breakfast, I put the item in a large box or sack. Then, at the end of the week, the kids have the option of buying it back for 25 cents per item or leaving it there for me to take to the Goodwill store, a ministry, or the church nursery. If it's hard for you to donate a toy that you know cost a lot, try to remember that you'll

probably be giving it to a child who *will* appreciate it enough to pick it up when asked.

- Next time your child "forgets" to put something away, like video games or sports equipment, put it away for him. When he asks where it is, tell him that he'll just have to look for it. Believe me, he will learn that it's a lot more trouble to find something that Mom has hidden than it is to put it away in the first place.
- If you have younger children who are messy, try this: Put their toys in a "rainy day" box to bring out later. This has the added benefit of making an old toy seem new again. Or set the toy somewhere out of reach but within sight for a predetermined number of days. This increases the impact of the correction by keeping the forbidden toy fresh in their minds.
- The next time you ask your child to clean up a mess and she comes back with, "But that's not mine" or "I didn't do that," say, "Fine, then for the rest of the day I will only wash the dishes I used and the clothes I wore, and I'll only prepare the food that I'm going to eat."
- Can you think of a worse punishment for an older child than having Mom or Dad pick out the clothes that she'll wear to school? The next time (after one warning) that you find your child's clothes on the floor instead of in the hamper or hung in the closet, tell her that you will need to pick out her clothes for the next day. You certainly won't try to embarrass her, but this will give you a chance to make her wear that adorable dress Aunt Myrtle sent for her birthday that she has never worn.
- This next idea is a stroke of brilliance, and I can't wait to try it with my own children. For every article of dirty clothing left

on the floor rather than placed in the hamper, have your child make five trips from the place where the clothes were dropped to the washing machine, hamper, or utility room. The child must pick up the clothes, walk downstairs, put the article in the hamper, take it back out, return to where it had been dropped, drop it again, pick it up again, and then repeat the cycle. And a pair of socks counts as two, which makes 10 trips!

• If things around the house start getting out of hand when it comes to everyone cleaning up after himself, declare a "Learn how to be an adult" day. This will probably be fun for your kids, but it will also give them an opportunity to learn how to pull their fair share of the load. They spend the entire day with you as your shadows while you teach them how to do everything that you must do every day. Take the time to explain in detail how to properly wipe a kitchen counter, load the dishwasher most effectively, add fabric softener to the laundry in the rinse cycle, thoroughly wash vegetables, and so on. If you end up doing this often enough, you can almost work yourself out of a job, or at least a few chores.

Rowdiness

• I heard from a mom who had tired of her three sons' ceaseless noises and sound effects—so she got creative. If her boys did not take their commotion outside, she would make them sit down and listen to the "Barney" theme song cassette for 10 minutes. For adolescent boys, it's torture!

• If your little one gets too hyper, come up with a code word to remind him to stop the action without embarrassing him. Whenever Tucker started getting too rowdy in a group, I would yell, "Hey, Batman." He knew that he needed to calm down before I had to take more drastic measures.

- Physical exercises, such as running laps around the house or doing push-ups or jumping jacks (even in the grocery store), can be a productive punishment. They also serve a dual purpose for ADHD children or active boys in general. This type of correction is not only sufficiently unpleasant, but it also drains some of the pent-up energy that probably fueled the offense in the first place. This can be an appropriate form of correction for laziness as well.

- When the kids run up and down the stairs after having been told not to, have them crawl up and down on their bottoms. Use the same principle for running through the house, only have them crawl on all fours to get to where they were going in such a hurry.

- Kids intuitively know that we're reluctant to correct them in public. Call their bluff. The next time your young one starts acting up in a restaurant or store, warn her first that if she doesn't straighten up she will have to stand in a corner in public. If she doesn't believe you and continues to misbehave, point to a nearby corner in the restaurant or store and require her to stick her nose there for five minutes.

Self-Importance
- For a while my brother Casey was getting just a little "too big for his britches." He had the misconception that my mother's primary function in life was to be his personal slave. To help

him appreciate her more, she made him go a day "without a mother." He had to walk to school, fix his lunch, prepare his dinner, figure out his own homework, and so on. He was quickly reminded how valuable his mother is.

- Surprise your child by doing something unexpected. If he is acting too arrogant to hear your instruction and wisdom, then stop in the middle of what you are saying and don't proceed. He will probably begin to beg you to continue, but don't give in. After all, he refused your counsel.

- In the fifth grade, my teacher passed around a card for the class to sign to send to a student in the hospital. I took up the whole bottom left corner of the card and signed it, "Lisa the Great." My mother not only required me to buy a new card, but she also had me write a letter of apology to the class and then apologize personally to my teacher for messing up the card. It was embarrassing, but it sure made an impact. Though I remember little of my childhood, I know I'll never forget that correction. Requiring apologies is very effective in curbing pride.

Sticky Fingers

- Haven just can't seem to refrain from touching everything she sees. One day before she headed to Grandmother's house, I explained, "I cannot be with you all day to remind you not to touch things that are not your property. Whenever you catch yourself picking something up, slap yourself on the hand for me." She thought this was so much fun, she kept it up even after she returned home.

Tantrums

- Does your child slam the door when she's angry? You might tell her, "It's obvious that you don't know how to close a door properly. To learn, you will open and close this door, calmly and completely, 100 times."
- If your child likes to stomp off to his room or stomp around in anger, send him outside to the driveway and tell him to stomp his feet for one minute. He'll be ready to quit after about 15 seconds, but make him stomp even harder.
- The same goes for throwing fits. Tell your child to go to her room to continue her fit. She isn't allowed to come out and she has to keep crying for 10 minutes. Ten minutes is an awfully long time, and it's no fun if your parents tell you to cry.
- Another way to handle temper tantrums is to simply say, "That is too disruptive for this house. You may continue your fit in the backyard. When you're finished, you are welcome to come back inside." When there isn't an audience, the thrill of throwing a temper tantrum is gone.
- If your child asks for something and then argues or throws a fit when you tell her no, tell her that no matter what she asks for, from that moment on the answer will be an *automatic* no until she can accept the answer "no" respectfully.
- I heard of a grandmother who was buying shoes for her 10-year-old grandson. He threw a fit when he realized he wouldn't get the more expensive pair. So she leaned down and whispered in his ear, "If you continue to embarrass me, I will kiss you all over your face right here in the middle of the store." He stopped immediately.

Whining

- No whining and no begging are allowed at our house. My children know that if they add "Please, please, please" when asking for something, my response is an automatic "No, no, no."
- Our children's piano teacher told me that when she was a little girl and would start whining about something, her mother would stand there, looking confused—as if she were speaking a foreign language. Then her mother would say, "I'm sorry but I do not understand 'Whinese.' Would you please speak to me in English?"

Chores

- If a job is not done diligently, have your child *practice* doing it. She'll learn to be more thorough if she's made to sweep the floor three or four times because her first effort wasn't good enough.
- If your children whine or argue when you dole out their chores, add another to each list. Once they hit extra chore number three, they'll get the point and stop complaining when they're asked to help out.
- Do you have to constantly remind your child to feed his pet? Mount a little box on top of the pet's house or cage and put your child's lunch money or lunch bag in it. If he wants his lunch that day, he must make sure his pet gets its lunch first.
- Whenever my brother Casey forgets to take out the trash the night before the garbage truck comes, my mother sneaks into his room and sets his alarm for 5:30 in the morning.

This gives him time to wake up and carry the can out to the curb. (This correction can work well for any job that is supposed to be done before going to bed.)

- Have you ever considered charging a 10-cent reminder fee when your child forgets a chore? Let's face it, a child who has been told since day one to set the dinner table is not really "forgetting" to do it. I require my children to keep a couple of their dollars in dimes in a jar. This way, it's much simpler to collect the fee for their "forgetfulness."

- When one of my children is acting disrespectful, disobedient, or defiant, I will instruct him or her to choose a chore from the Job jar. The jobs include scrubbing the toilet, organizing the pots and pans, moving and vacuuming underneath the furniture, weeding the garden, matching up odd socks, defrosting the refrigerator, and cleaning the closet, garage, or under the bed. And those are just a few possibilities. You could add ironing, vacuuming the refrigerator coils, scrubbing the inside of small wastebaskets, polishing the silver, cleaning the window wells, brushing the animals, cleaning the fireplace, shaking the kitchen rugs, vacuuming the couch, alphabetizing the spices, and using wood cleaner on the dining room chairs. Not only does the Job jar help to get my house clean, but it also keeps my little ones from complaining that they're bored. They know that with the Job jar, Mom will always have an antidote for boredom.

- Is it your child's job to take out the trash or the recyclables? Doth the can runneth over? If so, simply take out the trash for him . . . but leave the can in the middle of his bedroom floor. He may be more prone to take it out as the stench rises.

- If your child's responsibility is loading the dishwasher, and the prerinsing job never gets done thoroughly, explain to her, "If the dishes aren't clean, you must wash them again— by hand."
- I have a friend whose son's morning chore was to get the pooper-scooper and clean up the doggie gifts littering the backyard. The boy was not doing this job with much diligence, so his father came up with this creative solution: After the boy had completed the task, he would be required to run through the yard barefoot! From then on, their lawn was perfectly clean.
- You can really get your child's attention by ordering her to do meaningless chores, such as moving the woodpile to the other side of the yard or digging a large hole and then filling it up again.
- Tucker is the only boy in our household. Therefore, whenever I find yellow water in the toilet without any paper floating around, I know he's the culprit who did not flush. The same is true for leaving the toilet seat up. Whenever I discover the bowl in either state of male insensitivity, I grab the toilet-bowl brush and go looking for the offender. He is then required to scrub the toilet clean.
- The next time your child does not do a diligent job of scrubbing the dinner dishes, rinsing the spinach leaves, or wiping the table, insist that she go back and re-do everyone else's dishes, spinach leaves, or place at the table. But the less-than-spectacular job she did should be good enough for her things.
- I like the creative correction I received from a mom of three boys. One Saturday morning she gave them a list of chores to

have done by noon. At eleven o'clock they were still in their pajamas, watching cartoons, and hadn't even started on the chores. She didn't nag; she simply waited until the stroke of noon. Then she called a neighbor who had children the same ages as hers and offered to pay them to come over and do those chores. The neighbor kids jumped at the chance, rushed right over, and quickly worked through the list. When they were done, the neighbor kids were allowed to go into the boys' rooms and choose any toy they wanted in payment. Another idea would have been to pay with the boys' allowance for the week.

• If your kids have assigned chores and they ask you to do something special, simply respond with, "Did you wash the dishes?" or "Is your bed made?" or whatever chores should be accomplished by then. Whether they answer with "yes" or "no," you then respond with, "That's the answer to your question." Soon they will get the message not to ask you for anything special unless they have all their chores done first.

Creative Correction Ideas

Assigning Schoolwork

• Two summers ago I drove with the kids, my mother, and my grandmother in a camper from California to Texas. My grandmother, "Nanny," asked me not to spank the children while on the trip because it upset her. The kids were ecstatic about this. Whenever they did something that deserved correction, they would quickly remind me, "We don't want to give Nanny a heart attack." I wasn't about to let them snooker me that easily. I stopped at a bookstore along the way and bought three grade-appropriate workbooks. For every wrongdoing, they were required to do a certain number of pages in these workbooks. (Believe me, schoolwork in the summertime is a terrible punishment!) Since then, I have photocopied pages of math facts to bring with me on trips. The kids have memorized their addition, subtraction, multiplication, and division tables in hotels all across America.

- You can use the method I described above to correct a variety of problems. My brother Casey continually left the cabinet doors open whenever he removed a dish. Every time my mother discovered a door wide open, she would send Casey to the typewriter to practice typing a page or two from a book.
- It's particularly effective to match habits that need to be broken with skills that need to be strengthened. For example: *unmade bed* equals *practice instrument; shoes in the middle of floor* equals *reading five chapters of a book; toys or bikes left on the driveway or in the yard* equals *copy the names of states and their capitals.* You know what needs the most work around your house.
- If you have the Internet in your home and some kind of child-protection software such as CyberSitter, try this one: Have your child—with your or your spouse's help—do Internet research on a subject that seems appropriate for the correction. For ungratefulness, have your child research hungry children in Africa; for stealing, juvenile hall; for laziness, the ant. Get creative. Then have him do an oral

report at the dinner table. The same idea can be accomplished using an encyclopedia. Here's a similar idea: Give your child a list of words appropriate to the intended lesson and have her find and copy the definitions from the dictionary.

Time-outs

- The old standby of "standing in the corner" still works today. But make it tough. Require your child to stand up, with his nose stuck to the corner and no looking around. Set a timer, and if he asks, "Is it almost time yet?" reset it. (I had to buy a clip-on timer because I got so caught up in all the quiet time that I forgot they were in the corner.) I also add an extra minute for every word of argument or "explanation" on the way to the corner.
- You might want to establish specific corners for specific purposes. In one room, you could have the standard "punishment" corner. In another, you might designate a "chill-out" corner, where your child can calm down or reassess her attitude. You may even title another corner as the "thinking" corner, where she is to think about why her actions were inappropriate and then be ready to report to you afterward. You could also create a "prayer" corner, where your child can repent and ask for help from God.

  Don't have a corner handy? Tell your child to cover her eyes with one hand and hold the other against her nose until the time is up.
- If time-outs don't work, try a "time-in." This can be accomplished by sending your child to a designated spot where he

must complete a task that has a definite beginning and end. This could be putting together a small puzzle, stringing 50 beads on a piece of yarn, or tracing the alphabet. A time-in diverts his energies and encourages him to focus on something positive.

- Who says a time-out should be in short increments? As my kids have gotten older, their time-outs have grown considerably longer. It's not unusual for them to be banished to the reading chair for 45 minutes or longer. It buys me some peace and quiet, and the extended period hurts enough to be effective.

Using Scripture

- Have your child practice his or her printing, cursive, or typing by copying the appropriate verse (to match the infraction) a certain number of times.
- If you have a child who likes to draw, have her write out the verse and then illustrate it.
- Read a verse you're trying to teach to your children. Then have each of them tell you what they think it means in their own words.
- If your kids are older, have them copy the verse in a Scripture journal, along with their own paraphrase. You also might instruct them to record what their infraction was, along with the suitable scripture, the lesson they learned, and a prayer.
- For older children, give them a Bible reference to look up themselves. Then have them read it to you or write it out. To teach Bible study skills, show them how to use a concordance to find an applicable verse.

Miscellany

- Often whispering can be more effective than yelling. Try it next time you feel like screaming. Your children may actually hear you more clearly.

- Timers set definite boundaries. For example, with a timer, you can say, "I'm setting the timer. I want your room cleaned (or your shoes on, or the dishes unloaded) in 15 minutes. If you haven't finished by then, your correction is . . . ." This method not only spurs on easily distracted children, but it also leaves little room for arguing about a job that isn't finished and whether the correction is warranted.

- If you ever catch your child playing with fire or matches, take a few things that are important to him, like a couple of his baseball cards or some of her Barbie doll clothes, and burn them in a safe place. Remind your child that as important as those things are to him, his family is much more important. If he accidentally caught the house on fire, it not only would burn all his stuff, but possibly his family as well.

- If your children are just having too much fun in the bathtub to get out when told, turn on the shower with cold water. You'll be amazed at how quickly they obey.

- Make a homemade "Correction" can and fill it with tickets or slips of paper with various consequences written on them. Instead of giving your child a time-out, send her to the can for a slip. A few ideas might include no TV or computer for a night, early bedtime, or an extra chore. Toss in a blank piece of paper, a "mercy" ticket. This gives you an opportunity to talk about how God gives us mercy even when we deserve punishment.

- If the wrongdoing is simple childishness, I will sometimes let my kids draw two pictures, one indicating what they did wrong, and the other, what they should have done.
- A church service can get unbearably long for a little one, especially during the sermon. We've tried crayons and paper and books, but these items inevitably end up on the floor, with my little ones crawling under the pew to retrieve them. You may want to try this fun game the next time the preacher steps up to the pulpit. Hold your child's hand, and every time the preacher speaks the name "Jesus," see who can squeeze each other's hand first.
- Many children miss the school bus because they dawdle. If they are old enough, require them to walk to school the next morning. Or, if the school is not close enough to walk to, charge them a "Mom's Bus" fee (maybe 25 cents, depending on the age) to drive them there.
- Get an old, worn-out change purse and call it "Mom's Mad Money" purse. Warn your children that from now on, instead of getting angry, you're going to get even. Whenever they push you too far, remind them, "Okay, you're making me mad. Put a quarter in my 'Mad Money' purse." Soon you'll have enough to go to Starbucks. It may afford you just the break you need to keep from blowing your top.
- As I mentioned in an earlier chapter, when my children were younger, as soon as the phone rang, they suddenly needed my undivided attention. To break them of the habit of interrupting me every time I was on the phone, I told them to go to the doorway of their rooms as soon as the telephone rang

and sit quietly until I finished my conversation. This needs to become an automatic response so they're not tempted to interrupt. You do it only until they learn not to interrupt or if they start interrupting again. Partner with a friend and have her call you throughout the first day to practice this with your children.

- Every once in a while, ask your children to come up with the correction they feel is appropriate. They may surprise you.
- Have you ever tried a teaspoon of concentrated lemon juice as an antidote for a sour attitude?
- If your child catches himself and corrects a wrong behavior before you do, the correction is averted.
- When shopping with your children, establish the rule that if they ask for anything, the answer is an automatic *no*. Instead of saying, "I want . . . I need . . . I must have . . ." they are allowed to say, "That sure would be fun to play with" or "I like that dress." Occasionally you can surprise them by purchasing it for them, but not all the time. It takes a lot of pressure off you and makes the shopping trip much more pleasant.
- The next time your child begins a behavior that requires punishment, stop him in the middle of it and ask, "What are you doing wrong right now?" Wait for him to identify his sin, and then sincerely ask, "What can we do to help you correct this behavior?" If his idea is at all acceptable, pray with him and implement the change. This not only puts him in control of his behavior, but it also teaches him how to confess and repent, which are just fancy words for admitting what you've done wrong and then turning around to go the other direction.

- One way to keep your children's rooms from overflowing after Christmas or birthdays is to have them exchange one new toy for an old one. Then, together, you can take the old toys down to the nearest Sunday school, orphanage, daycare center, or charity. Share Jesus' words from Acts 20:35, "It is more blessed to give than to receive."

- Whenever you feel as though you've said the same things over and over to your child and the thought of saying them one more time frustrates you to no end, try writing your child a letter. Say all the things you would like to express, and the next time, rather than wasting your breath, have your child retrieve the letter and read it out loud three times to herself in her room. This also prevents you from saying something in anger that you might later regret.

- "If it had been a snake, it would have bitten you!" Do you remember your parents saying that when they told you to go get something and you came back two minutes later with, "I can't find it"? Of course, they would then walk directly to the place they told you to look and find it immediately. It's amazing how little some things change from generation to generation. My kids are still just as blind and susceptible to snake bites. But I've come up with somewhat of a solution to this problem. If my kids come back and tell me they can't find something and I'm sure they just haven't looked hard enough, I give them a choice. They can either try again or I will go look for it myself. But if I find it, I get to go into their room, choose any toy, and really hide it. They can't play with it again until they diligently search for and find it.

- After the birthday or Christmas chaos has subsided, take a morning and have your children bring all the gifts they received into the living room. For every gift, the family member who got it thinks about the person who gave it and then thanks the Lord for the individual and says a prayer of blessing for him or her.
- I know selfishness is rampant in all of us, but it's hard to see it rear its ugly head so dramatically in our children. When the stench of selfishness begins to permeate your house, may I suggest a drastic measure? Pull a couple of large suitcases out of your garage, go into your selfish child's room, and load the bags with all the many blessings your child has started taking for granted. Then send the stuff on a "trip" for a week or so. When it returns, perhaps your child will be a bit more grateful and a little less greedy for more, more, more.
- Pulling weeds is one of my very favorite, and Tucker's least favorite, forms of correction.

Correction Ideas from Proverbs
- Proverbs 13:18—"He who ignores discipline comes to poverty and shame, but whoever heeds correction is honored."

  Have your child remove money from her piggy bank.
- Proverbs 10:31—"The mouth of the righteous brings forth wisdom, but a perverse tongue will be cut out."

  A short pinch by a clothespin on the tongue can discourage foul language.

- Proverbs 12:24—"Diligent hands will rule, but laziness ends in slave labor."

  If one child is being lazy about doing his chores, he also has to do a chore from his sibling's list.
- Proverbs 13:4—"The sluggard craves and gets nothing, but the desires of the diligent are fully satisfied."

  If their chores are not finished by the time specified, the kids miss the next meal.
- Proverbs 21:25–26—"The sluggard's craving will be the death of him, because his hands refuse to work. All day long he craves for more, but the righteous give without sparing."

  If laziness is a problem, feed your child half the normal amount all day. She won't starve, but all day long she will crave more.
- Proverbs 14:23—"All hard work brings a profit, but mere talk leads only to poverty."

  Tucker loves to talk, especially when he's supposed to be working. We make *him* pay *us* when he talks incessantly on the job.
- Proverbs 19:22b—"Better to be poor than a liar."

  If you catch your child lying, take every cent in your child's piggy bank. (Use discretion. For Tucker, this would amount to, at most, $4. For Clancy, it could be more than $35 dollars.)
- Proverbs 30:17—"The eye that mocks a father, that scorns obedience to a mother, will be pecked out by the ravens of the valley, will be eaten by the vultures."

  You know that look—the look that indicates disrespect is lurking in your child's heart: It's the rolling of the eyes.

If your child does that to you, blindfold him for half an hour. It will teach him quite the lesson about the severity of disrespect.

- Proverbs 25:16—"If you find honey, eat just enough—too much of it, and you will vomit."

A good lesson in greediness is to shock your kids by buying a jar of honey and handing them a spoon. Let them eat as much as they want. They'll probably get sick of it very soon.

Chapter 6

Let's Talk about Child-rearing

everal years ago, Steve and I attended a five-day seminar in Chicago. Before we left, we farmed out our children, ages two, three, and four, to various friends' houses. Each child had a fabulous time with his or her buddies, but all three were glad when Mommy and Daddy returned. The reunion, however, was short-lived: Steve and I had to attend a meeting at church the very night we arrived home.

I realized the kids had probably gotten away with "who knows what" while we were gone and that they'd be frustrated we were leaving again. I was especially worried about the baby-sitter. Would she be able to handle them?

In an effort to work "damage control," I warned Tucker, "I really want you to do your best to obey the baby-sitter tonight."

"Well, Mom, I just don't know if I can do that," he admitted.

My eyebrows rose. "Why?"

With a straight face, Tucker said, "There's so much foolishness built up in my heart, I don't think there is any room for goodness and wisdom."

"Then maybe we need to step into the bathroom and drive that foolishness out," I suggested.

Tucker's eyes widened. "W-wait a minute," he sputtered. "I feel the foolishness going away all by itself—the goodness is coming in right now!"

I didn't know whether to laugh or cry.

TO SPANK OR NOT TO SPANK

You've probably guessed it: I want to discuss the topic of child-*rearing* in the literal sense. "To spank or not to spank," that is the question —and it's one of the most difficult parents must address. I won't attempt to answer this controversial question for you, or try to change anyone's mind. Instead, I'll give my opinion and then leave it up to you. You know what's best for your family. I anticipate that some parents—both for and against spanking—won't agree with me. That's okay. But I certainly couldn't write a book on correction and not address the issue of corporal punishment.

At the risk of sounding like a politician, I must confess that I can see the value in arguments from both sides. On the one hand, I know incredible children who have never been spanked a day in their lives. It's hard to argue with remarkable parents who raise extraordinary children without ever spanking them. On the other hand, I received plenty of spankings growing up, and I've never felt tempted to get violent because of them. I received them as the corrections they were intended to be.

Frankly, I've experienced the value of both points of view, even within my own family. As I explained earlier, my mom is very strict with my brother Casey. But she wasn't always so firm. For the first four years of Casey's life, discipline was rare because we were too busy enjoying this adorable late-in-life baby. Consequently, behavior that was cute in the beginning became obnoxious as he got older. He was having a hard time making and keeping friends. My mom and stepfather recognized that if something didn't change, kindergarten would be a nightmare. So they made a fresh commitment to discipline Casey—and that included spanking him. It took about a year for their correction to sink in, but soon Casey was a delight to everyone, not just to his adoring family. Thankfully, the power of spanking turned his little life around! I guess he just needed someone to draw the line for him and then give him a good reason not to cross it.

But that certainly wasn't the case with Tucker. As I hinted in the first chapter, the whole catalyst for this book—fueling my need for creative correction—came when my son was about six or seven years old. Suddenly, spankings, so effective in the past, just didn't work on him anymore. They actually made things worse. It didn't matter how calmly and lovingly I administered the spanking; it would send Tucker even further out of control, and we would *both* end up crying.

It all came to a head one morning when Steve called home from work. When I said, "Hello," he knew something was wrong.

"I-I've spanked Tucker twice already, and it's not even 9:30 yet," I blubbered.

Steve was silent for a moment. Then he said, "Why don't you both go to your rooms to calm down? I'll be right there."

This was not the first time Tucker and I had needed rescuing. When Steve arrived home, he and I decided something had to change. We couldn't continue like this. So we set the spankings aside for a while and instead concentrated on finding ways to help Tucker learn to regain self-control, which he seemed to lose every time his will was crossed. For starters, we refused to be drawn into a heated battle. Tucker was required to sit on his bed until he could join us for a calm discussion. Once we changed our approach, we quickly made an encouraging discovery: Tucker usually made the right choice after he settled down. Of course, it was still a battle to subdue our son, but at least we weren't inflaming his temper anymore.

I still occasionally choose to spank my kids, but it's no longer my first or only choice of correction, especially now that they're older. And while I am grateful for the gift of spanking, I consider it to be just another option, or tool, in our parenting toolbox. In fact, I have purposely positioned this chapter after chapter five—which contains a variety of ways to administer correction—to drive home my point.

THE AGE FACTOR

Whether spanking works or is the best approach depends not only on the child and the circumstances, but also on his or her age. When my kids were little, for example, I sometimes felt it was more effective to administer a spanking than to try to reason with them. I can remember giving four-year-old Tucker an impassioned and encouraging talk on the need for self-control. It was designed to bring about a great change of heart in my son and had been a deep and meaningful conversation . . . or so I thought.

The moment I finished talking, my son piped up. "Mom," Tucker began, "only one word makes sense out of everything you just said."

"Oh, which one was that?" I asked, curious.

He furrowed his brow. "I forgot."

A spanking might have been kinder than my long-winded lecture, and definitely more memorable!

Thankfully, as my kids have matured, my "talks" and other modes of correction have had some impact. But in their early years, discipline was certainly a challenge. For example, when my children were toddlers and constantly getting into things, it seemed my only alternatives for discipline—other than spanking—were distracting or confining them. Both of these choices helped to a degree, but they definitely had their limitations. I could only toddler-proof the house so far; there were still things, such as phones and VCRs, that needed to remain accessible. Constantly diverting my tots' attention from something off-limits was a superficial cure. It only postponed the need to teach them that we can't always have everything we want. Besides, it kept me hopping! Yet the other alternative—keeping them confined to their playpen for half the day—seemed even more cruel than a slap on the back of their hands.

So I chose to spank. And for many years it worked, even on Tucker. Using corporal punishment while my children were young actually afforded our whole family more freedom in the long run, because it established boundaries and reminded the kiddos who was in charge—freeing me up to try other, more creative corrections as they matured.

WHAT DOES THE BIBLE SAY ABOUT IT?

As we saw in the previous chapter, God's Word frequently addresses the subject of raising children. Corporal punishment is no exception. For example, Proverbs 13:24 reads, "He who spares the rod hates his son, but he who loves him is careful to discipline him." I wholeheartedly agree, and I'm sure you do, too—if we love our kids, we should correct them.

I believe children also understand this (though they may not admit to it!). Somehow, they intuitively know spankings are good for them, and that they receive them not only because they deserve it, but also because their parents love them. Let me see if I can convince you.

One evening, when Haven was only two and a half years old, Steve and I left the kids with a baby-sitter. Our instructions were clear: The girls went to bed at 7:00, Tucker at 8:00. When we arrived home at 8:30, the children were in bed, but even from the family room, we could tell that Haven wasn't asleep. There was screaming coming from her bedroom. She was in the midst of a full-blown temper tantrum, and the baby-sitter, Shawna, said she'd been acting that way all evening.

When I went to talk with Haven, I expected to be met with more screaming and crying. But instead she said, "'Pank me."

"Did Miss Shawna spank you?" I queried, confused.

"No. 'Pank me," she urged once again.

We went back and forth like that several times until I finally realized Haven wasn't talking about the baby-sitter. "Do you want Mommy to spank you?" I asked, my jaw dropping in astonishment.

"Yes!" said Haven, and she jumped out of bed for her correction. Afterward, she locked her arms around me in a bear hug.

As this story reveals, correction *can* reach the heart of a child. And it should! Corporal punishment is most effective when our kids know what God says about discipline. It helps them to understand why they are being punished.

For this reason, I've quoted Proverbs 22:15 to my children about a hundred times. It says, "Folly is bound up in the heart of a child, but the rod of discipline will drive it far from him." The companion verse is Proverbs 29:15: "The rod of correction imparts wisdom, but a child left to himself disgraces his mother." My kids know from these verses that spanking not only drives out the foolishness in them, but it also produces positive benefits, such as bringing them wisdom. This helps us all focus on the good that will result from an otherwise painful situation.

PUTTING THE PRINCIPLES INTO PRACTICE

Unfortunately, knowing and doing don't always go hand in hand. Haven might have shown in the story I shared above that she understands the meaning and need for correction—but that doesn't stop her from being disobedient occasionally. Recently, my older daughter defied her grandmother's instruction to put the Popsicle back in the freezer until after dinner. I stopped my work and called to her.

"Haven, meet me in the bathroom!"

A few minutes later, I found her there.

"Now, Haven," I began, "why are you getting this correction?"

Her head hanging, she mumbled, "Because I went ahead and ate the Popsicle even though Grandmother told me not to."

"Why was that wrong?" I persisted.

"Because Grandmother is my authority and I need to obey her."

I continued. "Why do you think she told you not to eat the Popsicle?"

Haven stared at the floor. "Because we're going to have dinner soon and it might ruin my appetite."

"Haven," I told her, "I'm going to need to spank you because Proverbs 23:13–14 says, 'Do not withhold discipline from a child; if you punish him with the rod, he will not die. Punish him with the rod and save his soul from death.' There may come a day when Grandmother tells you not to eat something because she knows it could make you sick. You must be in the habit of obeying her. Do you understand?"

"Yes, ma'am," she said quietly.

I beckoned her toward me, where I was seated on the toilet lid. "Now, lean over my lap."

After I spanked her—eight times for her age—I invited her to sit on my lap. Cradling her in my arms, I said, "Haven, I love you and forgive you, but you need to ask Jesus to forgive you for not obeying Him. Remember, He is your ultimate authority."

Haven nodded and, at my urging, bowed her head. "Dear Jesus," she prayed, "please forgive me for disobeying Grandmother. Thank You for forgiving my sins. Please fill me with Your wisdom and help me to obey. Amen."

After the prayer, we kissed, hugged—and moved on.

A WORD OF CAUTION

If you decide to spank your children, be careful: You could be setting yourself up for controversy, because some parents abuse the privilege of spanking. I was reminded of this one afternoon when I took Tucker to a homeopathic doctor, looking for help with his allergies. She sat us both down on a couch in front of a portable camera, then asked if she could film Tucker during the course of the appointment. She explained that she learned a lot just by watching children's body language and would review the tape later for further insight. I had no objection and consented.

Everything was going smoothly until about an hour into the

interview, when the doctor said, "Tucker, you haven't mentioned your father yet. Tell me about him."

Tucker's face became animated. "When my dad spanks me," he began, motioning with his hands, "it's like he's a major league baseball player trying to hit the ball out of the park!"

Sitting next to him on the couch, I felt my palms begin to sweat. *I know he loves to exaggerate*, I thought, *but this doctor doesn't!* There was nothing I could do, though. If I interrupted to set things straight, it would look as if I were trying to cover something up. So I just sat still, praying that he wouldn't say anything else.

I should have known better. Tucker was just getting started.

"When he's not spanking me, he's yelling at me," my son continued.

The doctor's eyes widened.

Meanwhile, I sat there, helpless. Like a bad home video, a string of terrible events played out in my mind: It would take us about an hour to drive back to Los Angeles. By that time, the doctor would have called Child Protective Services, and they would be waiting on my doorstep. I tried to shake the picture from my mind.

Thankfully, the appointment ended without incident—but I still prayed all the way home. When we turned onto our street and I saw that our driveway was empty, a wave of relief swept over me. Hallelujah! There were no CPS officers around!

Later that night, after I'd had a chance to recover, I asked Tucker, "Why did you make up that story about Daddy?"

He shrugged. "I don't know. I was just having fun for the camera."

You can be sure that Tucker and I had a serious discussion about exaggerating things in general and his father's discipline in particular. I also told him that some things, like spanking, were to be discussed only with family and close friends, not the general public.

We live in a sad world where it is necessary to have organizations like Child Protective Services. In the majority of cases, these services save children's lives. Nevertheless, it was disturbing to know that, had the doctor believed Tucker's claims, the CPS could have paid a visit to our house. I'm sure they would have witnessed a safe and loving environment and let it go from there. But the report would have remained on my record for two years or more, depending on the opinion of the investigator.

With that in mind, I think it's important for parents to know what the law is in regard to corporal punishment—especially nowadays, as parental rights are diminishing. The law in California says you can legally spank your child on the buttocks, using an open hand, but *never* to the point of bruising. That is considered child abuse, and if a teacher or doctor ever sees bruises on your child, he is required to report it.

Let me offer a few more words of caution: Make sure you don't spank as a last resort or because you've already told your child something five times. It's too tempting to use spanking as a release for anger and frustration rather than for correction. To help avoid this, I send my kids to a predetermined place to receive their spankings. It allows both of us time to calm down (and gives me a minute to wrap up whatever I'm doing). If you feel you may lose self-control or if you have a propensity toward violence, don't spank at all. There are many other effective options.

Last week, I spoke with a lovely Christian mom in Oklahoma who said she could never "hit" one of her children—it would crush her. I resisted the urge to tell her that I don't "hit" my children, either. There was no need to get into an argument. She is making the best choice for her family. If she feels that spanking is a subtle form of child abuse, there is no reason she should put herself through that guilt and agony.

I imagine that some of you are much like the mom I described. When you think about spanking, you picture an irate father beating his child with a belt. Well, I'm uncomfortable with that picture, too. It doesn't at all reveal the positive, loving correction I've found spanking to be. In some ways, I find writing this chapter to be a risk. I would never want someone to read my advice and interpret it as a license to harm a child. If you choose to spank, please be careful. Corporal punishment must be motivated by love.

May I wrap up this discussion with another picture? The one that sticks in my mind is that of my three-and-a-half-year-old son sitting on my lap after a spanking and a hug and voluntarily praying, "Dear Jesus, thank You for taking away my sins. Thank You that spankings drive away the foolishness in me. Please help me not to do bad again. Amen." After Tucker offered that sweet prayer, he turned, gave me a big hug, and thanked me for the spanking.

I believe that when handled correctly, spankings can be a gift from God—and that picture gives me all the evidence I need.

Let's Talk about Child-*rearing*

Toolbox

Below I've listed a few guidelines for spanking. My intent is to give tips to assist you, not to offer you hard-and-fast rules. I know that every household is different.

Spanking Guidelines
1. Never spank out of anger.
2. Send your kids to a predetermined place for correction. It will not only give both of you time to calm down, but it will also immediately begin the discipline, even if you need to get something out of the oven, hang up the phone, or find a break in whatever you're doing.
3. Talk with your child first about what he did wrong. Ask him why he is receiving the correction. This takes the burden off you and reminds him that Mommy or Daddy isn't being mean; he simply needs to be punished for his disobedience.
4. There may be times when, after hearing your child's side of the story, you decide the offense doesn't warrant a spanking. It's okay to change your mind and come up with a more appropriate correction. This will also reinforce to your children that they are being heard.
5. Ask your child to lean over, stand up, or lie down, however it works best. The main purpose is to avoid wrestling with your child. She needs to willingly submit to the punishment. For example, at our house, Clancy prefers to stand up and lean both hands against the wall, while Haven would rather bend over my lap.
6. Where to spank: Steve and I spank on the bottom—but never the bare bottom—because it has the most padding. Sometimes,

if the hand is the offender (i.e., hitting, pinching, throwing rocks, and so on), we'll spank the palm.

7. As children get older, it may be prudent to have dads administer spankings to sons, and moms to daughters.

8. Number of times: The number of "spanks" we give corresponds to the child's current age. This makes birthdays bittersweet, but it works for us.

9. The majority of your corporal punishment should be accomplished by age five and gradually diminish until age 10. It should be extremely rare after that.

10. Always hug your child when you've finished the correction.

11. Have your child ask for God's forgiveness through prayer. This will help her grasp the concept that God is the one to whom she is ultimately responsible. I sometimes pray, too, if I still feel that I need to address the issue.

12. Finally, forget about it. God has forgiven your child, so move on.

Administering Correction in Specific Circumstances

1. I caution against spanking children in public. If you must, go to the public rest room and wait until it is empty or, better yet, head to the car. Once, in desperation, I hopped on the elevator and waited until everyone got off—then gave Haven a quick swat between floors.

2. Steve and I also hesitate to spank our children when guests or service people are in our home. You never know how they might feel about corporal punishment or whether they think

it's their duty to inform the authorities. Perhaps you could keep a little "tally sheet," if necessary, and correct your child later, after the company leaves.

3. If you do not have time to stop and take care of the offense quickly, feel free to say, "We'll take care of this later." Sometimes a little stewing can soften the hearts of our young ones!

4. When driving, you may need to pull over to the side of the road a couple of times before your children realize that you mean business when you give them an instruction. (This is much safer than the age-old "backhand" from the front seat that children of my generation remember so well.)

As I mentioned in the first part of this chapter, spanking can be a valuable tool, but it shouldn't be our only form of discipline. There are countless other ways we can mold and shape our children—and those corrections are often more effective than spankings. Sometimes a swat on the bottom is a parent's best and only choice, and sometimes the situation calls instead for a creative correction.

Chapter 7

WWIII: The Sibling Conflict

few years ago, Pastor Jack Hayford had a brainchild called *Church on Sunday*. This one-hour cable show, produced by our church, was to be shown on Sunday mornings as an outreach to the city. I was asked to host the children's portion. My mother offered to watch the kids for me while I taped my Sunday school vignettes, but a few days before the taping, she had to cancel. She'd forgotten about a quilting class she'd signed up for during the same time. Unfazed, I assured her it wouldn't be a problem; I'd just bring the kids with me. After all, I was supposed to be a "teacher" reading Bible stories to children. My kids would act as my students. This could be fun!

Still, I wanted to make sure my little ones knew this wasn't a time for games. On the way to the taping, I explained to them, "I want you to follow the director's instructions. This is important—we've been given a real opportunity to reach out to people who wouldn't normally go to church on Sunday and tell them about the love of Jesus."

Tucker, unfortunately, didn't get the message. He grinned at me in the rearview mirror. "Let me see if I've got this straight," he offered from the backseat. "This show is going to be on TV. I'm going to be in it. That means I'm gonna be a star!"

"Yeah, that's what it's all about, Tucker," I said, grimacing. "Your rise to fame." I sent up a quick prayer for God's help and mercy.

Several minutes later, we arrived at the church, got our makeup on, and were put into position. I was seated in a chair with about a dozen children gathered around me, including my three little darlings. After the director yelled, "Action!" I introduced the program.

"Hello, boys and girls," I began, smiling. "Today we're going to read one of my favorite Bible stories . . . ."

I had just opened the Bible when a little blond girl in the back squealed. "Mom," Clancy whined, "Haven's sitting on my foot, and she won't get off!"

The director shook his head. "Cut!"

Trying to stay calm, I kept smiling at the children. The director again called, "Action!" and I inquired, "Do you children know the story of—"

"Move over, Clancy," Haven interjected. "I can't see the pictures!"

"Cut!" said the director once more, running his hands through his hair.

I shot each one of my angels the meanest mommy look I could muster, and after the director's cue, I started the story: "In the town of Galilee lived—"

"Tucker, stop!" a third voice interrupted from the back. "You're pushing me over!"

The director rolled his eyes and looked at me. "Cut!"

I wished we all would just disappear; I also determined that once we got home, some of the kids' privileges would vanish, too.

The taping took much longer than it should have that day, and it was all because my kids were fighting and bickering.

I think sibling rivalry is the most convincing argument for birth control (and I'm only partly kidding). I've never met a pair of siblings that didn't quarrel at least once in a while. You could probably add some colorful stories about your children, too! I like this one:

A Sunday school teacher was discussing the Ten Commandments with her five- and six-year-olds. After explaining the commandment to "honor thy father and thy mother," she asked, "Is there a commandment that teaches us how to treat our brothers and sisters?"

Without missing a beat, one little boy answered, "Thou shall not kill."

This conflict between brothers and sisters has its roots in the very first sibling relationship—that of Abel and his brother, Cain, whose philosophy was (literally!) "Eliminate the competition" (see Genesis 4:8). I wish the problem could have stopped with Cain and Abel, but because we human beings are sinful, sibling rivalry will always be an issue.

Steve and I certainly have had to deal with our fair share of sibling squabbles. Clancy, who is only 13 months younger than Haven, was nicknamed "Me-Me," because as a toddler, she was extremely jealous of her older sister. She earned the moniker before she could even talk. Anytime someone complimented Haven, Clancy patted herself on the chest and demanded, "Me! Me!"

If Grandfather said to Haven, "That's a pretty dress you have on," Clancy would squeal and tug at her own dress, protesting, "Me! Me!" If Grandma Cauble complimented Haven by saying, "What a lovely bow you're wearing," Clancy, who hardly had any hair, much less a bow in it, would nonetheless insist, "Me! Me!"

Then, somewhere along the way, things got turned around. Nowadays Haven is the one shouting, "Me! Me!" without saying a word. I think I know when things changed. When Clancy's hair finally did come in, it was blond and curly—and Haven, whose hair is brown and straight, noticed right away. And I probably didn't help matters. I don't have naturally curly hair, or naturally blond hair, for that matter, so I made a big deal over Clancy's goldilocks.

One morning when Haven was three, I was having fun scrunching up Clancy's curls with some gel. I looked over and saw Haven looking into the mirror and tugging at her hair. Later that day, she gave herself a "haircut." I empathized with my oldest daughter, so when I took Haven to the hair salon for damage control, I asked my stylist to cut Clancy's hair, too—into a pixie cut. I knew Clancy didn't care, and I figured that if Haven couldn't have curly locks, at least she would have the longest hair.

Unfortunately, that didn't solve the problem. Maybe the issue started with her hair; maybe it's "middle-child syndrome"; whatever it is, the conflict hasn't gone away.

THE BATTLE LINE

As parents, we walk a fine line as we try to build one child up without inadvertently tearing another one down. But no matter how careful we are to avoid making comparisons, our children will always find ways to compete. To help ease the effects of sibling rivalry, Steve and I have encouraged our kids to find their own special niches, the place where they can be the best at something. We try to encourage them to develop a skill, hobby, or activity. When kids are recognized for something positive, they are less likely to try to get attention by doing something negative. In our family, this clamor for negative attention shows itself as "kindling strife" (see Proverbs 26:21). Steve and I can always tell when Haven is feeling insecure: She starts aggravating her brother and sister. If I have the time, energy, and forethought, I'll pull her aside and give her lots of affirmation.

Of course, Haven is not the only guilty party. All three of my children seem to love to aggravate one another. I figure that it must be a kid thing. Children must find some feeling of pleasure or power that can come only from "getting somebody's goat." Though I don't understand it, I know I don't have to put up with it. At some point, we as parents have to draw the battle line—and then step away. I'll try not to praise one child without also pointing out something worthy in the other; I'll try to fill up a child with love when his "tank" is empty. But I'm not going to take the full responsibility of negotiating peace in the middle of a war zone.

These are the ground rules at our house: No hitting, biting, kicking, pulling hair, or any other forms of physical retaliation. No name-calling, humiliating, sarcasm, or verbally wounding another person. No stealing, destroying, or borrowing personal property without permission. Breaking these rules will result in laps, push-ups, interrogation, or solitary confinement—sometimes literally!

Unfortunately, I've seen enough John Wayne movies to realize that even if there is a temporary cease-fire and all is quiet on the battlefront, the war can still be raging within each child's heart. Recently, Haven and Clancy slept over at their grandma's—and the entire night, they engaged in a quiet tug-of-war. When I talked to the girls on the phone the next morning, I found out from Clancy that her sister had deliberately been sticking the foot of her sleeping bag on Clancy's pillow.

"Why would you do that?" I asked when Haven got on the line.

"I don't know, Mommy," Haven admitted quietly. "I want to do the right thing, but I always end up doing the wrong thing."

The apostle Paul said basically the same thing, and he was a grown man (see Romans 6:18). In his letter to the Roman church, he explained that there was a war going on within him. He wanted to obey God, but he couldn't. Paul didn't have the power to win the war, and because we're sinful, neither do we. But Jesus does! He won the war for our children when He died on the cross and forgave their sins, giving our kids His Spirit to help them overcome challenges . . . even the challenge to love their pesky siblings.

PEACE IS POSSIBLE

If you feel that your children will never be at peace with one another, don't despair—with God's help, it *is* possible. As Paul explains in Romans 8:6, "The mind of sinful man is death, but the mind controlled by the Spirit is life and *peace*" (italics added). The same Spirit who raised Jesus from the dead is available to help our children conquer the problems in their lives.

We must teach our children to call upon Jesus, especially when they're feeling weak. When Haven finds herself fighting a losing battle, she sends up a quick prayer. Before her lips form the words "Help me, Jesus," He is there to give her the strength and power to overcome her weaknesses. Even if she stumbles, she knows He'll be there to help her up again.

One night about a month before Haven's sixth birthday, I was putting her to bed early; she'd been antagonizing her sister all day.

Haven's lip quivered. "Mommy," she cried, "I feel that I'm always stumbling."

I smoothed her bangs from her forehead and said, "Honey, I know it feels that way. But the truth is, you're walking in the Spirit—following God and His commands—much more than you're stumbling."

She brightened a bit. "You mean, I'm walking in the Spirit 80 percent of the time and I'm walking in the flesh 20 percent?"

My eyebrows shot up as I nodded. "How did you know that?"

"Oh, that's easy!" Haven said. "Eight plus two equals 10. And 80 plus 20 equals 100."

I think until she can reach 100 percent in heaven, 80 percent is pretty good. But we'll keep working on that 20 percent!

The Power of Friendship

As I mentioned earlier, we as parents can help ward off sibling conflict. Focusing on the positive in each of our kids, not comparing them, and helping them develop skills at which they can be "the best" are just three ways. But there will still be times—that "20 percent"—when our kids will decide that the smell of a good fight is just too intoxicating to pass up. It is in that arena that we must act as referees. We may have to simply separate them and send them to separate corners. But how can we keep them *out* of the ring?

Since it's more satisfying to throw a punch at an enemy than a friend, try to strengthen the friendships between your kids. Sometimes at dinner, we'll go around the table and say one positive thing about each family member—something we've noticed about him or her that is particularly attractive, maybe a strength or a gift. The idea is to take the time to intentionally build one another up in love.

You can also teach your kids to demonstrate their love for their siblings by praying for them. If I'm putting Clancy to bed, and Tucker's been a real bother of a brother all day, I'll say, "Why don't you pray for Tucker tonight? He had a really hard day." Prayer keeps things in perspective and fosters love for the other person.

At the same time, look for opportunities in which your children can serve each other. For example, if I'm busy and I notice one of my kids is struggling to do something or is calling for me, I may suggest, "Haven, can you go help your little sister?" Afterward I'll affirm her, letting her know what a sweet big sister she is.

You can also encourage loving relationships between your kids by helping them to focus on the long-term. Tell your children about one of the best friends you had as a child, and describe all the fun things you did together. Then tell them how long it's been since you've seen or talked to that friend. Point out to them that friends are great, but family is forever. Ask your kids this: Would you rather invest all your energy in watering and tending a flower that, while beautiful, lasts only a season? Or would you want to spend more of your time cultivating a tree that will grow throughout your entire life, one that can bring you joy during your childhood and shade in your old age?

I often tell my girls how much I wish I had a sister. I remind them that brothers and sisters are gifts from God—and they should cherish those gifts. Of course, our children won't automatically know how to cherish an expensive present: We as parents need to teach them. Here is an example of how I once handled it.

At the beginning of Tucker's fourth-grade year, he and Haven began fighting like two alley cats. I tried all the usual tactics to help them get along, but nothing was working. One morning it got especially out of hand. I took Tucker—the chief culprit—upstairs and expressed my concern.

"Tucker," I told him, "I'm really worried about you and Haven arguing so much. I'm afraid that if you two don't resist this, your fighting might become divisive and cause permanent damage."

Tucker's eyes were wide. "How do I stop?"

"Well," I instructed, "James 4:7 says, 'Submit yourselves, then, to God. Resist the devil, and he will flee from you.' So the first thing you need to do is pray and ask the Lord to forgive you for giving in to your urge to fight and not trying to be a peacemaker anymore."

When Tucker had prayed for God's forgiveness, I concluded, "Now, you need to pray for God to help you resist a spirit of division."

"That's my kind of prayer!" Tucker jumped in. "Can I resist a spirit of multiplication next?"

My son, the comedian!

Sometimes it's not easy to teach my kids to value one another; other times I'm amazed at the deep bond of love and friendship between them. Last month, Haven and Clancy were at a friend's birthday-swim party. It was an event full of games, contests, and prizes. The year before, Haven had won the swim race, and she really wanted to place first again this year. She did, and I was ecstatic for her.

Clancy, however, was one of the only girls who hadn't participated in the contest. "Why didn't you race today, honey?" I asked while putting her to bed that night.

She shrugged. "I didn't want to."

"But why?" I persisted. "You're a good swimmer, too."

She lowered her voice and confessed, "I didn't want to take a chance on winning, because then Haven would've been disappointed."

Touched, I wrapped my arms around her. "I think *both* my daughters are winners," I told her.

Of course, that kind of compassion and love doesn't happen all the time at our house—and before Tucker and Haven read this and string me up by my toes, let me say that Clancy has been known to lob a few grenades of her own. There have been days when our house has felt like the battleground of World War III, and I'm sure you as a parent can identify. But we don't have to wait for a miracle, those moments that seem few and far between, when our kids actually choose to love one another.

In the following "Toolbox" section, I've come up with several strategies to foster healthy, happy sibling relationships. By working with our kids, we can help keep sibling conflict from escalating into nuclear war—and keep peace on the family horizon.

WW III: The Sibling Conflict

Toolbox

Strategies to Defuse Sibling Conflict

- I've noticed a couple of tiny "mommies" and a diminutive "daddy" running around our house. They show up long enough to reprimand the others about behavior that is not permissible. But they tend to speak in rather sharp tones. Sometimes I'll say to a miniature parent: "Are you Haven's mommy? You're sounding like you are, so would you please prepare her lunch today?" (You can, of course, substitute any chore that you as the mom or dad would normally do.)

- Tucker has learned the art of delegating from his father. This is a useful skill for Steve to use at the office, but Haven and Clancy don't quite interpret it that way when it comes from their brother. They call it as they see it: being bossy! Jesus said, " . . .Whoever wants to be great among you must be your servant" (Mark 10:43). This is a good verse to quote before requiring the self-proclaimed boss to serve his "employee." Have the bossy child ask his sibling, "What would you like me to do?" Then have him do it!

- When my children were little and Tucker would take one of Haven's toys without asking, I would allow Haven to go into Tucker's bedroom and pick out any toy she wanted to play with for the day.

- A little boy named Kyle went to his first day of school with a brand-new box of crayons. Another little boy in his class swiped the box and broke them all in half. Kyle went home furious that afternoon. His mother comforted him. Then she said, "Broken people do broken things. Why don't you pray for that little boy?" This can be done with siblings. We often break the hearts of those we love the most—and children should learn to pray for their loved ones, especially when they've been hurt by one.

- If one of my girls breaks the other's toy, the other girl is allowed to choose any of her sister's toys to replace the broken one.
- If your child has a special or new toy that he can't bring himself to share, don't force the situation. Simply explain to him that he may play with that toy only during "quiet times," when he is alone in his room. If he wants to play with it at any other time during the day, he must be willing to share it. Otherwise, it wouldn't be fair to the other kids because they would have to sit around and watch him play with such a "cool" toy.
- Things got so crazy one day with fighting at our house that I made the kids go a whole day without the benefit of one another's company. The next morning, from the moment they woke up, they weren't allowed to talk, eat, or play with each other or have school in the same room. By the next day, they were so desperate to be together that they called a truce.
- A fun and effective technique for dealing with sibling conflict is to make your children laugh and have fun with their siblings, even while they're fighting. There are many creative ways to do this. For example, if your children are fighting or arguing, put one child on each side of a sliding glass door with a bottle of glass cleaner and a paper towel. Challenge them to clean the door while trying the make the other child laugh. Whoever is able to maintain a straight face wins the argument.

Here are some more ideas: Require the two siblings to

go "toe to toe." Have each child face the other with their toes touching; they must remain that way until they're no longer angry. Or send them into a room and don't allow them to come out until they've made up a song or a joke about their argument. You can also make them hold hands (this is especially effective in a public place). Finally, you can require squabbling children to stop and sing in their most operatic voices, "I love you truly, brother (or sister) dear." It's so much more fun to laugh than to fight!

- Use a pair of toy handcuffs to join two siblings who can't seem to get along. It's really fun to watch them try to eat dinner like this, or read a book, or take the garbage out, tasks I'll often assign them. They are forced to figure out a way to work together before they are set free.

- If your children get into a high-decibel argument, transfer it to the backyard. Make each child stand at opposite ends of the yard. Then have them yell, "I love you!" back and forth 20 times. This releases some of the pent-up anger, and it's a lot better than some of the other words they may be tempted to yell. After this, allow them to continue the argument, if they choose, but with no more yelling. Nine times out of 10, all the energy is diffused and the disagreement is forgotten.

- Hugs, even forced ones, are good at breaking down barriers.

- When the level of tension has reached a plateau, it's time to strengthen the friendship. Throughout the day, whenever one sibling runs into the other, whether it's passing in the hall, coming out of the bathroom, or doing their chores, require them to greet each other with the words "I love you, and you're my best friend." This gets a bit redundant and usually doesn't come straight from the heart, but somehow it still makes a difference and the fighting dissipates for a while.

- Isn't it amazing how two children can tell entirely different stories about the same event? When this happens, I restrict them to the same room until they can come up with one version of the story. This forces them to think about the events that actually occurred, and each child is motivated to confess her "sin" in order to be released from the deliberation room.

- Hurtful words are usually easier to remember than compliments. When my friend Terri's children speak unkindly to one another, she requires them to come up with a list of seven nice things to say about their sibling before they can play again.

- Car rides can be torture with multiple children. We've all drawn the imaginary line down the middle of the backseat only to hear, "He's looking out *my* window." So for Steve's sanity and my own, we bought a TV/VCR combo that can be placed between the front seats of our van. Each child has a set of headphones, so it is peaceful, enabling Steve and me to have an uninterrupted conversation.

- When our kids were little (and before the installation of the car TV/VCR), we played story tapes and Scripture song tapes whenever we got in the car. This helped everyone think positive thoughts rather than negative ones.

- After years of resisting, I allowed Steve's parents to give each of the kids a Game Boy for Christmas. They are only allowed to play them in the car, at doctor's offices, and in restaurants, but they are such effective diversions that I wonder why I didn't give in sooner.

- When Tucker's actions didn't show love toward his sisters, I printed out five different translations of 1 Corinthians 13 (the love chapter) and had him read each one aloud. Of course, halfway through we were all in hysterics as he read each translation in a different voice. Nonetheless, it got the truth into his heart. (Now, if only it would transfer to his actions!)

  Another way to encourage your child to love his sibling is to have him read 1 Corinthians 13 aloud and insert his name wherever the word "love" is written. (For example, "Tucker" is patient, "Tucker" is kind, and so on.)

- If you overhear your children arguing, step close enough to let them know you're listening. Say that you will give them a few more minutes to work it out on their own. If they aren't able to do this, however, you will work the problem out for them, and it probably won't be fun for either child.

- If your kids are quarreling, say loudly enough for them to hear, "I hope I'm not hearing bickering and fussing." This should stop them immediately, since they know your theory: Children fuss because they don't have enough to do; fighting children should be put to work!

- I issue a $1 fine to an older sibling who is tormenting or playing too roughly with a younger one. What really makes this hurt is that I make him or her pay the fine to the younger sibling, not to me.

- Boys love to wrestle. I know this is normal, but sometimes it can get out of hand. When that happens, send them to a "penalty box." This can be a bench set aside for unnecessary roughness or just a place to cool down after they've ignored your request to "Chill!"

- If you have a son who insists on getting physical to solve disputes, buy him a pair of boxing gloves. The next time things begin to "come to blows," pull out the gloves and put them on the boy. Don't allow him to take them off for the rest of the day. This makes simple tasks like eating dinner, brushing one's teeth, and putting on pajamas rather difficult. You can even cook popcorn for an after-dinner snack. (Be sure to pull out the video camera!)

- One rule around our house is that you can't play with friends if you are treating them better than your own family. If one child has a friend over, she is not necessarily required to include her sibling in everything—but she must be kind. If common courtesy is not extended, her friend has to go home.

- If my daughters are able to get along and are "kind and compassionate to one another" (Ephesians 4:32) for seven days straight, they are allowed to invite a friend to sleep over. If they argue, pick, or snip, then the clock is turned back to day one.

- It is my responsibility to create a peaceful environment for my family; I don't like having conflict in the house. If my kids are bickering, I'll often explain this to my children. If they are unable to cooperate with one another, they must play in the backyard, whether it's 30 degrees or 100 degrees outside. Of course, on those kinds of days, they seem to be able to work things out more quickly.

- Many sibling conflicts can be avoided before they begin by establishing who gets to be "Kid of the Day." (This should be decided in advance, determined by the day of the month, perhaps.) Special privileges could include riding in the front seat of the car, controlling the remote at cartoon time, and answering the phone all day.

- Most of the time when one of my children accidentally, purposely, or "purpodentally" (accidentally on purpose) hurts a sibling, the offender is so intent on running in and explaining why he or she shouldn't get in trouble that the hurt one gets left in the dust. I have had to walk my kids through the steps of compassion. First return to the hurt child and ask, "Are you okay? Can I get you anything?" Follow up with a Ziploc bag of ice held to the sore spot or gentle rubbing of the hurt area. A prayer would be nice to round things out, but I'll be happy with a sincere apology, even if it truly was an accident.

- You know how bickering can just wear you out. It's highly stressful to listen to fighting all day long. The next time your kids can't seem to get along and you're at your wit's end, call them over to do some damage control. Assign one of them to your neck and shoulders, one to your feet, one to your hands, and so on. Their job is to massage the tension that their bickering has caused right out of your weary muscles. This helps get them all working together for the common good of Mom and temporarily brings unity where there has been division. (Really, that's just a semi-spiritual rationalization to get a massage.)

- Apology Pills! Come next Valentine's Day, buy a couple of extra bags of candy hearts. Keep them in the kitchen drawer, and if one of your children needs to wave the white flag for forgiveness, he or she leaves a candy heart on the dresser or nightstand in the sibling's room. It may not be a full-blown, face-to-face, down-on-your-knee apology, but it's a much easier way to get kids in the habit of taking that first step with humbling initiative.

• When taking kids on a long road trip, give them each a roll of quarters ($10) in a clear Ziploc bag. Each time they argue with one another, they pay you a quarter. Once you reach your destination, the money left in the bag is their money to buy souvenirs.

• Oh, the power of praise! Do you ever feel as if you are scolding your children all day long for bickering? Wouldn't you rather sing their praises all day? Try this. Instead of reprimanding the one who's causing the strife, encourage the child or children who are playing without arguing. Children enjoy being noticed and singled out for good behavior. Perhaps the reward of Mother's praise will be enough to keep the peace.

• I just love this idea I received from a first-grade teacher. I can't wait to use it in my own home for my little "newscasters." The teacher explained that she has a classroom full of budding CNN anchors who love to tattle. They had discussions about the difference between tattling and reporting. (For example, you tattle when someone is disobeying, you report when someone is being hurt.) In an attempt to nip the tattling in the bud, she requires the tattler to complete a Tattle Report. It must be in the child's best handwriting and have as few spelling errors as possible. After the teacher has marked the mistakes, the student must recopy the paper. This practice has dramatically reduced the amount of needless tattling.

- Our pastor has taught us for years that if you want to be a leader, you must practice being a servant. This is a wonderful principle to teach when you have more than one child. "Can I push the grocery cart?" "You pushed it last time!" "Nuh uh, it's my turn." Sound familiar? Try establishing *Leader of the Day.* This child gets to bring in the mail, unlock the door with Mom's keys, push the grocery cart, choose the cereal, and all those other opportunities of privilege. The flip side is that the leader also does the dinner dishes, folds the laundry, takes his or her bath last, and does other random acts of kindness.
- What is it about car rides that brings out the worst in our kids? The next time your kids are arguing, look for a parking lot to pull into. Tell them to get out of the car and work out their differences. They will either be totally freaked out and drop the discussion right away, or they will step out into the elements and realize that whatever they're arguing about is not as important as being in the air-conditioned or heated car. It's amazing how quickly they can call a truce.
- A good way to cut down on the arguing about who got the bigger piece when sharing food is to let one child divide the treat and the other choose the first piece.
- I received the following e-mail from a very creative parent: "My older daughter had taken a toy from her younger brother without asking and was playing with it. When he saw her playing with it, he asked her nicely to put it back. When she didn't respond to his request, it turned ugly. When I intervened and asked why she had taken the toy without asking and wouldn't return it, she said, 'Because he wasn't playing with it, and the only reason he wants it is

because I'm playing with it now.' I told her that I thought that was a logical rule and that we should implement it immediately. I then instructed her brother to please go up to her room and get any toy that she wasn't currently playing with." I can imagine that new rule has not been implemented too many times since then!

- Another mom suggested that I might want to offer my bickering children an opportunity to clear things up on their own and resolve their conflict or they could each receive a tiny pinch of horseradish to help them "clear the airways."

Helpful Ideas from the Bible

- Matthew 5:9—"Blessed are the peacemakers, for they will be called sons of God."

  Ever since my kids were tiny, I have put a lot of emphasis on being a peacemaker. To help drive home this point with your kids, keep a small puzzle going on top of a corner table. Whenever you catch one of your children acting as a peacemaker, allow him to put a "peace" of the puzzle together. Then explain that Jesus wants us to be unified, like the finished puzzle, and living in harmony. Many pieces must come together in the puzzle before we can have a finished picture—in the same way, it takes all of us working together peacefully to represent the whole picture of God to a fragmented world.

- Luke 17:1–2—"Things that cause people to sin are bound to come, but woe to that person through whom they come.

It would be better for him to be thrown into the sea with a millstone tied around his neck than for him to cause one of these little ones to sin."

Got any old hand or ankle weights in the garage? Have your child wear them around his ankles or carry them around for the day as punishment for being a bad example to a younger sibling.

• Matthew 20:28—" . . . The Son of Man did not come to be served, but to serve, and to give his life as a ransom for many."

Every so often I have one child act as the servant to her siblings. Build this up to be a privilege. This is her opportunity to be most like Jesus. The designated servant gets to prepare and serve breakfast, open car doors, pick up the other child's toys, and do anything else she can to show love for her family. Remind the served children of the difference between a slave and a servant. They are not allowed to order the servant around; the servant decides how to serve her family. Not only does this teach the children about serving others, it also builds up the sibling relationship.

• Romans 12:20–21—"'If your enemy is hungry, feed him; if he is thirsty, give him something to drink. In doing this, you will heap burning coals on his head.' Do not be overcome by evil, but overcome evil with good."

Relax. I'm not about to suggest that you gather up a bucket of burning coals. I am proposing that the next time a "tattler" comes your way, help her put together a delicious snack to serve her tormentor. This is probably not the revenge your child had in mind, but you can always console her by assuring her that she is actually "killing them with kindness," as my grandmother always says.

- Ephesians 4:2–3—"Be completely humble and gentle; be patient, bearing with one another in love. Make every effort to keep the unity of the Spirit through the bond of peace."

   Tie the arguing siblings' ankles together as though they're in a three-legged race, and don't let them part until the issue is resolved or dropped.

- Here's a way to torture your kids until they get along. Whenever you hear them fighting, begin singing a Bible verse about loving each other. My favorite is Ephesians 4:32: "Be kind one to another, tenderhearted, forgiving one another, even as God in Christ forgave you" (NKJV). I also like the one from Psalm 133 that goes, "How wonderful it is, how pleasant, when brothers live together in harmony."

- James 3:18—"Peacemakers who sow in peace raise a harvest of righteousness."

   Sunflower seeds are the latest craze around the little-league ball field. I can't stand them because I find shells in the van for days. One day I bought a bag at the snack bar and told my children that they could have them when they got home—but they would have to earn them. I called them "seeds of peace" and said that, for the rest of the day, I would hand out seeds whenever I noticed one of them being a peacemaker. Oh, that was a glorious Saturday!

- Proverbs 17:1—"Better a dry crust with peace and quiet than a house full of feasting, with strife."

   This verse works wonders for bickering at the dinner table. Simply remove the dinner plates of the arguing siblings and replace them with the heels of the bread loaf, served on a napkin. Use your own judgment as to whether the meal is eventually served to the quarrelers.

- Proverbs 18:18—"Casting the lot settles disputes and keeps strong opponents apart."

   Keep some dice handy for those occasions when you don't have time to be a "just and fair" judge. Make it quick by saying, "Okay, whoever rolls the lowest number wins the argument. End of story."

- At the beginning of the day, build a small house out of LEGOs with each of your children while teaching them Mark 3:25: "If a house is divided against itself, that house cannot stand." Then throughout the day, whenever one of them makes a remark that brings division into the home, that child must take off one of his or her LEGO pieces. Conversely, if one of them chooses to be a peacemaker and bring unity into the home, that child earns a piece back. At the end of the day, whoever's house has the most pieces left gets a reward.

Chapter 8

God's
Topsy-Turvy
Truths

$\mathcal{I}$ was happily scrapbooking in the dining room, the table hidden under piles of supplies as I selected photos to include in my in-laws' fiftieth wedding anniversary album. The celebration was only a few days away—and I had another decade to document. I was thankful to have a few minutes' peace. I'd only finished two pages when Haven burst in from the backyard.

"Mom," she complained, "Tucker threw his glove at me and almost hit me!"

This was not something I wanted to deal with now. Sighing, I said, "Okay." I got up from the table and leaned out the door to the backyard. "Tucker," I called, "please come in here."

Tucker charged in, his face red. "It was her fault!" he said quickly.

Scowling, Haven shook her head. "No, it wasn't!" She looked at me. "Mom, don't listen to him!"

Ignoring their pleas, I pointed to the couch and said, "I want both of you to come over here and sit down." Usually, I would have asked Haven to tell me her side of the story and then give Tucker equal airtime. But today I wasn't in the mood to hear any long, drawn-out defenses. Instead I threw them a curveball.

When they were seated together, I asked, "Haven, what was your sin?"

Her mouth dropped open in surprise. "Nothing!" she claimed. "He tried to hit me."

"I didn't ask what his sin was, I asked what *yours* was," I reminded her.

She folded her arms and mumbled, "I threw the ball over the fence when it was his turn to bat."

I turned to my son. "And Tucker, what was your sin?"

"I just tossed my glove toward her because she—"

"I didn't ask what *she* did," I cut in.

"Okay, I threw my glove at her." He slumped back against the couch.

Satisfied, I studied my little ones and began, "In Luke 6:41, Jesus asked His followers, 'Why do you look at the speck of sawdust in your brother's eye and pay no attention to the plank in your own eye?'" I looked intently at the kids before continuing. "I'm going to interpret that to mean that you need to take a look at the sin in your own life before you come tattling to me about what somebody else is doing wrong," I said. "Haven, I think you need to ask Tucker to forgive you for the plank in your eye. And Tucker, you need to ask Haven to forgive you for the speck in yours."

Reluctantly they obliged. Then I sent them back outside with the warning that I didn't want to hear any more fighting. I was eager to steal a few more minutes working on my photo album.

Ever since my children were small, I have endeavored to teach them how to best handle conflict. (Obviously, as my story reveals, those words of wisdom don't always sink in!) The principle, however, is this: If they feel someone has sinned against them, they have the opportunity to make one of three choices: (1) They can get angry and sin back. (2) They can appeal to an authority (Mom or Dad) and seek justice. (But this can be done only after they've spoken the truth in love to that person. If the offender repents, they must forgive and forget.) (3) They can selflessly pardon the offender and "turn the other cheek."

I tell my kids that if they choose the first option and sin back, they will receive correction, along with the primary offender, if applicable. If they pick option number two—go to an "authority" after trying to make peace—they will get the temporary blessing on earth of justice served, without receiving correction. But if they choose the third option—the answer to the question on everyone's bracelet, "What Would Jesus Do?"—they will be rewarded, both on earth and in heaven. From Steve and me, they'll receive hugs, kisses, and the first and biggest serving of dessert; but from God, they'll receive His richest blessings in heaven.

Your kids may consider it strange or backward to choose the selfless option and love the person who wronged them. Well, it may seem odd in the world's eyes, but that's how God operates. He runs an upside-down kingdom. And if we can teach our children God's topsy-turvy principles while they are young, they will stand a better chance of realizing that it's really the *world* that's backward.

INSTILLING GOD'S TOPSY-TURVY TRUTHS

Throughout the New Testament, Jesus teaches that the moment we choose to "lose" is actually the moment we "win." That is, when we decide to sacrifice our pride, money, toys, or agendas to follow God's commands, He will multiply what we lost by infinity. His blessings in heaven cannot be compared with anything we will receive on earth. These paradoxes of faith are sprinkled all through the Bible. Here are three of them: " . . . Whoever wants to become great among you must be your servant" (Matthew 20:26); " . . . He should become a 'fool' so that he may become wise" (1 Corinthians 3:18); "For when I am weak, then I am strong" (2 Corinthians 12:10b).

If you think that only a child would fall for that kind of logic, you're right. Jesus thought so, too. That was why He said to His disciples, "Unless you . . . become like little children, you will never enter the kingdom of heaven" (Matthew 18:3). Our kids need to know that God's words are also written for them, not just Mom and Dad. I'm not referring simply to Sunday school stories like "Jonah and the Whale" and "Daniel in the Lions' Den." These are great lessons, but most likely your children already know them by heart.

Challenge them! You don't have to keep the lessons confined to Sunday school. What was your pastor's main message? Teach it to your kids over Sunday lunch. Or buy them the tape and play it at bedtime. Believe it or not, Tucker has listened to Pastor Jack Hayford's sermons since he was four years old. Pastor Jack is often way over my head, but Tucker loves him. Never underestimate what your kids can grasp. What did God teach you in your devotional time this morning? Share that with your children over breakfast. They, too, must deal with issues such as anger, greed, and fear.

It is imperative that we show them the truth because our kids are growing up in a world that feeds them lies every day. Most of what society teaches is in direct opposition to God's truths. In the book of Matthew, Jesus says those who are meek, sad, merciful, poor in spirit, and peacemakers will inherit God's kingdom. That is certainly a far cry from the assertive, popular, powerful, self-reliant, and prosperous people that the world puts on pedestals.

Our children need to understand that true success, true joy, comes only through God—and only by living out His upside-down principles. Throughout this chapter, I have outlined several concepts that we should instill in our kids, such as being separate from the world, taming the tongue, practicing the Golden Rule, and cultivating a giving spirit. By teaching our kids to embrace these hardcore, complex biblical truths, they will better be able to live out their faith in this crazy, backward world.

BEING SALT AND LIGHT MEANS BEING DIFFERENT

The Bible tells Christians to expect opposition and peer pressure—and even to welcome it (Matthew 5:11). So let's prepare our children early for the persecution they are sure to face. Warn them that they may be teased for going to church, or mocked for wearing a "WWJD" bracelet; that they may be called a "chicken" for choosing not to participate in something they know is wrong, or shunned for not watching certain television shows and movies. Remind your kids that when they are persecuted for following God, for standing apart from the muck of the world, they will be richly blessed later, in heaven (Matthew 5:12). That's God's promise to His children—and yours and mine are no exception.

Even now, our little ones are influencing their world. Their friends and neighbors can see there's something different about them. So let's assure our children that it is good to be different. If they have made Jesus their Lord, they have been "sanctified," set apart, by God (1 Corinthians 6:11). The Lord of the universe considers them special. Teach your kids this truth, not to make them proud, but to build them up before the world attempts to tear them down.

How might we teach our kids to be set apart? Don't tolerate anything in your child's life that might harm his or her relationship with God, even if that means banning seemingly "good" things. I have nothing against television; as a matter of fact, television holds a special place in my heart. But if TV influences your child toward greed, lust, or sassiness, turn it off. The same goes for the Internet, videos, books, sleepovers, and so on. All these things can be great fun, but if they tempt your child to sin, they're not worth the risk.

The same principle applies to friendships. If you are the parent of young children, you should carefully choose which friends your kids can play with. It is your responsibility to protect them when they're little. So look carefully at your children's playmates. What kind of language do they use? Are they kind? How do they treat their parents? These questions are important because friends will influence your little ones, for good or bad.

Our family is fortunate to live around the corner from a cul-de-sac full of wonderful kids, and Steve and I know each of the nine families personally. Make sure you know the child *and* his family before you let your kid go shoot hoops with the nice little neighbor boy down the street. You never know what kinds of things might be happening at his house.

As your kids get older, train them to choose their friends wisely. Teach them, as Jesus taught us, how to know a person by his or her fruit, whether it is good or bad. I have made a point to talk openly with my kids about whom they decide to befriend, and as a result they have been careful about the friendships they sustain. Once, when Tucker was five years old, I was driving him over to a friend's house to play. I liked this little boy and his family, but I knew they were somewhat lenient about the choices they allowed their son to make.

"Tucker," I warned him as we drew closer to the house, "don't walk down any paths that you know in your heart aren't wise. Remember, Proverbs 13:20 says, 'He who walks with the wise grows wise, but a companion of fools suffers harm.'"

Tucker nodded. "I know, Mom," he tried to reassure me. "Sometimes Spencer [not his real name] says and does things that are foolish, and I shouldn't start doing them, too. So I'll tell him, 'My mom says I can hang around you, but I shouldn't be a fool like you.'"

I grimaced. "Well . . . I wouldn't use those exact words."

Maybe we need to focus more on that tongue and practicing discretion.

TAMING THE TONGUE FOR GOOD

Speaking of taming the tongue, it's the next upside-down principle I want to address. It is critical that we teach our children, particularly while they are young, how powerful their words can be and why it's so important to use them to foster good rather than evil. Yet in a world that encourages lying, cursing, gossip, insults, and sarcasm, this can be a difficult principle to instill.

The Bible has a lot to say about the capability of the tongue to produce life or death. All through the New Testament, Jesus commands us to speak words of goodness, truth, love, and faith. We are to glorify God with our words by building others up. And Jesus means business. In fact, He even warns, " . . . Whoever shall say, 'You fool,' shall be guilty enough to go into the fiery hell" (Matthew 5:22 NASB).

Now, my kids have been known to call each other names, so that particular verse really caught my attention. When I first read it, I thought, *Just calling someone a fool is going to put my children in danger of the fire of hell? Isn't Jesus overreacting a tiny bit?* Wanting to give Him the benefit of the doubt, I studied this verse a little more in depth. After some prayer and reading, I realized Jesus is not saying little Clancy is going to hell if she calls her brother a "fool." Rather, He is reminding us that on the day of judgment we will all have to give an account for every careless word we've uttered (Matthew 12:36–37). I come from a long line of talkers, so this scripture sent chills up my spine!

How can we put God's upside-down command into practice, to speak only positive words? Proverbs 18:7 says, "A fool's mouth is his undoing, and his lips are a snare to his soul." Listen closely for any traps your children may unwittingly set for their souls by speaking careless words. "I can't do anything right!" spoken in discouragement needs to be replaced with "I can do everything through [Christ] who gives me strength" (Philippians 4:13). The words "I hate you!" should never be left hanging to wreak future havoc. When things cool down a bit, the trap must be sprung with the words "I love you. Will you forgive me?"

As soon as our little ones can say "I'm sorry," we should encourage them to do so when they've wronged someone. As our children get older, however, "I'm sorry" doesn't always fly. They wise up and realize it's easy to say those words just to placate Mom and not because they're really contrite.

One day, when Tucker was about four years old, he accidentally stepped on Haven's foot. It soon became obvious he wasn't going to say anything, so I reprimanded him. "Tucker, apologize to your sister. You stepped on her foot."

Tucker never took his eyes off the video he was watching. "Sorry, Haven," he said offhandedly.

I put my hands on my hips, disappointed. "Say it as though you mean it," I ordered him. "Where is the love in your heart?"

He thought about it for a second and then replied, "Oh, it's off to the side of my heart."

Do you see why I now expect more than a simple "I'm sorry"?

But let's take Jesus' command one step further. If we truly want our children to learn to use their words for good, we must train them to be the *initiators* of reconciliation. And nothing could be more upside-down than teaching our little ones to be quick to admit their faults and ask for forgiveness. When apologizing, have them be specific: "Will you please forgive me for (fill in the blank)? I was wrong." This assures the other person that the offender knows exactly how he hurt her, and besides, confession really *is* good for the soul.

Haven has this teaching down cold. Whenever a tattler comes through the back door, Haven is fast on his heels, pleading, "I'm sorry! I'm sorry! Will you please forgive me?"

Most of the time, the tattler will choose to ignore her because he would rather see her get her "just desserts." But before I give that child the satisfaction, I ask, "Haven, was there something you were trying to say?"

If she can sincerely ask for forgiveness and make amends, I let it go. "That was easy," I'll say. "Now run along and play, and next time, you two work it out between yourselves."

LIVING OUT THE GOLDEN RULE

The Golden Rule! I don't know if there is a more appropriate scripture that we could use to train our children. And in this competitive, ego-driven world, the principle of putting others before oneself truly is upside-down.

Even when our kids were toddlers, Steve and I tried to teach them to live out the Golden Rule. We found that the easiest, most effective way to do this was when they were fighting over a toy. When Clancy, for example, swiped Haven's doll, we didn't just ask, "Okay, who had the toy first?" or "Who does the toy really belong to?" or even, "You play with it five minutes, and then I'll let the other child play with it for five minutes." Steve and I had been teaching the kids Jesus' command to "give to the one who asks you, and do not turn away from the one who wants to borrow from you" (Matthew 5:42), and we wanted to experiment with taking that verse literally. So we said to our toddlers, "If you are playing with a toy and someone asks you for it, give it to them." The only stipulation was the other person had to ask. If they grabbed, the deal was off.

Though our experiment didn't always work, it wasn't any more difficult to teach our children this method than the typical "Let's everyone share" approach. And this lesson is much more valuable, as it encourages them to consider the needs of others first.

I think our efforts to write the Golden Rule on the hearts of our kids have largely paid off. For instance, a few weeks before Clancy's sixth birthday, I took her shopping for a new dress. She fell in love with the first one she saw, so much that she insisted on carrying it all over the store while we double-checked to see if she liked anything better. But despite seeing dozens of others, she had her heart set on that particular one.

As we approached the cash register, I noticed that the dress was dusty and rumpled from being dragged all over the floor of the girls' department.

"Clancy," I said, "hand me that dress and let me go get another one in your size. This one has dirt all over the bottom."

But Clancy tightened her grip. "Oh, no, Mommy," she said, her jaw set firmly. "I don't want some other little girl to have to get a dirty dress."

That statement sums up the Golden Rule.

STORING TREASURES IN HEAVEN

By a show of hands, how many got sucked into the Beanie Baby craze? My hand would be up if I weren't typing. Those toys were a weakness of mine; but I bought them only for the kids—and I never paid over retail for one, though I was tempted to for "Spangle." My bedroom is decorated in Americana and . . . . Lisa, get ahold of yourself! (Slap, slap.) Okay, I feel better now.

I like to collect things. Over the years, I have accumulated everything from antique dolls to porcelain tea sets. You would think that losing all those collectibles in a 6.8 earthquake would teach me a lesson. It did: I no longer amass anything breakable!

Having confessed all this, I realize I haven't been a good example to my children. I'm supposed to be preparing my family for heaven, and meanwhile I'm trying to pack things I can't take with me. God has commanded us to live freely and not place too much importance on the things of the world (see Matthew 6:19–21). But as with every other upside-down principle, we as parents must also have our minds focused on heavenly treasures, rather than on the little figurines in our dining room hutch.

I know an incredible woman named Joyce, whose husband told me something I have never forgotten. He said that once a year, Joyce goes into her closet and picks out her favorite dress to give away. She has done this for years, and as her two boys have gotten older, they have followed Joyce's example by giving up their favorite outfits as well.

Recently, I shared this story with my kids and then asked them what their favorite possession was. Tucker answered first.

"My baseball card collection," he said proudly.

"If God asked you to give it to Him," I questioned, "could you do it?"

Tucker nodded. "Sure."

I had an idea. I leaned forward and looked carefully at my son. "I received an e-mail this morning from a friend whose neighbor's house burned down last week," I told him. "I'm gathering up some homeschool materials to send to the mother. But the 12-year-old boy lost all his baseball cards in the fire. Would you like to put any of yours in the box?"

Tucker hesitated for just a minute and then ran upstairs. When he came down, he was carrying his favorite Mark McGwire and Sammy Sosa cards.

I hugged my sweet son, who was willing to give up his prized possessions for a stranger. Then I made a mental note to add my favorite dress to that package.

SERVANTS IN AN UPSIDE-DOWN WORLD

A few months ago, Steve, the kids, and I were driving in the van on the way to church. The children were arguing over a book that one of them insisted was her personal property, so I took the opportunity to remind all three of them, "Jesus says, 'If someone wants your coat, let them have your shirt also.'"

Giggling, Haven piped up, "Yeah, but that would be immodest."

With that in mind, let me add a word of caution: It is vital to train our children to follow godly, upside-down principles, but in doing so, we must be careful that they don't become critical or self-righteous, puffed up with knowledge (see 1 Corinthians 8:1). I place so much emphasis on making right choices that my kids have become quick to notice other people's decisions. "Look, Mommy, that girl is dressed immodestly," Haven will say. Or Clancy might point out, "Mommy, that man is smoking!"

When this happens, I take the opportunity to teach them to combat the temptation to judge. I'll say, "Oh, you're right, Clancy. We need to pray for that man." And if it's appropriate, we will pray for the person right then and there. We whisper, "Dear Jesus, please help that man not to get sick and give him the willpower to break the habit of smoking. Amen." Praying enables us to take the worldly temptations of judgment and gossip and turn them upside down. Instead of criticizing, we ask for God's blessing on a life. Doing this has helped to keep my children grounded as they focus on the spiritual needs of others.

If our kids are going to make an impact in the world, they must understand God's Word and how His upside-down commands can be lived out day by day. Our boys and girls will be the leaders in the next generation. But to be godly, successful ones, they must first learn to be servants. In the "Toolbox" section of this chapter, I have included some practical ways to teach our kids to be just that: servants in an upside-down world.

God's Topsy-Turvy Truths

Toolbox

Ways to Be Servants in an Upside-Down World

Give

- Luke 6:38—"Give, and it will be given to you. A good
measure, pressed down, shaken together and running over,
will be poured into your lap. For with the measure you use,
it will be measured to you."

  To illustrate the principle that we can never outgive
God, I gave each of my kids a handful of M&M's. I told
Haven to take her handful of candy to the kids playing
down the street and give it all away. I told Tucker to eat his
handful, and I instructed Clancy to close her hand and hold
the candy tightly until Haven returned. When Haven got
back, I instructed her to cup both of her hands and I poured
double the amount into her palms. I then gave Clancy permission to open her hand and eat her M&M's. She couldn't,
of course, because they were all "smooshed." (Not that she
was above licking her fingers!) After she washed up, I
explained the lesson: If we live with our hands open, the Lord
is able to continually give back to us, by the same measure we
choose to give away. If we think only of ourselves, we will
receive a limited blessing. If we hoard what God has given us,
we will lose what little we had in the first place.

Pray for Your "Enemies"

- Matthew 5:44—"Love your enemies and pray for those who
persecute you."

  We have one culprit in our household who finds great
pleasure in aggravating. I'm not going to name any names
because I'm confident this child will soon grow out of it. But

God works in mysterious ways, and this aggravating has driven the other two children to their knees. I cite Matthew 5:44 to the aggravated siblings. Then I explain, "If your brother or sister is pestering you, then stop right where you are and pray for him or her." This not only keeps the "pesteree" from grumbling and gossiping, but it also takes all the fun away from the "pest." And perhaps those prayers will help the child who's doing the aggravating to mature more quickly!

Put Others First

• Matthew 20:16—"The last will be first, and the first will be last."

I wanted to teach my kids this upside-down scripture, and I figured if it was ever going to fly, I'd need to start early. So, from the time my children were itty-bitty, I have asked enthusiastically, "Okay, who wants to be last this time?" They each want to be last because they know what that means in our house: Being last is best! The last piece of pie is the biggest, the last dip of ice cream overflows the cone, and the last in line gets an extra turn.

Care for the Less Fortunate

• Luke 14:12–14—"Then Jesus said to his host, 'When you give a luncheon or dinner, do not invite your friends, your brothers or relatives, or your rich neighbors; if you do, they may invite you back and so you will be repaid. But when you give a banquet, invite the poor, the crippled, the lame, the blind, and you will be blessed. Although they cannot repay you, you will be repaid at the resurrection of the righteous.'"

To help your child to become more sensitive to those less fortunate, ask him to identify the child in his class that most needs a friend. This could be a child who is new in school or perhaps one who is always overlooked. It might be the boy who is picked last to play baseball or the little girl who makes the lowest grades. Encourage your child to invite that child over to play after school one day. Then "prepare a banquet" for him or her. Stop by the toy store on the way home and pick out something for the kids to play with together and then let the new friend take it home. Cook a special dinner with dessert and center the table talk around the guest of honor.

Tithe

- Leviticus 27:30—"A tithe of everything from the land, whether grain from the soil or fruit from the trees, belongs to the LORD; it is holy to the LORD."

  Giving away money is a lot easier to do if it's not yours. And there is no better time in life to teach the value of giving offerings and tithes than when your kids are young and broke. Reach into your pocket or purse and hand them some change to put in the offering can when they are in Sunday school. Then, when they get their first birthday dollar, make a big deal about it and say, "Great! Now you get to give Jesus a dime from your own pocket."

Fast

- Matthew 6:17–18—"But when you fast, put oil on your head and wash your face, so that it will not be obvious to men that you are fasting, but only to your Father, who is unseen; and your Father, who sees what is done in secret, will reward you."

I don't think it's ever too early to teach kids the principles of the sacraments. Almost every year before Easter, Steve and I fast along with our church congregation. Last year, I wanted my kids to participate, but obviously not by abstaining from food (they need the nourishment). So I explained to them that fasting didn't necessarily have to mean not eating. I offered a couple of ideas from which they could choose to join with us. I said, "How about fasting from cartoons or snacks or video games?"

They all had their own ideas. Clancy piped up: "I would like to fast from spankings!" Haven jumped in, saying, "I would like to fast from schoolwork!" And of course Tucker had to announce, "I would like to fast from wearing underwear!"

We ultimately chose, as a family, to fast from television and instead introduced the "chapter break." We discovered there were many opportunities throughout the day that were just long enough to squeeze in a single chapter from a good book. We learned to keep a book handy and whenever we were tempted to turn on the "tube," we read a chapter or two from the book. We made it through *Stuart Little* this way—and we discovered on a small scale a little more about denying ourselves something good for something better.

Keep the Sabbath

- Exodus 20:8–10—"Remember the Sabbath day by keeping it holy. Six days you shall labor and do all your work, but the seventh day is a Sabbath to the LORD your God. On it you shall not do any work, neither you, nor your son or daughter."

It's interesting how seriously we take the other nine commandments but how quickly we'll toss this one aside. I'm usually busy doing something all the time. Because of that, I rarely take the time to sit down and read, take a nap, or work on a scrapbook without feeling guilty. Recently, I began resting on the Sabbath—and I cannot describe what an indulgent pleasure it is to take a day off! It may be topsy-turvy in this workaholic world, but it makes sense: Our bodies need one day of rest.

We can teach this to our kids by example and in other practical ways. For instance, if they keep the Sabbath, they'll rejoice at having no schoolwork on Sunday—but that also means they must be diligent the other six days of the week. Any reports that are due on Monday must be finished by Saturday, or they'll have to be turned in incomplete.

Of course, it's important for each family to decide how they should honor the Sabbath. But consider as a family taking a day of rest and following another of God's upside-down principles. I think you'll soon be hooked.

Don't Make Promises

- Matthew 5:34,37—"But I tell you, Do not swear at all. . . . Simply let your 'Yes' be 'Yes,' and your 'No,' 'No'; anything beyond this comes from the evil one."

It's certainly upside down, but we never let the "I promise" thing get started. As a matter of fact, if I slip up, my kids are quick to catch me. They say, "Let your 'yes' be 'yes'

and your 'no' be 'no.'" When we follow up a declaration
with "I promise," it can indicate that we feel that we are not
believed or taken at our word. It is important for a child to
feel trusted. By eliminating suspicion, we can create an
atmosphere in which we expect only the truth.

Shield Yourself from Evil
• Matthew 5:27–28—"You have heard that it was said, 'Do
not commit adultery.' But I tell you that anyone who looks
at a woman lustfully has already committed adultery with
her in his heart."

The world our children are growing up in is filled with
images that can lodge deeply in their souls, only to creep out
at a future time and ensnare them. I suppose this is nothing
new. More than 3,000 years ago, Job said, "I made a covenant
with my eyes not to look lustfully at a girl" (Job 31:1). We
can teach our children—both our boys and our girls—to set
"eye gates" and shield themselves from impurity.

I remember a family vacation we took with the cousins a
few years ago. We drove through Las Vegas, and I think I spent
the whole day warning Tucker, "Look at your shoes." It became
a family joke. Soon my sister-in-law was instructing her husband, "Look at your shoes." It was funny, but my instructions
to Tucker were serious: There is no sense in letting the specter
of lewdness lodge in our kids' hearts, only to haunt them later.

Keep a Pure Thought Life
• 2 Corinthians 10:5—"We demolish arguments and every
pretension that sets itself up against the knowledge of God,

and we take captive every thought to make it obedient to Christ."

To help Tucker keep his mind pure, we came up with a plan. Whenever undesirable thoughts would enter his head, he would recognize that they were not from him and reject them. Later we came up with a strategy to get on the offensive. The plan was, whenever an impure thought popped into Tucker's mind, he would immediately start praying for someone's salvation.

I had forgotten all about this until one day, when I reported to him that I had heard that the Dallas Cowboys' quarterback, Troy Aikman, was getting married.

Tucker replied, "Yeah. I've been praying for him."

I was surprised. "Oh, you have?"

"Sure," he said. "Whenever one of those yucky thoughts pops into my mind. I'm going to keep praying for him until he gets saved, and then I'm going to pray for John Elway."

I wouldn't be surprised if the devil decided to back off a little before Tucker prays the whole NFL into heaven!

Master Your Emotions
- Jeremiah 17:9—"The heart is deceitful above all things and beyond cure. Who can understand it?"

  There will be times in our children's lives when they will be tempted to follow the world's philosophy: "If is feels good, do it." There will be other times in life when they must do things they don't feel like doing. It is important to teach our children as early as possible that our feelings are a gift from God, but that they can't always be trusted. From the first time they whine, "I don't feel like it," remind them, "Be the boss of your feelings!" This phrase will become even more valuable as our children get older.

Confess Your Sins and Pray

• James 5:16—"Therefore confess your sins to each other and pray for each other so that you may be healed. The prayer of a righteous man is powerful and effective."

I have been surprised at how much Tucker, who just turned nine years old, has already had to deal with the lust of the flesh. Thankfully, he can't keep anything hidden in his heart. He just can't rest until he's brought it out into the light and we've asked Jesus to overexpose the picture. Last summer, when he was still eight, I was putting him to bed when he stopped me at the door.

"Mom," he said, "I need to confess something."

I returned to his side. "Sure, what is it?"

He detailed what happened earlier in the day. "When Grandmother and I were riding bicycles at the beach today," he began, "we stopped in a souvenir store. I saw some cards with immodest girls on them. I knew that I shouldn't, but I went over and looked at them anyway."

I consoled him. "Tucker, it was wise of you not to keep that secret. There was nothing wrong with your being tempted to look at the beautiful girls. God made women, and He did a pretty good job! But you need to ask God to forgive you for disobeying His voice. He whispered in your heart not to go over to the cards and look at them. He was trying to protect you, and you ignored Him."

I then prayed with him—and afterward, we both felt better.

Let Go

• Matthew 5:21–22—"You have heard that it was said to the people long ago, 'Do not murder, and anyone who murders will be subject to judgment.' But I tell you that anyone who is angry with his brother will be subject to judgment."

One phrase we say frequently around our house is "Just let it go." Often we get angry when we don't get what we want or think we deserve. In the heat of the moment, we believe we have to fight for what's rightfully ours! Yet in reality, what we want is usually not worth fighting for at all. That's when it comes in handy to have Mom around to suggest, "Just let it go." If my suggestion is met with "But that's not right. I had it first!" I offer them a choice: "Would you rather be right or righteous?" This reminds them that it's good to be right, but it's godly to be righteous.

Chapter 9

Grace 'n' Failure

For more than 20 years—and virtually every day—*The Facts of Life* has been on television around the world. This, for me, is both a blessing and a curse. The financial blessings from residuals ran out a long time ago. But the show has continually allowed me to develop new friendships, and it makes millions of people smile each day. *The Facts of Life* has given me a huge platform to share God's love with generations of girls. Sometimes I'm awed by how much God has been able to shape me—and others—because of it.

Yet it wasn't an entirely rosy experience. Who of you would relish having your awkward adolescent years archived and displayed for the world? I'm still approached by girls in the mall who say, "Blair! You don't look as fat as you do on TV!" Am I supposed to say, "Thank you"? Actually, there's really nothing *to* say. Those girls don't mean any harm; they're just calling it as they see it. Anyone who followed the show for even a little while watched me quickly balloon up. Adolescence, for me, was a cruel "fact of life." Unfortunately, someone forgot to inform me that a television star isn't allowed to go through puberty. Or, if she does, she had better hide it—especially if she's been cast as I was, to play a perennially beautiful, rich, and thin ingenue.

I began "blossoming" (i.e., gaining weight) toward the end of the second season. In hindsight, I realize I was eating out of loneliness. I was 17 years old, and all my family and friends were in Texas. My mother was trying to raise my 13-year-old brother, Cody, and couldn't just pick up and move everyone. So every three weeks, I flew home, indulged in my mom's home cooking, and ordered pizzas with my girlfriends. Then I headed back to my job in California and, homesick, tried to fill the void with food.

My plight was certainly understandable, but there were millions of dollars riding on my character looking a certain way and, consequently, there was very little room for compassion. The producers swooped down on me like a swarm of Africanized bees. They hired nutritionists, therapists, and hypnotists. They sent me to fat farms, exercise trainers, and health spas. They even brought in a scale and had me weigh myself every morning in the middle of the rehearsal hall, while they all gathered around to see if I had gained or lost any weight.

I don't blame them for any of the measures they took. They were just doing their job; I was *not* doing mine. I didn't fulfill my side of the contract. They had hired me to fill a particular role, and I filled it to overflowing. As is typical of human nature, the more they pushed, the more I ate. And the more I ate, the lonelier I felt. And when I was alone, I had to face my failure. Finally, at my lowest point, a friend asked me a question that changed my life.

"Lisa," he said, "you sound miserable. How much time are you spending with the Lord?"

I raised my eyebrows. "Well, I pray every day," I began. "I read my Bible every night before I go to bed, and I go to church every Sunday."

"I don't mean what you're *doing* for the Lord—I mean how

much time are you spending just being with Him and getting to know Him?" He gestured at the two of us. "You know . . . like friends do."

I wrinkled my brow in thought, then admitted weakly, "I guess not very much."

"Why don't you try a new diet?" he encouraged. "You can eat anything you want for the next two weeks. The only stipulation is that you must set your alarm early every morning and spend time with God before you go to work."

I nodded, eager to try it. This was the best diet I'd ever heard of, and I thought I had tried them all. For the next 14 days, I woke up every morning and went to the bathroom. (I lived in a studio apartment with my grandmother, and it was the only room where I could turn on the light and not wake her.) Closing the door, I grabbed my Bible and sat on the commode—with the lid down! Some days I would read God's Word and feel as if He were speaking directly to me. Other times I felt so bored I could barely keep my eyes open. But I knew my time with God was feeding my soul.

I also spent time in prayer, envisioning Jesus sitting beside me, on the rim of the bathtub. Often I started my talks with God by saying, "I love You." Then I spilled everything: how much I missed my family and how I wished that I could go home, how I wanted to find a girlfriend in California, how sorry I was that I'd failed so many people. As I prayed, the pangs of loneliness and hunger began to subside, and I discovered the truth of Jesus' promise: "I am the bread of life. He who comes to me will never go hungry" (John 6:35).

My favorite part of the "diet" was the time I spent sitting quietly, just being with Jesus. I wouldn't say anything, and most of the time He wouldn't either. Sometimes I even fell asleep. But I knew

He was there. I could sense His presence, and it filled the emptiness in my soul.

My life turned around during those two weeks, and it has never been the same since. Though I wish I could say I suddenly dropped 20 pounds and never had to count another calorie, the truth is that physically I stayed the same; however, I was different on the inside. Over time, my hormones evened out, and I lost the baby fat. But more importantly I lost the emptiness I had been trying fill with food.

I'll never be able to go back and erase *The Facts of Life* tapes that forever captured my posterior for posterity. I don't know if I'd want to, even if given the chance. If I hadn't been intensely lonely, I might never have known intimate friendship with Jesus. If I hadn't been insatiably hungry, I might never have been filled with the Bread of Life. If I hadn't failed a dozen diets, I might never have decided to "taste and see that the LORD is good" (Psalm 34:8).

LEARNING FROM FAILURE

It is in the face of failure that we can see redemption on the face of God. That is as true for a seven-year-old as it is for a 70-year-old. God catches us, His children, when we fall, no matter how old or young we are. And before He lifts us back up again, He teaches us a lesson.

A wise parent will let her children stumble and fall. My mom could have hopped on the first plane to California—and she was often tempted to do so—but she knew I needed to work through my pain, and that I couldn't do it if she rescued me every time I was lonely. She knew I would learn a lot when I was on my face before the Lord. I did. And I have found that to be true with my children as well—literally.

One week after Tucker got his braces off, I walked in the door to find his daddy holding a bag of ice on what was left of his front tooth.

Before I could even ask, Tucker blubbered, "Mommy, I know why this happened. Daddy told me not to hang on the basketball rim, but I did anyway. Then I slipped and fell on my face. I know this will cost you a lot of money to get my tooth fixed, but it will have been worth it, because I learned why it is so important to obey your parents."

Sometimes we just need to let our children fall. And as I have discovered, they will learn from their stumbling. I'll admit it's not easy for me to see my kids struggle. If I could have spared them the pain, I would have. (Lord knows I've tried!) But now I'm glad I failed. I'm glad they failed. That pain has brought us all closer to God.

In school, you only fail a test when you don't know the answers. How do you find the answers? By looking them up! When our children fail, we can teach them to look up—up at God—to find the answer. My friend Myrene once told me, "Remember to teach your children to pray through all conflicts, large and small. This reminds them that it is ultimately God who shapes us into His image, not our trying to be good enough. The more we invite God into our children's lives—from scraped knees to lost shoes to science tests— the more our children will naturally turn to Him and develop their own relationships with Him."

You'd be surprised how many times each day we have the opportunity to invite God into our children's lives. For example, did your child get into trouble at school? That's certainly a cause for correction, but more importantly it's an opportunity to teach her respect for authority, or diligence in schoolwork, or the reasons for following rules. Has your son suddenly been spouting colorful words after playing with the new kid on the block? Teach him about coarse talk and using the Lord's name in vain, reminding him that his words can be used for good or evil.

When hard times come knocking, we as parents should welcome conflicts, struggles, and failures. As I've said in earlier chapters, I would much rather invite them in while my children are still living at home, where I can guide and help them, than later in life, when I'm not around to help point them in the right direction.

FACING FAILURE

We can help prepare our children for the hard choices they will surely have to make. What were some of the lessons you learned growing up? Share stories of your own failures (but use discretion). Haven used to ask every guest we had over for dinner, "Tell me something you did bad when you were a kid." Somehow it made her feel better to hear of other people who had failed and lived to tell about it. She learned many vicarious lessons this way.

Explain to your children that each of us has weaknesses and strengths. Help them identify and give thanks for their strengths, while asking the Lord to help them to be strong in their weaker areas. Teach them to compensate for their vulnerabilities.

Ever since she could talk, Haven has been tempted to repeat words that she is not allowed to use. One afternoon, Clancy ran inside.

"Mommy," she called, "Haven said *butt!*"

I summoned Haven, who was four years old at the time, and asked, "What's going on?"

"I just said *bud-uv-it*," Haven said innocently.

I folded my arms. "And what does *bud-uv-it* mean?"

"It's a new word that means 'Praise the Lord!'"

"And where did you hear that word, Haven?" I queried.

She didn't hesitate. "Grandmother taught it to me to love God."

I leaned in a little closer to my imaginative daughter. "Oh, really?"

Haven received two corrections that day—one for saying a word she wasn't allowed to use, and one for lying. Then we came up with a plan. Whenever she heard someone else use inappropriate language, or she was tempted to use it herself, she would praise the Lord in its place. This worked well—after all, Haven provided me with the idea.

Our kids are going to face plenty of failure. We can't expect them to be mature Christians in tiny bodies. The Bible describes Jesus as a child, saying, "And Jesus grew in wisdom and stature, and in favor with God and men" (Luke 2:52). Even Jesus had to grow intellectually, physically, spiritually, and socially—and so will our kids.

Childish inclinations are perfectly natural. In aspiring to build godly children, we must be careful not to make them feel bad about themselves for just being children. It is often quoted that "the good is the enemy of the best." Yes, that is true. But hey, let's not forget to point out and reward the good! Then, and only then, should we strive for the best. When encouraging holiness, I will often say to my children, "It is perfectly natural to feel the way you do. But with God's help you can be more like Jesus." Then I tag on our little slogan: "Would you rather be natural or super-natural?"

It takes time for our children to mature. If we just keep feeding our kids what's good for them, they will grow into spiritually strong and morally healthy adults.

AMAZING GRACE

Don't get discouraged during the growth process. The good news is that our kids are most receptive to experiencing God's grace when they have felt the pain of their own failure. The Bible says, "If we confess our sins, [God] is faithful and just and will forgive us our sins and purify us from all unrighteousness" (1 John 1:9). What greater reason could there be for rejoicing in failure? We can tell our children all day long how much God loves them, but they'll better understand His love after they've messed up and He's forgiven them, completely erasing their mistakes forever.

That forgiveness and God's promise of salvation is grace. The absence of punishment is His mercy. To make those concepts real, we must demonstrate God's grace and mercy at home. Our children need to see us apologize and freely forgive our spouses. And they need to see us humbly ask for their own forgiveness when we fail them—the kids—in some way, too. We need to show them that when they voluntarily confess their sins to us, as opposed to waiting to see if they get caught, we're more likely to be merciful toward them (i.e., not punish them). This gift of mercy is priceless: When they've received it from us, they will be more likely to extend mercy to others, growing up to be more compassionate adults.

Of course, we can't force our kids to be full of grace, compassion, and mercy. Only they can learn these truths for themselves. As parents, we can do only so much—the rest we must leave up to God. But far from being scary, that's part of the beauty of Christianity: Through the power of His Holy Spirit, Christ can help us to become more like Him, something we'd never be able to do on our own (see 2 Corinthians 5:21). It really isn't a matter of trying harder to be better parents. It's not even a matter of our children trying harder. We must teach our children to pray, "Lord, I can't do what Your Word commands me. I need Your grace—please fill me with it. Help me to overcome my sin and become all that You have created me to be."

Our job as parents should start with and continue in prayer. We can teach our kids how to pray when they're little—and then pray that those prayers will stick when they're older. In the "Toolbox" section of this chapter, I've written a few sample prayers that your children may find helpful to say alongside you when they find themselves in need of grace and power in the midst of failure.

Grace 'n' Failure

Toolbox

Prayers for When They Sin

Aggravating

Children seem to love aggravating one another—especially their siblings! Therefore, we need to help them overcome this temptation.

> Dear God,
>
> I confess that I was just stirring up strife. Thank You for forgiving me when I admit my sins. Thank You for also helping me when I can't seem to help myself. I need Your help now, God. I want to stop aggravating others, but I still keep doing it. I could come up with excuses, but I know that sometimes I just cause trouble for no good reason. So I'm counting on You to help me stop. You told me all I needed to do was ask You. Thanks for Your help. I love You. Amen.

Anger

Anger is easy to recognize when it's expressed through physical retaliation or hurtful words. But we must also address anger when it shows up in passive forms, such as in pouting and giving "looks that could kill."

> Dear God,
>
> I am angry because _____. Please help me to just "let it go." I choose to bless my enemy, and I trust You to take care of the revenge part. Please forgive me for my sin. Lord, when I don't get my way, help me to remember that all I have to do is ask You for what I want or need. And if it is something You want for me, You'll

give it to me. Thank You that I don't have to fight for
what I want. Remind me that my job is to concentrate on
serving others and obeying my parents, and You'll take
care of the rest. Amen.

Arguing

Our children need to be in the habit of obeying without arguing. Unfortunately, forming good habits can be as difficult to do
as breaking bad ones. That's why it is so important to start early
and be consistent. I can think of few efforts that will reap greater
rewards.

> Dear God,
>
> Please forgive me for thinking that I am smarter than
> my parents. You have given me a big brain, and I know I
> have good reasons for wanting things my way—but I
> also want the wisdom that comes from trusting and obey-
> ing my parents. Help me to be slower to speak, quicker
> to listen, and even quicker to obey without arguing.
> Amen.

Bad or Perverse Language

As parents, it's often hard to know when our sons are "just
being boys" and when they have crossed the line to crudeness, or
what I call "potty mouth." It's easy for boys to go from "bodily
function" humor as kids to being men of "unclean lips," so at our
house, we've adopted an interesting approach. Proverbs 18:20
reads: "From the fruit of his mouth a man's stomach is filled; with
the harvest from his lips he is satisfied." Therefore, our rule of

thumb for "boy" talk is, "Don't speak about anything you wouldn't want to eat." Yuck!

> Dear God,
>
> Please cleanse my mouth. Make my words wholesome and pure, like a freshwater stream. Please forgive me for polluting the life You have given me with words that are dirty. I want my lips to be glorifying to You so that I can tell others about You and Your clean, living water. Amen.

Cheating/Deceiving/Stealing

All three of these sins stem from the desire to get something the easy way. But, as I tell my kids, deception isn't worth it, because "you may be sure that your sin will find you out" (Numbers 32:23).

> Dear God,
>
> I realize that You see everything and that I can't get away with anything around You. Please forgive me for even trying. I understand that I deserve correction. Help me to receive Your punishment through the hands of my parents. I know that You correct me because You love me. "Catch me" with Your light if I try to hide my sin again. Amen.

Complaining

God hates complaining. So do I, and I bet you do, too! There's nothing worse than a child who complains, when inconvenienced, that his life isn't perfect. The children of Israel were famous for it. They had the presence of God and all of His resources available to them—and still, they always found something to complain about. Let's guard our kids from this.

Dear God,

I don't want to be like the children of Israel, who wandered in the desert for 40 years, complaining about how bad their life was even though they had many blessings. Help me to focus on what I do have instead of what I don't have. And help me to be grateful for You. I'm sorry that my attitude has been so bad. Help me to be content and patient in every situation and to rejoice in all things. Amen.

Disobedience

I have left a blank space so that this prayer may be applied to whomever the child has disobeyed.

Dear God,

Please forgive me for disobeying _____. I understand that he/she has been placed in authority over me for my protection. I now choose to submit to him/her and obey. Please help me to obey Your commands because I love You. I want to love Your rules, because I know that when I'm following them, I'll feel the happiest and most blessed. Thank You for Your forgiveness. Amen.

Disrespectfulness

Proverbs 9:10 reads: "The fear of [respect for] the LORD is the beginning of wisdom." It is important to train our children to respect the Lord. The amount of respect they have for their heavenly Father will be determined in large part by how they view their earthly parents. With that in mind, we must not allow our kids to display a casual attitude toward our authority.

> Dear God,
>
> I'm sorry that I was disrespectful. Would You please forgive me? I want to honor my parents, mostly because You say that it is important, but also because I want to live a long, good life that is blessed by You. Please help me to trust my parents' wisdom and to be respectful toward them even when I disagree with them. Help me to remember that they love me and that they, like You, only want what is best for me. Amen.

Impatience

Children really believe that the whole world revolves around them. So when they are asked to wait for something, they don't understand why we don't just stop everything and take care of their desire. We must train them early to be patient—it will soften the blow when they eventually realize that life doesn't always unfold the way we'd like.

> Dear God,
>
> I want what I want, when I want it! I guess that sounds kind of demanding, huh? Please forgive me, Lord. I understand that when I get upset, I'm basically saying, "What I want is more important than anything else." Please help me to be more patient, and help me to be able to wait with my mouth closed. Thank You. Amen.

Jealousy

Comparing is dangerous. And it's one of the oldest tricks in the book. Satan told Eve, who lived in paradise, that she was missing something from her life, and he convinced her to eat the forbidden fruit. How sad that our children have inherited this same desire to be and have something other than what God has intended for them. Let's help them to combat this desire now.

> Dear God,
>
> I know that it makes You sad when I want to be different from the way You created me. Help me to see myself through Your eyes because I know You think I am perfect just the way I am. When I want something that someone else has, I'm not being content with what You've already given me. Please forgive me.
>
> If You think I need something more than what I have, You'll take care of it. Lord, You know what You are doing—You have everything under control, and You know exactly what I need. Help me to remember that. Amen.

Lying

We all know that lying is a big no-no. But do we understand why it's such a big deal? One of the reasons is that lies originate from Satan—whom Jesus called the "father of lies." We must be quick and sure to keep our children from falling into the trap of deception.

> Dear God,
>
> I'm so sorry that I lied. Please forgive me. I'm Your child, and I want to follow Your commands for my life. I

want Your way and not my way, especially if I have to lie to get what I want or to protect myself. I realize You are always watching and that I cannot hide anything from You. I know that You hate a lying tongue, so please cleanse my lips—please forgive me. Thank You, Jesus. Amen.

Making Excuses/Shifting the Blame

It's much easier to blame someone else than it is to say, "I'm sorry." But it's hard to do only before we've said it. Afterward it feels so good to "come clean" that you wonder what the big deal was.

Dear God,

Please help me to be quick to ask forgiveness and apologize. Rationalizing might help me to avoid getting correction, but it doesn't get my heart clean like confession does. I want to be forgiven even more than I want to be right. I shouldn't have done/said what I did. Please forgive me. I'm glad it's okay to make a mistake. Thank You for giving me a second chance when I admit that I've messed up. Amen.

Out-of-Control Tongue

The tongue is a small part of the body, but it contains the power to bring life or death. Proverbs 21:23 reads: "He who guards his mouth and his tongue keeps himself from calamity."

Dear God,

I let my tongue run loose again. Please help me to better control it. I want my words to bring life, not death.

You say that my words come from my heart. Would You make my heart more like Your heart? Please forgive me for the things I have said that are not pleasing to You. And where my tongue has hurt someone else, please make it better. Amen.

Rebellion

Rebellion is when our children consciously make the choice to go their way instead of God's way—not the impulsive disobedience that is so often the characteristic of childhood. God says, "For rebellion is as the sin of divination [witchcraft]" (1 Samuel 15:23). Those are strong words, but they indicate the danger that comes with choosing to walk away from God's ways.

> Dear God,
>
> I must be honest: There is a part of me that doesn't even want to pray this prayer. I like doing what I want, and sometimes it's hard for me to give that up. Please give me the desire to obey You. Please soften my heart. I choose, as an act of my will, to ask You to forgive me and change me. Amen.

Selfishness

Selfishness is the cause of most childhood (and adult!) misbehavior. This makes it a worthy focus of prayer.

> Dear God,
>
> I tried to be king of my own life. Please forgive me. I don't really want my own way all the time, because I know

that Your way is best for me. Lord, You are my king and I will follow You. Help me to deny myself and sacrifice what I want for You and for others. I know that I don't have to look out for myself because You will take care of me. Thank You. Amen.

Sibling Conflict

Boy, I could write a book on this subject, except for the fact that I'm too busy acting as referee for my three children! If we ever needed prayer, this would be the reason.

Dear God,

I want to get along with _____, but I just can't seem to keep it up for very long. It's really hard sometimes, and I need Your help. The next time I'm in the middle of a big argument, remind me that I can be a peacemaker. I may lose the battle, but I'll win Your smile, and that's more important to me than anything else I'm fighting for. Amen.

P.S. Between You and me, I really do love my brother/sister. Thank You for letting me grow up and live with my best friend(s).

Tattling

Sometimes kids need to tattle and have a parent step in and keep things from escalating out of control. But often tattling is simply a way of getting someone else in trouble. When that's the motive for tattling, it's important for the parent to address the tattler's heart.

Dear God,

Please forgive me for trying to get _____ in trouble. I know that judging is Your job, not mine. I will leave that up to You from now on. Remind me to think about my own response and make sure that everything I'm saying and doing is pleasing to You *before* I complain about someone else's sin. Please teach me to speak the truth in love so that we can help each other walk in Your ways. Amen.

Teasing

I often point out to my kids that when they say, "I was just joking!" they usually could have said, "I shouldn't have done/said that." Often we try to cover up our sins by laughing instead of admitting, "I'm sorry. I was wrong." Let's teach our kids to be more sensitive.

Dear God,

I got a little carried away and crossed the line between having fun and being unkind. I'm sorry—I didn't mean to hurt anybody. Please help me to remember that getting a laugh is not more important than someone else's feelings. I want to have the self-control not to go too far next time. Will You please help me? Thank You, Lord. Amen.

Ungratefulness

It's such a dilemma for parents these days. We want to give our children everything, but then they begin to expect it and become ungrateful. In the Old Testament God dealt with this same issue over and over again with His children.

Dear God,

I'm sorry that I have acted so spoiled. Remind me to stop every once in a while and thank You for the things I take for granted. I'll start right now: Thank You for giving me a warm bed. Thank You for loving me. Thank You for giving me clothes and food. Thank You for making nature beautiful to look at. Thank You for _____ and _____. When I think about how much You've given me, I realize my attitude is ungrateful. Please forgive me. I really do appreciate my life. Thank You for everything. Amen.

Unkindness

If we can teach our kids to be kind, we've come a long way toward raising children who exhibit the love of Jesus. Each day, our children have opportunities to choose kindness. Let's help them.

Dear God,

I'm afraid that I've hurt somebody You love very much. I'm sorry. Help me to do better next time. Make my heart tender like Yours so that I think first about how my words and actions might make someone else feel. Please fill me with your love so that I can be kind to those around me. Thank You. Amen.

Prayers for Strengthening Virtues

Choosing Salvation

The single most important decision our children will make is whom they are going to serve. If they do not make a conscious choice, they will serve themselves or the world by default. It is our privilege as parents to teach them of God's love for them, demonstrated through the death and resurrection of His Son, Jesus.

Dear God,

Thank You for loving me so much that You sent Your only Son, Jesus, to die for my sins. I know that I'm a sinner, and I'm thankful that You want to have a relationship with me, that You want to be my Lord. I believe that Jesus died on the cross for me, and that His blood covers my sins and allows me to be clean in Your sight. I also believe that you raised Him from the dead on the first Easter. Because of Jesus, I can approach You. Thank You for forgiving my sins and for allowing me to live in heaven with You forever when I die. Thank You for sending Your Holy Spirit to help me obey You and to help me to live life to the fullest here on earth. I love You, Heavenly Father. Amen.

Delighting in Correction

You may think it's impossible for your children to *delight* in correction. But "delighting" is different from "enjoying." We can train our children to realize that correction is for their benefit and, subsequently, to welcome it.

Dear God,

I understand that You have given Mom and Dad the responsibility to protect me and train me. Thank You that they love me enough to teach me to live by Your Word. I want to be wise and listen to their instruction. I know that I may not like it when they correct me, but I need their correction. After all, it isn't nearly as bad as what could happen if they weren't teaching me to follow Your Word. Thank You, Lord, and thank you, Mom and Dad. Amen.

As we discussed in an earlier chapter, if you choose to spank, it is important to complete the correction with a hug and a prayer. The following is a suggested prayer that will help to remind your child that you love her and that your love is the reason for this form of correction.

Dear God,

Thank You that my parents love me and that because they love me, they correct me when I sin. Thank You that the spankings drive out the foolishness in my heart. Please fill my heart with goodness so that I can please You. After all, I want Your blessings in my life! I'm so glad that You not only forgive me, but that You also forget about whatever I've done wrong. I like that and I like You. Amen.

Diligence

Because most of us don't live on farms anymore, our children don't have as much opportunity to learn diligence by default. We have to consciously espouse excellence and hard work as virtues that are worth pursuing.

Dear God,

I admit that I like things to be easy, and when things

are too hard, I sometimes would rather give up or do just enough to get by. But I know You have created me for more than that. You see me at my highest potential. I want to be all You have made me to be. I want to tackle everything with Your help, knowing that You are watching me. I want to give You my best. Whether I'm at school, doing chores, or deciding how to spend my free time, I want to be striving for excellence. Amen.

Resisting Peer Pressure

Peer pressure can come in a variety of forms. It can manifest itself in an attraction to the things of the world, to friends who would bring our children down, or to doing things our children know are wrong. It is mostly an overwhelming awareness of and attraction to what the crowd says is acceptable or cool.

Dear God,

Please help me to have the courage to stand up for what I know is right. Help me to resist the pull to be like the world even though it makes me feel accepted. I want to choose friends who will encourage me to stay close to You, Lord. Please help me not to make decisions based on what other people will think, but instead on whether my choices make You smile. Forgive me when I have sought other people's approval before Yours, God. Amen.

Seeking the Lord

As we encourage our children to seek the Lord with all their hearts, we'll have to nag and scold less and less. When our kids learn to follow God, they will be parented more and more by the Holy Spirit, who can change them from the inside out.

> Dear God,
>
> I want to be more like You. Please change me into Your image as I spend time talking to You, reading Your Word, and listening to You. When life gets busy, help me to remember that there is nothing more important than being with You. As I grow up and the cares of this world try to capture my interest, keep my focus on what You say. I love You, Lord, with all my heart, soul, and strength. Amen.

Self-Control

It is not unusual for our children to need extra help when it comes to self-control. Often little boys especially need to ask God for the strength to overcome impulsiveness, hyperactivity, and sometimes anger.

> Dear God,
>
> I keep doing things that I don't want to do. Please forgive me and help me to stop and think before I act or say something I will regret. I haven't been doing a very good job of controlling myself. Please help me to change. Fill me with Your power and strengthen me so I can make good choices. Thank You. Amen.

Sharing/Giving

It's hard to teach children to understand that there is more joy in giving than in receiving. But we can start by encouraging them to give and share. Then they'll understand how good it feels to sacrifice to make someone else happy.

> Dear God,
>
> You are the giver of all good gifts. Thank You for giving me so many! You have said the more I give away, the more I'll get. That's hard to understand, but I choose to believe You. I want to give that a try—again. Please forgive me for being greedy. Help me to remember how good it feels to share the gifts You have given to me. Amen.

Spiritual Warfare

Sometimes we can tell that the opposition our children face goes beyond what is natural and reasonable. During these times, our children can utilize the weapons of warfare that have been given to them to fight the battle in the invisible realm (see Ephesians 6:10–18).

> Dear God,
>
> I realize that I need help to fight this battle, that without Your help, I'll lose. Jesus, help me to overcome the devil's power in my life. Help me to put on the armor of God that You've provided me. I've done all I can. Now I'll stand and watch You win the victory for me. Thank You, Lord. Amen.

Chapter 10

In the Beginning

When Focus on the Family asked me to write an additional chapter for the trade paper release of *Creative Correction,* concentrating on toddlers and preschoolers, I was excited but a wee bit nervous. I have three children in junior high these days, and although there are some uncanny similarities between the "tweens" and the "twos," I wasn't sure I could still come up with a realistic and effective toolbox for the early years. Would I still be able to relate to that mom in the throes of diapers, pacifiers, and temper tantrums?

To refresh my memory, I opened my journals from those days not so long ago and was flooded with familiar emotions. As I lingered over those precious recollections, I was at times surprised, at others shocked, but often encouraged. I had to laugh out loud when I read the following entry dated March 7, 1995:

*I'm sooooo tired. Not really physically, although that too. Mostly, emotionally stressed. Just in case five years from now I forget, let me just now state for the record: **Raising three preschoolers is exhausting!** Today we started a whole new sticker chart for serving one another. They get one sticker every time they do something to make someone else happy, and they* *get one taken away if they aggravate or talk harshly. When they fill the chart, they go to Target and get a toy. So far, so good. I decided this morning to not count on doing anything for myself. That means no treadmill, no bath, no cleaning, no computer, etc. This has really helped reduce a bit of the frustration.*

Perhaps you can relate to one or both of these entries dated around the same time:

The kids are still sick, and I am so stressed. It's really not the fact that they're sick that's so hard. It's what it does to them emotionally. Most all self-control goes out the window. Everything is an issue. It's exhausting. I can't just let them get away with it because they're sick. It usually takes two weeks for the cycle to end, and by that time bad habits would have set in and I would probably be a nervous wreck. So the alternative is about 100 spankings, 200 "Go sit on your beds," and 300 lost privileges. This morning I was almost in tears. It was 9:30, and Tucker had already gotten too many spankings to count. I called Steve at work, and he started to pray for me over the phone and ask God to help me. I really resented that. I said, "I don't want your prayers for God's help; I need your help!" *He left work to come home and rescue me—and Tucker.*

February 26, 1994
I'm very sleepy, I'm tired of taking care of sick kids, and Tucker seems out of control. All boundaries and rules have disintegrated because he's sick. I have no idea when Steve will be home. And there are four hours and 15 minutes before I can put the first one to bed. There's a sneak preview of a movie tonight that I've wanted to see, but I can't go. Tucker just informed me that his ear hurts really badly. The doctor's office is closed. I

feel fat and unmotivated. And there's nothing good to eat in this house. Other than that, it's been a great day. Except for the big argument Steve and I had before he left this morning.

Does the entry below sound like a typical day with toddlers around your house?

Yesterday while I was on the phone talking to my mom, the kids took the spray chalk and spray "painted" everything in the backyard. I had specifically instructed Tucker that he could only "paint" the old skateboards. He then proceeded to paint the trampoline, the playhouse, the bikes, the furniture, and the girls. When Steve got home, I was on the phone, Clancy had Indian war chalk all over her face, and Haven was running around in the backyard stark naked, with spray chalk all over her body.

Just when I thought I had drowned those toddler traumas down deep in "De Nile," I came across this short journal entry:

*At one point today, Tucker was mad about hitting his head, and he lashed out at me while he was crying, "Don't just stand there; do something!" After applying a bag of ice to his noggin to prevent swelling, I applied a tiny drop of Tabasco sauce to the tip of my finger and then to the tip of his tongue to prevent disrespect. He then proceeded to yell out the window for all the neighbors and social workers to hear, "**Somebody help me!**" very loudly, over and over again.*

What's amazing to me is how little has actually changed, in some ways, over the years of parenting. As I reread a prayer that I wrote on behalf of my preschoolers, I realized I could have written that same prayer yesterday:

> *Dear Heavenly Father,*
>
> *It's as if there is a cloud around the children. In the olden days, children respected and obeyed their parents. It couldn't be because they spanked them more or it would be child abuse. Then why don't my children have more respect for Steve and me and obey us better? The only reason I can come up with is the spiritual realm around them. I keep them pretty much sheltered from the culture of the world, so it just must be invisible and everywhere. This is the main reason I'm fasting. I feel like I've done all that I know to do. I've spanked, encouraged, given stickers, appealed, had mercy—everything—and I've been consistent. I'm now going to concentrate my energy toward battling the air around them. Jesus, I ask You to please show me how to do warfare for my kids and family. Dismantle whatever is surrounding them of disobedience or disrespect or greed or pride or selfishness or anything else of evil. Start with me and Steve if You must. Whatever. I just want to see my kids have a fair chance to respond righteously. I am convinced that only You can change and shape their hearts. So I'm praying to You and asking You to do this. Clear the spiritual air around them of all darkness, and breathe the fresh force of Your Spirit upon them. Give them a heart after You. Encourage them to love and desire righteousness. Put respect and trust into their hearts for us and authority. Give me wisdom about anything I can do that I'm neglecting. The rest I must leave in Your hands.*

The final entry I want to show you was written about a year before I began writing *Creative Correction:*

"The struggles that you're going through now—don't discard them. Listen to God as He teaches you so that you can teach others. You see, a time of suffering teaches us something we never knew before and may prepare us for a time for counsel that we will give someone years from now." (by Max Lucado)

This was the quote of the day on the daily calendar we keep in the bathroom. It just so "happens" that I had asked God to show me specifically that He was in charge of today. Ironically, it turned out that I had a really, really tough day—especially with Tucker's behavior. I believe the Lord was telling me up-front that the things I was learning by raising a child like Tucker were lessons that He would use to enable me to help other mothers.

How true that last journal entry has turned out to be! I continue to write and speak, not from a point of parenting perfection, but from the perspective of a fellow mom in the trenches. So let us tackle the toddler years together.

THE MOST EFFECTIVE TOOLS
FOR TODDLER TRAINING

As exhausting as toddlers and preschoolers can be, the simplest forms of correction usually work the best with them. So, although I've added a Toddler Toolbox at the end of this chapter, I want to cover what I have discovered to be the most effective tools up front: spankings, routine, choices, redirection, tone of voice, and lots of *lovin'*.

Let's start with the most traditional avenue of correction—spanking. Unless you skipped to this chapter, you already know how I feel about spanking. I believe it's a wonderful tool when administered with love and self-control, but I don't see it as the *end-all* (no pun intended) for every behavioral challenge.

One of the most common scriptures used to support the use of corporal punishment is Proverbs 22:15: "Foolishness is bound up in the heart of a child. The rod of correction will drive it far from him" (NKJV). Although I believe the term *rod* in this verse is best interpreted literally, the same word is also used in the Bible when referring to the staff used by a shepherd to guide, protect, and even comfort his sheep.

We would be wise to use the rod in the fullness of its meaning. We can address foolishness by guiding our children with our words, protecting them by enforcing boundaries, and comforting them with loving encouragement. But there will also be times when a quick swat on the bottom of our little lambs is exactly what is needed—especially when they are being rebelliously "baaa-d." (So sorry, I just couldn't resist.)

I like Tucker's response when I was trying to convince him one day of the importance of spanking. "Son," I said, "someday you'll come to me and say, 'Mommy, I disobeyed you and I need a spanking to drive the foolishness out of my heart.' And then you'll thank me for loving you enough to correct you."

His answer was quick: "Well, today is not *someday*. I don't want a spanking!"

When my children were smaller, we used corporal punishment quite often to lay a foundation of respect for authority. Proverbs 9:10 explains, "The fear of the LORD is the beginning of wisdom." The word translated *fear* in this text means "a reverential awe or healthy respect." I don't think there's anything wrong with my children "fearing" me enough to be in awe of my commands and respecting the place of authority God has given me in their lives.

If, while they're young, they obey me for the sole reason that they're afraid of what will happen if they don't, that's okay with me. That is the *beginning* of wisdom—not the end—but it's a good beginning. From there we can enjoy the benefits of Proverbs 19:23: "The fear of the Lord leads to life, and he who has it will abide in satisfaction; he will not be visited with evil" (NKJV).

THE POWER OF ROUTINE

Thankfully, the majority of the time there are many other, and better-suited, options for correction. The first question to ask of ourselves when determining what kind of correction is necessary is, have we been consistent in keeping our little ones on a schedule or routine? Often our children don't need a spanking, time-out, or a 3-2-1 countdown—they need a nap.

Or, as Tucker so succinctly pointed out to me one day, sometimes it is me who needs it even worse. At the end of a long day, he came up to me in the kitchen and asked, "Are you tired of giving spankings?"

I wearily confessed, "Yes, Tucker, I'm really tired."

He observed, "Yeah, you look like you need a nap."

Children respond well to consistency and routine. Their little bodies need a certain amount of sleep each night, rest every day, regular meals, in-between snacks, indoor time, outdoor time, play periods, quiet periods, self-focused and others-focused intervals, uptime and downtime.

I wrote a letter to Haven on her second birthday and included her daily schedule at that age. Perhaps it will help you to "see" what I'm talking about when it comes to the importance of a routine in your toddler's life:

Haven, your schedule for the day goes like this:

7:00- You sit in Daddy's or my lap in the La-Z-Boys and watch Barney. *He's a big, purple dinosaur, and you love him.*

7:30- "Breakfast." You do not like milk. It's very "yucky." But you want chocolate milk every morning. Your favorite breakfast is "Banana Nut Crunch" cereal. This is not a kiddie cereal. It happens to be your daddy's favorite too.

8:00- "Separate room time." I put you in Clancy's room with the gate in for you to play by yourself. I put a Barney *cassette on, and you either "cook" or "read" or play with your dolls.*

9:00- "Together time." This is the time you and Tucker get to play together in your room. I do a lot of refereeing during this hour. A lot of "no grabbing," "no hitting," "SHARE!" etc. But most of the time you're both begging for together time.

10:00- Sesame Street *time. You and Tucker sit in the La-Z-Boys in the living room and watch* Sesame Street. *You're not allowed to get up until it's over, but you don't even try.*

11:00- "Snack-time" and "outside time." You and Tucker go play in the backyard while I bring out a little snack. It's usually Kool-Aid or juice and fruit snacks or cookies, or some other fun surprise. You both have several riding toys, or you play cowboys or dig in the sandbox. You're very adventurous.

12:00- "Free time." You watch videos or we run errands or go to Grandmother's house.

1:00- "Lunch."

1:30- "Nap time."

3:30- "School time." You like to do puzzles and color. You already know the "alphabet song." And you're learning your numbers right along with Tucker. You know a lot of songs because you sing a lot and have memorized many of the "Hide 'em in Your Heart" Bible verses.

4:00- "Together time with all three of you." Sometimes this works and sometimes this doesn't.

5:00- "Reading time." You really like this. You pick a bunch of books. Then I read one to you, and then I set the timer and you and Tucker sit on the couch and read for 15 minutes, and then I read another one.

5:30- "Daddy's home." Yea! Daddy plays with you while I finish getting dinner ready.

6:00- "Dinnertime."

6:30- "Bath time." Daddy gives you all three a bath at the same time in the big tub. You love it.

7:00- "Bible and bedtime." You sit in my lap, and then we read two books and a Bible story before hopping into bed with one last drink of water. Then we pray for you and sing a praise song.

So that's your day at two years old. It might sound pretty rigid, but you must remember it's the ideal and it rarely ever happens just like on paper.

When our children's bodies are adjusted to a schedule, we can more easily determine if crankiness, hunger, or boredom are contributing to their negative behavior.

CHOICE AND CONSEQUENCES

We can also give children as young as two years old a choice before inducing a war of wills. The battle cry for toddlers is "I can do it all by myself." They are bursting inside to exercise their independence. This is what makes the "twos" both terrible and terrific.

Let's capitalize on this desire to be in control of their lives by offering them choices. For instance, "You can either wear the red shirt with Mickey Mouse on the front or the pink one with Barbie." "Lunch is your choice today; will it be peanut butter and jelly or fish sticks?" "Do you want to obey Mommy and stop throwing a fit, or do you want to go in your room with the baby gate up until you can settle down?"

As they get older, we can play the game "Choice or Consequences." This comes in handy when they start negotiating for a third or fourth option after being given only two. You, as the game show host, simply remind your contestant child that you have offered only door number one and door number two. If the child insists on arguing, you will give in and introduce door number three, but he or she isn't going to like what's behind that one.

Sometimes we can avoid confrontation altogether by taking a few precautionary measures. Much has been written on the importance of toddler-proofing your home for safety reasons. I recommend you take an additional sweep through the house to temptation-proof it. There's no reason to "tempt them beyond what they are able to bear."

I wrote in an earlier chapter that I'm not normally a big fan of redirection, simply diverting children's attention to something more fun in order to avoid the inevitable conflict when we try to teach them the meaning of the word *no*. As I read the early chapters of Genesis, it doesn't appear that God, as Father of Adam and Eve, was too concerned about distracting His children from the Tree of Knowledge of Good and Evil with something more colorful and exciting. Instead, it says that He placed it in the middle of the garden and basically told them, "Don't eat it or you will die."

We know that they were as prone to pushing the limits as our own children. And because they were not willing to take no for an answer, sin and death entered the world, and we're still suffering the consequences. Tucker grasped this concept at an early age. He was still a preschooler when I told him not to do something and he did it anyway. On the way to the bathroom for correction, I heard him say, with a heavy sigh, "I wish Adam had never sinned!"

But in the Garden of Eden, even though God said that one tree was off-limits, He also provided plenty of alternatives. We as parents can do the same thing. To offset the drawers and cupboards that are off-limits to our toddlers, we can provide other drawers full of fun plastic lids, bowls, and rags that they can rummage through. Or if we have breakable ornaments on our Christmas trees, why not provide a "baby" tree decorated with plastic ornaments?

Look for ways to provide acceptable alternatives for your toddlers in situations that strictly require them to stay away from dangerous things. Even a baby can begin to learn the lesson that was so hard for Adam and Eve to grasp!

A CHANGE IN TONE AND A LOTTA LOVIN'

Creative correction in its most basic form might be a simple change in the tone of voice you use with your toddler. A firm "no" works wonders, even producing tears in more sensitive children. (I only had one of this kind of kid.)

We instinctively use an excited tone when "encouraging" our children to clean up their toys or do something even less thrilling. We say in our highest-pitch, singsongy voice, "Hey, I have a good idea. Let's get off all your clothes as fast as you can and get into the tub so you can hop in bed on time!"

Even a whisper is an effective way to stimulate obedience. When tempted to yell, we can go the other extreme and whisper. This will probably startle our toddlers out of a stupor when the droning of our constant commands has lulled them into a trance.

I would encourage you to always strive to discipline in a pleasant, loving voice. Even when our toddlers can't understand what we're trying to teach them through discipline, they can comprehend our hearts loud and clear by the tone of our voice.

This brings us to the hands-down most important and effective form of correction for any age—lots of lovin'! It's amazing how much 15 or 20 minutes spent playing on the floor with your three-year-old will do to settle down a toddler. That same amount of time coloring with your daughter can yield better results than a hundred time-outs. Play toy cars with your son and watch him delight to obey and please Mommy and Daddy.

We need to remember that negative behavior can sometimes be a desperate cry for attention. It was no coincidence that my little ones always acted up the most when I was on the telephone or had my face glued to a computer screen. The most stressful days were always the ones in which I shortsightedly put my children on my "To Do" list.

If you catch yourself becoming frustrated because your toddlers are being naughty and won't allow you to *check them off* and move on to other important tasks, it's time to pull out the most lethal punishments. This could mean tackling them and kissing them all over their bodies, pausing long enough to particularly persecute them on their tummies. Or it could mean tormenting them with a good dose of Tickle Torture. Or you may just have to grab them and hug them until they beg and squeal for mercy.

Above all, thank God for the privilege of being a parent. Don't worry, they won't walk down the wedding aisle sucking their thumbs, they will be best friends when they get older, and I never thought I'd hear myself saying this but it's true . . .

Enjoy them while they're young, because they grow up before you know it.

Toddler

Toolbox

Security Objects

- When Haven turned three years old, we decided it was time for her to give up her "bappy" (pacifier). She was way into the movie *Snow White and the Seven Dwarfs* at the time. It just so happened that we had a friend in our church who used to play the character Snow White at Disneyland. For Haven's third birthday, we threw her a Snow White party, complete with a special appearance by the Disney princess herself. We told Haven that this would be a good time to give her beloved Snow White her beloved "bappy." In exchange, Snow White handed her a stuffed doll to cuddle at night. You probably don't know a real Disney character, but what about Barney, a favorite cartoon character, or good ol' Uncle Ralphie? (As a side note, Haven's bite had begun to round out because of the pacifier, but it returned to its natural shape within days of her giving it up. She also wanted me to write that she went into the kitchen and cried real hard after giving it away.)

- I read about one family that threw a "Bye Bye Binky" party, complete with balloons, cake, and presents. Over the next few days, whenever their son asked for his pacifier, they reminded him of the big celebration when he threw his "binky" away and took one more step as a big boy.

- One mother recommended soaking all the pacifiers in lemon juice so they weren't quite as appealing.

- Another friend poked tiny needle holes in the end of the pacifier so the sucking sensation was less satisfying.

- How about introducing a visit from the "Passy Fairy"? When your child says she's ready, have her leave her pacifier under her pillow for the "Passy Fairy" to come and trade for a "big girl" prize.

- A delightful little Muppets book called *Bye-Bye Pacifier* would be a fun way to prepare your little one for the inevitable.
- I heard of another mom who snipped a little bit off the end of the pacifier each night. Finally the child woke up one morning, announced, "This is broked," and threw it away.
- For another family, merely giving the child a new pacifier was all it took to break the habit.
- I received a tiny, square "blankie" at Tucker's baby shower. He loved it and grew very attached to it. Then one day I lost it. Panicked, I ran to the nearest Wal-Mart and bought a large blanket, then bought some wide, satin ribbon at the fabric store. I cut the blanket into 18-inch squares and sewed the satin border around them. Tucker never missed a beat, and I always had backups available for laundry day and extras at Grandma's house, in the diaper bag, and in the minivan.
- I used a variation on this theme to help Tucker break a habit: sucking his thumb. Whenever he was able to go a full day without sucking his thumb, he could mark a day off on the calendar. When he was able to go 21 consecutive days (they say that's how long it takes to break a habit), he earned a trip to Toys "R" Us to pick out the action figure of his choice.
- Tucker was a thumb-sucking, blankie-clutching, hair-twirling toddler. Thankfully, the thumb thing and the hair habit went hand-in-hand. Once he gave up the sucking, he

also let go of the hair. But the blankie was another story. Have you ever read the Golden Book *The Poky Little Puppy*? We put our own spin on this little tale, and I began to cut off an inch at a time of his beloved blankie until there was just a tiny swatch left to hold. By that time all the satin was missing, and that was his favorite part to rub anyway. One morning, the leftover piece of his "geekie" was lost in the covers, never to be found. He cried for a couple of nights and then never mentioned it again. (I did keep one of the "extra" blankies that I had made and put it in his baby box.)

Creative Correction

- When you tell your child to do something and she doesn't obey because she's being distracted by a toy or a video, she has to give up the distraction. Gently take the toy away or remove the video and explain, "I know you want to obey Mommy, but this dolly is making it very hard. So I will set her aside so you can obey me."

- Going to bed early can be a painful correction when you're little. The only problem is, younger children have a difficult time associating something they did wrong earlier in the day with the punishment in the evening. Try making a clock out of a paper plate, a brass brad, and some construction paper. At the beginning of the day, set the hands to your toddler's regular bedtime. Throughout the day, whenever he throws a toy, runs away from you, hits his brother, or does whatever behavior you're working to improve, move the clock hands back five minutes. At the end of the day, the time on the paper plate is his bedtime.

- The younger the child, the easier it is to find creative corrections. For instance, if your child gets a bad report from her daycare or preschool teacher, she is not allowed to use ketchup at dinner. (And, what a coincidence, you were serving tater tots tonight.) Think of other "simple pleasures" that might be effective to withhold in order to teach an important lesson.

- I love the following story a young mother told me when she finally found something that reached her son's heart enough to have him stop and think about his choices: his beloved toy car collection. She explained, "Whenever I need him to do something (or stop doing something) and he doesn't obey, I remind him that I will need to add one of his cars to my collection for the day. If he doesn't comply, I take one of his vehicles and put it on the island in the kitchen, and he can't have it back until the next day. Here's another bonus: My husband can immediately tell what kind of day I've had by the number of toy cars and trucks on the island." I love the last part of her story: "It's a great way to start the following day on a positive note. My son cheerfully gathers all his toy vehicles."

- If you have a toddler who loves to touch *everything*, especially if it's on the coffee table, for example, try using a flyswatter—to spank the coffee table. The sound will startle her enough to get your point across about the items' being off-limits, and you won't even have to touch her.

- Does your daughter have a baby doll or your son a favorite action figure or stuffed animal? The next time you're trying to teach your child a lesson, demonstrate with the toy. "It's time to clean up your toys. Hey, look, Spiderman is cleaning up with you." Or, "Baby Susie-Q is going to sit over here with you for your time-out. See, she's already waiting for you."

- Psalm 34:12–13 says, "Whoever of you loves life and desires to see many good days, keep your tongue from evil and your lips from speaking lies." If your preschooler tells a big fat whopper and you know it, remind him of this verse. Then tell him to go look in the mirror, open his mouth, stick out his tongue, and watch it until he can come back and tell you the truth.

Rewards

- Rewards for toddlers can be so simple. I know of a mom who lets her two-year-old blow out the bathroom candle every night he allows her to brush his teeth without struggling with her and wiggling around. Can you think of other small pleasures your little one enjoys that could be used as a reward?
- Pennies work well with preschoolers who don't yet have a concept of the value of money. Pennies can be given rather freely, and as they add up, little eyes get bigger—especially if the pennies are placed in a transparent jar. Dole out pennies for every toy picked up, for every time they say thank you, or whenever they share a toy. Then let them pick out a toy with the money. (Thankfully, young children's toys are relatively inexpensive, so this works!)
- Pennies are such a big deal to a three-year-old. Once you get past the "put everything in their mouth" phase, try the 10-penny method. Begin the day by giving your son 10 pennies to put in his pocket or your daughter to carry around in her

purse. This makes children feel especially big, and they just hate to part with even one red cent because of punishment. At the end of the day, let them spend their hard-earned money on a tiny treat.

- Get two glass jars and fill them half full with marbles. Label one "The Sad Marble Jar" and the other "The Happy Marble Jar." When your children do something that makes God happy (follow His commands), transfer a marble from the "Sad" jar to the "Happy" one. If they do something that makes God sad (break His commands), do the opposite. The idea is to empty the "Sad Marble Jar" and fill up the "Happy Marble Jar." When that happens, head out to McDonald's for a "Happy Meal."

- We learned from Mary Poppins that a spoonful of sugar helps the medicine go down. Well, I say, "So does a handful of chocolate!" Next time you head to the drugstore to pick up a prescription for your little one, pick up a bag of M&M's as well. After the teaspoon of the dreaded pink stuff is swallowed, quickly follow it with an M&M chaser.

- I kept a large container of jelly beans on the kitchen counter that I named "Good Manner Beans." Whenever my kids remembered to say please, thank you, yes sir, no sir, yes please, and so on, I would let them grab a jelly bean. They would also get a "Good Manners Bean" for having nice table manners and for displaying good manners when meeting new people. They would suddenly become even sweeter than the candy, and because they received only one at a time, I could offer them anytime without worrying about spoiling their appetite.

- I love to use food as a reward, but I understand that many people believe this sends the wrong message to your child about the place of food in our lives. So here's an alternative. Whenever your toddler does something that deserves a reward, allow her to feed the doggie a treat. That way you aren't teaching your child bad food habits—just the dog!
- It's hard to beat the age-old gold star! There's just something about earning one of those little stickers that makes a child feel especially proud about doing the right thing. A whole chart full of gold stars can do wonders for a child's self-esteem.
- Here's a fun, simple, and somewhat educational reward. Buy a box of pipe cleaners and some wooden beads at a craft store. Allow your preschooler to thread a bead on the fuzzy stick for each good choice she makes throughout the day (thus exercising fine motor skills while simultaneously earning a reward). At the end of the day, have your young student count the number of beads she has strung, and let her trade them in for a special treat.
- Have you seen those huge candles that look as if they would take years to burn? Buy one and name it the "Victory" candle. Then, whenever your child does something deserving special recognition, light the Victory candle and celebrate all day long.
- Buy a calendar and draw a happy face with a large smile on the date. If your child goes all day without throwing a fit, leave the face smiling. But if he loses his temper, draw a frown on top of the smile. When connected, the two curves form a circle, resembling an open, screaming mouth. Encourage your child to go seven days in a row to earn a "happy week award."

Perhaps the award can even be a toy from a McDonald's Happy Meal or other fast food prize. The idea is to save the toys from the lunch sacks to be earned at a later time for good behavior. This keeps the privilege of the drive-through meal without taking the free toy for granted.

- Do kids ever outgrow the joy of stickers? Sticker albums are easy to find, and stickers are relatively inexpensive to buy—a perfect combination for that little something extra to say, "I noticed that you made a good choice."

Public Outings

- Tell your preschooler that it is time to "hide your thumbs" when it looks as if there might be too many tempting things to touch. Having her thumbs safely tucked into her fists makes it a lot harder for your child to pick up things that shouldn't be touched in a store.
- If your grocery store has those large tiles covering the floor, then while waiting in the checkout line, assign each child a square to stand in until you get all your bags packed and ready to go. Make a game out of not stepping on or over the lines. Later on, this would make a good object lesson in being careful not to "cross the line" when an authority figure draws an imaginary but nonetheless very real one.
- If your little one balks at holding your hand while in a parking lot or crossing the street, give him a choice. Remind him, "I can either hold your hand or hold your hair." Independence isn't quite so appealing on those terms.

- Any parent of tiny tykes knows that the moments after getting out of the car at the supermarket can be stressful and potentially dangerous. One idea is to have your children immediately "toe the line" in between parking spaces. When they're toddlers, physically place their feet on the line and instruct them to watch their feet to make sure they don't move.
- Another idea is for children to keep one hand touching some part of the car until you take their hand to walk across the parking lot. Give them the goal of growing taller than the hood of the car, at which time they can simply stand beside the car and wait for you until you're ready to go.
- Be sure to pack crayons for your next visit to the pediatrician's office. The paper on the examination table makes a great artist board as you patiently wait for the doctor to arrive.
- To reward good behavior in the grocery store, try this instead of heading to the gumball/candy machines at the exit: Pick an aisle and let them choose any one thing they wish. For example, you could make the cereal, snack, or cookie aisle the last one you visit on the way to the checkout stand.
- Do you shop someplace where they have the little rides at the entrance? If so, hand your child a quarter as you enter the store. If she can hold on to it the whole time, and she doesn't lose it by touching something, running off, or disobeying Mommy, she can put it in the coin slot all by herself and enjoy the ride as much as you enjoyed the stress-free shopping trip.

Potty Training

- With all three of my children, we utilized the *Toilet Training in Less Than a Day* book. And it worked—that is, after one premature attempt and one "train" wreck. The first time I tried to potty train Tucker was right before his second birthday and just after the birth of his baby sister Haven. He was definitely not ready, and then I got pregnant with baby Clancy and didn't have the energy to try again until he was just over three years old. (At that point we had three kids in diapers, and I could no longer afford putting off the inevitable.) On the second attempt, I made a big deal with Tucker about potty training day coming up soon. When the big day arrived, he was so excited that he could barely contain his excitement. "Where's the potty train? When is the potty train going to get here?" Needless to say, the disappointment upon discovering that potty training had nothing to do with a locomotive prompted us to postpone the big day until the following week. When that day arrived, I dropped off the two babies with Grandmother and put on my apron, with my pockets loaded with tiny, tasty goodies. The refrigerator was stocked with all kinds of yummy drinks, and I devoted the next few hours to alternately filling up his juice cup and encouraging him not to fill up his new superhero underwear. By the time Daddy got home that evening, he was completely potty trained—even through the night.

- Is there a special video that you know your toddler would love, perhaps the newest *Veggie Tales* or *Ribbits!* video? I heard from a mom who bought a special video for her son and allowed him to watch it every time he left a BM in the potty. "In three days," she exulted, "he was totally poop-trained."

- The majority of the time, accidents while potty training are just that—accidents—and shouldn't be punished. On rare occasions, though, you know that your child, who is completely potty trained, is just having too much fun to stop for a quick trip the bathroom. If this becomes a habit, try putting the distracting game or toy on the potty until the next time your child can successfully make it to the bathroom on time.

- One mother told me that she and her husband allowed their son to wear Dad's Army Achievement medal while potty training. As long as he stayed dry, the medal was proudly pinned to his shirt. If he had an accident it came off, but only until the next successful trip to the potty. Then it returned to its place of honor on the boy's chest. Even if you don't have an official medal, you could buy one of those big blue ribbons at a party store to use for the same effect.

- Most little ones *love* their superheroes and favorite cartoon and movie characters. That's why they want to wear them on their underwear. Use this to your advantage and encourage them not to get Superman or Barbie wet. If they do, let your children help you clean their underwear up by rinsing them out and hanging them to dry.

- One mom had two great ideas. She wrote, "When my children were being trained, I would give them three M&M's or chocolate chips (whatever I had handy) each time they would go on the potty. When the younger ones came along and were being trained, I would also give the older kids the same treats each time their siblings 'left' something in the potty. This helped me recruit some helpers who were periodically asking the younger one, 'Do you need to go potty now?' It also had the added benefit of making sure they didn't feel left out while the younger one got all the attention. One other thing I did (and it probably sounds weird, but it worked!): When the child would sit on the little potty chair, I would put his feet in a tiny tub of warm water. It usually made him go, probably like it does us when we get into a warm swimming pool and have to get right back out to go to the bathroom!"

- I like this e-mail I received: "When I used to have a daycare in my home, I had several little boys who were being potty trained, and they would often miss the toilet. (It seemed like every time.) I came up with the idea of having a small bowl of one-inch paper boats that I would fold up the night before. The boys would then put one of the boats in the toilet water, and boy, did their aim get better as they tried to sink the ships!"

- On a personal note, it has been my experience and many professionals' advice that nighttime bed-wetting is completely involuntary and therefore should be handled with understanding and encouragement, never punishment. There are many ways to help your child control her bladder while asleep, from nose sprays to panty alarms, and I would encourage you to look into those further. I understand that getting up night after night can be exhausting, but on your way to your child's room, say a quick prayer for patience and mercy to extend to your little one who is already feeling bad enough about the accident.

- I love the creativity and humor exhibited by the mom who got tired of repeating the phrase "Flush the potty and wash your hands," only to have the words fall on deaf ears. One day she switched it around and told her son, "Flush your hands and wash the potty." That time the instruction stuck, and to this day he still laughs every time he washes his hands after flushing.

Eating

- From the very first meal in the high chair, hold your babies' hands together and pray with them. There's nothing cuter than the first time they join in the prayer with a loud "Amen!"
- Many children are reluctant to eat their veggies, but they love to make noise, and the louder the better. When serving raw vegetables as a snack, have them plug their ears (which amplifies the sound) and listen to themselves crunch. Join in with them and see who can make the loudest chomp.
- If you believe your child should eat at least one bite of everything served, institute the "No, thank you" bite. Each person at the table, including Mom and Dad, must take one bite of each food served. If the person doesn't like it, he or she simply says, "No, thank you. I would not like any more." This encourages kids to try new things but also teaches them how to decline politely.
- "I'm not hungry!" Ever hear that at mealtime? You could take them at their word and refuse to serve snacks until the next meal. Or you could implement the "bites for years" rule. They have to eat as many bites of food on their plates as years they've been alive. The tinier the body, the less they really need anyway.

- Preschoolers love their independence. But they must remember that it's a privilege that is earned. This will work in many situations, but in regard to table manners, if your child regresses at mealtime and begins to play with his food or silverware, it must be time to spoon-feed him again. This is a major setback and hopefully enough incentive for a child to "mind his manners" at the next meal.
- When teaching your preschooler good table manners, set 10 M&M's on a bread plate beside her. Throughout the meal, if she commits a "manner infraction," she must pay you, as the "Manners Police," one M&M. At the end of the meal, she gets to eat the remaining M&M's for dessert.

Timers

- Invest in a timer; it will save you time and emotional energy! Say the kids are playing in their room and you know you need to leave in 15 minutes. Walk into the room, announce that they have five more minutes to play, set the timer, and walk out. When it goes off, return to the room and declare, "The timer went off; now it's time to clean up." Set the timer for five more minutes and encourage them with, "Let's try to beat the timer by picking up all the toys before it rings!" Set the timer for the final five minutes and instruct them, "Find your shoes, grab your coat, and be ready to leave by the door before the timer wins." This simple tool eliminates so much of the stress associated with trying to coax our little ones into moving faster than the normal, frustratingly slow toddler-speed.

- Sometimes I'm the one who needs the timer. I know that I disappoint my children by promising them that I will read them a book, help them find their backpack, or watch their tricks on the trampoline "as soon as I'm finished" with whatever I'm doing. Of course, one thing leads to another, and I often end up not keeping my promise. If you find yourself in a similar situation, it would be a good opportunity to tell your children to go fetch the timer, put it beside where you're working, and set it for 20 minutes. Then when the timer rings, no matter what you're doing, stop and go enjoy the privilege of being a parent.

- You can make use of this timer idea throughout the day. Buy one of the clip-on kinds and tell your children, "Fifteen minutes to brush your teeth, get dressed, make your bed, and come down for breakfast." "You play with the toy 10 minutes, and then let your sister play with it for 10 minutes." "Give Mommy 30 minutes of quiet while I sit down and read this magazine." "Okay, I'll play with you for 10 more minutes, and then Mommy needs to cook dinner." "Five more minutes to play in the tub, and then it's time to wash up." One of the great things about this is that it makes the timer the bad guy instead of you. "Oops, the timer rang. I guess we have to stop now."

Sibling Conflict

- Your little ones are never too young to learn how to atone for a wrong done against someone. It can be as simple as teaching them to bring the person they hurt a drink of water or offering a hug with a sincere "I'm sorry."

- As they get a little older, you can teach them to pray for the brother or sister they hurt.
- We've all heard of placing a misbehaving child in time-out. How about sending the toy that causes the contention to time-out? This works especially well when sharing is involved. The two children can either work out a way to play with the toy peaceably or decide that the toy is unimportant and play without it.
- Sibling rivalry often enters the picture the moment the new baby arrives home. To thwart some of the natural feelings of jealousy because the baby requires so much attention, try filling a special basket full of toys and books that can only be played with while you are nursing the new baby. This makes it a special time for both children.
- Tired of figuring out a way to solve the "tattle battles"? Most of the time the things our kids are fussing about don't really matter anyway. So just get silly! Come up with some crazy way to reconcile. Tell them they must say "Oka, dinka, doo," shake hands, then go find something else to play with together. Or their sentence can be to say "I love spinach bubble gum" three times, tickle each other's tummies, kiss their own toes, and forgive each other. Usually they're giggling by this time and have forgotten what was so important to tattle about.

Preschool at Home
- I was so impressed with the following e-mail that I received from a mom who subscribes to my Internet e-letter:

Pre-k and kindergarten doesn't have to be such a "formal" thing. Your child can learn everything he needs to be ready to begin first grade just by reading and playing with you! He can learn the alphabet and counting from the hundreds of ABC books. Learn "phonemic awareness" from Dr. Seuss and other rhyme books. When you build with blocks or are just doing household things, there are all sorts of concepts you can teach him just by talking about what you're doing! Like how many, add, take away, tall/short, near/far, in front/behind, over/under, large/larger/largest, small/smaller/smallest, before/after, inside/outside, open/closed, up/down, upside-down/right-side-up, around/through, hot/cold, colors, numbers (not just 1, 2, 3; also first, second, third, etc.), shapes (dishes, cups and glasses, lampshades, and toilet paper rolls are circles; doors, tables, boxes, the TV set, windows, and books are rectangles; roofs, toys, Christmas trees, bridges, and other things may contain triangles), textures (soft towels, hard table, scratchy blanket, smooth windowpane, slippery soap, wet and dry laundry). Even what public school would call "critical thinking problems" can be addressed, such as: "We're having soup for lunch. What do we need to set the table?" "Grandma is coming for supper. How many places do we need to set?" "We bought two cans of beans at the store, but we already had three cans in the pantry. Now how many cans do we have? If we put one can of beans in the chili, how many cans would we have left?" If you'd like to have a more or less structured "school time," that would include your fun coloring and activity workbooks, cutting, pasting, and drawing. Read him a story and have him draw a picture that illustrates it: "listening comprehension"; have him retell it: "oral language skills, story sequence"; ask him about why the character did this or that or how the character felt: "character's emotions"; what might come next: "inference, prediction, extending the story." All of these come under comprehension skills for pre-k and kindergarten, and they don't require much "boughten" curriculum to do it! Have fun, and happy home-preschooling!

Aggressive Behavior

- Do you have a pint-sized screamer and you're at a loss as to how to get her to calm down? The next time your little loud one lets loose with shrill anger, immediately pick her up and place her in a playpen or room with a baby gate across the door. Listen closely for the first signs of extended silence, then swoop in with excitement and lift her out to freedom.

- If your preschooler launches into a fit, carry him into a room with a mirror and sit him down in front of it. This can accomplish two goals. First, a temper tantrum is a bit embarrassing to watch, especially if it's your own. Second, often the distraction of watching himself throw the fit will get his mind off the reason he was mad in the first place.

- Sometimes temper tantrums are more about frustration than anger. In these cases, offer your preschooler a place to "march out" her frustrations. If your little one reaches her tolerance threshold and begins destroying things she's building, throwing things, or lashing out, teach her how to march up and down the hall while making he-man grunting noises. Both of these actions act as stress relievers and make the child feel in control of the situation again. Follow up by teaching your child to ask for help. After a while, before your trip to the hall, you can ask, "Do you need help or would you rather 'march out your angries' first?"

- If your little one has a problem with hitting, immediately pull him away from the other child and have him sit on his hands until the timer "dings."

Biting/Spitting

- Trying to find some way to correct biting or spitting? Set a timer and have your child put her hand over her mouth for a reasonable amount of time after any kind of "mouth offense."
- Okay, this may sound a bit extreme, so take it or leave it. But if you have a child who bites and is definitely old enough to know better, pick up some of those Listerine breath strips at the checkout stand in the grocery store. They're mighty powerful and have quite a "bite" to them when placed on the tongue. Half the strip would make a strong impression on a child who tends to bite other children when angry.

Bedtime

- If the lure of the "after bedtime adult world" is too glamorous for your preschooler to resist, maybe it's time to pull out the trusty baby gate again. Explain that if he leaves his room after being put to bed, except to go to the bathroom, the baby gate goes up tonight and the next night. Keep it in place until he can set his own internal boundaries.
- When Haven was little, she was tormented by nightmares.

One of her favorite songs was by the contemporary Christian singer Carman and titled "No Monsters!" By listening to that song, she learned to take authority over her fears and, if she awoke frightened in the night, to say out loud, "Get out in the name of Jesus Christ!"

- If your child is frightened at night, read John 1:5 to him: "The light shines in the darkness, and the darkness has not overcome it" (ESV). Then place a small flashlight under his pillow and show him how the light drives away the darkness. Use this opportunity to teach him that Jesus is the light and that if he's afraid of the dark, he can invite Jesus to come drive out the darkness.

- Haven also loved to sleep with a Bible under her pillow.

- Perhaps you can offer your preschooler a little more incentive to get to bed on time and stay there. Make him a deal— explain that you cook breakfast at seven o'clock in the morning (or whatever your schedule is) and that if he gets his full night's sleep, he can wake up and help you cook. But if he dawdles before bed or repeatedly crawls out of bed, he will have to stay there until you're finished cooking, and then he can join the family at the breakfast table.

- I know a family who cut up foam squares, a different color for each child. On Sunday morning, they handed out seven color-coded "tickets" to each girl. Throughout the week, the girls were allowed to get out of bed at night without punishment if they turned in a ticket. Once they were all gone, they could not come out of their rooms. The reward was that, come Saturday morning, they could turn in any leftover tickets for 15 minutes per ticket of cartoon viewing.

- It is sometimes hard to get toddlers back to sleep after they've awakened from a bad dream. After praying with them and hugging them, have them turn their pillows over and lay their heads down on the "good dream" side.

Practice Good Behavior

- Train your children to immediately obey your command "Stop your words." Start by having them tell you what just happened in the cartoon they were watching or to tell their favorite fairy tale. Every few sentences say, "Stop your words," and then hand them a small treat like an M&M, Cheerio, or jelly bean. By the end of the story, they will have collected a handful of goodies and begun a good habit that will come in handy later. For instance, the next time they begin whining, fussing, talking unkindly, lying, or any other similar infraction, simply repeat, "Stop your words." Then either ask them to rephrase their request without whining, think about what they're saying before they get in trouble, speak in a kinder tone, or whatever is needed.
- From the time your babies are six months old, you can train them to "put your hands on your head!" It will be a game to them but not for you when it comes time to change diapers or put them in the car seat while you buckle them up.
- Most churches have child care, nurseries, and separate services for children, but some don't, and some parents just prefer to bring their young ones into the main service with them. If you're bringing your child into the auditorium for whatever reason, prepare her for sitting quiet and still for a long period by practicing at home. Tell Susie that she is going to

sit on Mommy's lap while you listen to a sermon on the radio. When she gets antsy, be ready with some kind of action to remind her to settle down. For instance, you might gently squeeze her on the thigh and whisper "Sit still" in her ear. If possible, do this several times before requiring her to do this on a Sunday morning. When the big day comes, sit her on your lap, just like at home. If she gets wiggly, gently squeeze her leg. You may not even have to whisper in her ear; she will remember your fun practice sessions. Be sure to include lots of snuggling during the sermon.

• How many times do you end up saying "Don't touch" to your toddlers? How about adding the phrase "Walk away"? By adding those two simple words, you may not only avoid the need to repeat yourself because the temptation is still right in front of them, but you also teach them a good principle about walking away from temptation.

• Toddlers love a fun game of "Freeze!" Put some music on and dance around, then turn the music off and shout, "Freeze!" Next, allow them to run through the house or around the living room until you yell, "Freeze!" Practice in the backyard, front yard, a friend's house, and finally in the grocery store. The point of this exercise, besides hearing their delicious giggles, is to establish the response before the consequences of disobedience are no longer a game.

• As I mentioned in an earlier chapter, my children suddenly need my undivided attention as soon as the phone rings. Train your little ones to sit in the doorway of their rooms and read or play quietly as soon as it rings. This needs to become an automatic response. Partner with a friend, and have her call you throughout the first day to practice this with your children.

- Kids love to perform. From the time my kids were babies, we played an "acting" game. I would say, "Show me your sad face," and they would immediately get all pouty-looking. Then I would say, "Show me your mad face," and they would scrunch up all angry-like. We even expanded their repertoire to include their "confused," "surprised," and "scared" faces. My favorite, of course, was their "happy" faces. What's fun about this little show is that you can start it up in the middle of one of their fussy periods, and it gets their minds off their sour moods long enough for you to end up with the "happy" face.

- A good night's sleep is very important, for children as well as moms! When the time comes to graduate from the crib to a real bed, spend a couple of nights practicing first. Rehearse pulling up the blanket if you get cold, finding stuffed animals and pacifiers under the covers, reaching for the sippy cup of water on the nightstand, turning on the light and going potty quietly—any scenario you can think of. Then practice waking up and pulling out a favorite book from the basket by the bed and reading until Mommy comes in to start the day.

- I have some adorable pictures of all three of my kids sitting in their "reading chairs." They were two, three, and four years old at the time. They loved this period every day when they were required to sit and read quietly for 30 minutes. It gave me a break during the day, and it was good practice for them on how to pass the time with a good book—or 10.

- They also spent an hour every morning for "I like being with me" time. When they were babies, they entertained themselves in the playpen with a collection of toys. As they got older, they spent many a fun morning "cooking" in their play kitchens, building with blocks, and destroying their rooms by playing with each and every toy for about five minutes at a time and then leaving them on the floor. But that was okay because I usually got another 15 minutes or so of peace while they cleaned everything up.

- I told my kids the story of the missionary father whose son was playing in the sand when the dad yelled, "Hit the dirt!" The boy had been trained to obey right away, without hesitation, so he lay down immediately. The father had just enough time to aim his gun at the poisonous snake hanging down from the tree branch above the boy. Now, every once in a while, I will yell to the kids, "Hit the dirt!" to practice the importance of obeying first and asking questions later.

- During the next Christmas or birthday celebration, take a picture of your child opening each gift. After you have the photos developed, go through them with your child and remind him who gave him each gift. Then ask him what he wants to say to that person to thank him or her. Next, you can transcribe his words on the back of the photo or on a separate note and send both to the gift-giver. Not only will the gift-giver enjoy seeing the excitement on your child's face when he opened the gift, but it will also be much easier for your child to associate the gift with the giver when he isn't being distracted by the next package to be opened.

- Toddlers love to be able to see their progress. Get an old board game like Candyland and place a token at "Start." Explain to your preschooler that you're going to move her token one space every time she obeys throughout the day, but she will have to go back a space when she disobeys. When she "wins" the game, you will actually sit down and play the game with her.

Cleanup

- Do you remember the road trip game "I'm going on a trip and I'm going to pack . . ."? Here's a variation on the theme. Tell your toddlers, "I'm cleaning up the room and I'm picking up . . ." Each time they put something away, you have to remember what it was and add it to your mental list that you continue to repeat. Kids so enjoy the idea of their parents playing a game with them that they hardly notice that they're cleaning up their mess.
- If you have younger children who are messy, try this: Put the toys that they didn't pick up as instructed in a "rainy day" box to bring out later. This has the added benefit of making an old toy seem new again. Or set the toy somewhere out of reach but within sight for a predetermined number of days. This increases the impact of the correction by keeping the forbidden toy fresh in their minds.
- Here's an idea from a very organized mom: "The biggest stress saver/training idea that I implemented with our boys at the toddler level was our 'Toy Check-Out Closet.' We had a handy closet in our house with built-in shelves. Since toy pickup (or the lack thereof) was the bane of my existence, I put all the toys into see-through lidded bins and placed

them at toddler level in the closet. I made each of our boys a checkout card from colored paper (one red . . . one blue), drawing a ball and bat and truck on each one. When one of them wanted to play with a toy, he had to bring me the card, and I would check him out the toy he desired. That child's card was placed in an envelope on the door to remind us all that that child had a toy checked out. Each toy had to be checked back in before another could be taken out. This not only lowered my stress in the cleaning department, but it also taught the boys to play with what they had out and to be responsible for cleaning up when they were finished."

- Sometimes cleanup inspiration can be as easy as changing things around a bit. Try telling your toddlers, "Okay, go clean up three things, and then come back and tell me what they were." When they've done that, say, "Now put away two things and come back for a report." Next, "Almost done! Now see how many things you can find that aren't in their place, and once you've found their 'homes,' come tell me where they 'lived.'"

- We kept a "shoe basket" by the door leading to the garage. This made it easy to toss the shoes into one place when they were taken off. It also cut down on the amount of looking for the one lost shoe that is inevitably under somebody's bed when you're rushing out the door.

- Our goal is to teach our toddlers to clean up their own messes, but there will be occasions when we just don't have time to wait for them to pick up all the toys. On days like that, we can quickly run through the house collecting their belongings and toys left lying around. We can then put them in a box, tub, or—even more fun—a bird cage and call it the "Clutter Jail." When your toddlers want to play with them again, they must pay you a kiss for every imprisoned item.

Time-outs

- Sometimes it's Mom who needs the time-out when her children have disobeyed—again. If you feel your frustration level spilling over and onto your child (who is acting like a child again), perhaps you could both sit down and take a time-out together. Instead of using a timer, try counting to 20 out loud. This gives you time to calm down, and your toddler also gets some counting practice.
- Remember the mood rings from the 1970s? Here's a twist: Designate a mood chair in your home. Whenever your child seems to be crying for no good reason, is whining and fussy, or is just feeling ornery, send him to the mood chair. Give him the freedom to express whatever emotion he's feeling as long as he remains in the chair. But if he wants to get up, he must adjust his attitude to a more pleasant mood.
- "It looks as if you need a *think about it* time-out." When your preschooler hears you repeat this phrase, she knows that means it's time to climb up on the sofa and think about what she has done. She will be allowed to come down and play only after she has told you what she has done wrong and is willing to fix it. This could mean giving a toy back, cleaning up a mess, or simply saying, "I'm sorry."
- If you have a youngster who refuses to stay in the time-out chair, try bringing the car seat into the house and strapping

him in. He'll probably be more willing to stay seated without restraint next time.

Routines

- To keep your child's morning and evening routine "handy," try this. Trace your hand on two pieces of construction paper, a yellow piece for the morning and a blue piece for the bedtime routine. On each finger, write one thing that needs to be accomplished. Write the first thing to be done on the thumb, for instance, *Make your bed.* Once your child completes this first task, she gives you a "thumbs-up" and proceeds with the rest: *Get dressed, Eat breakfast, Brush teeth,* and *Morning devotions.* Upon closing her children's Bible, she gives you a "high five" to indicate that her morning routine is complete. This is repeated in the evening for the nighttime routine. The only difference is, instead of ending with a "high five," you put your "fives" together for a bedtime prayer.

- We wanted to establish a daily routine for our children while they were still little. The biggest obstacle we faced was the fact that they couldn't read the fancy chart I had made. So, I asked their grandfather to draw pictures illustrating the task that was to be done next to a picture of what the clock would look like at that time.

- A similar idea is to create a daily planner by taking a picture of your child engaged in the activity listed on the schedule, as well as a picture of the clock at that time. Buy a small photo album and put in the pairs of pictures, one page per pair, in the order in which the tasks are to be accomplished throughout the day. First thing in the morning, the child opens her daily planner, does the first task, and then turns the page. The last page has a picture of the child in bed with a snapshot of his or her bedtime on the clock.

- Your morning routine could include filling six sippy cups each morning for each child and placing them on the lowest shelf in the fridge. You can fill two with milk, two with juice, and two with water. This is so much easier than pouring drinks all day long, it cuts down on your "waitressing" job, and it ensures that your kids get a healthy balance of liquids every day.

Choices

- Choices are a big deal to toddlers and are an effective way to encourage good behavior. Getting-dressed struggles? "You can wear either this shirt or this one." Cleanup contention? "You can pick up this mess while singing either the *Barney* song or the *Bob the Builder* one." Rushing to leave? "I can put your shoes on for you and carry you out to the car, or you can put them on all by yourself and meet me in the car seat."
- Choices can be as simple as letting your child pick between doing the right thing or receiving the consequence. "You can give me the toy or I can take it from you." "It's your choice—do you want to stop whining and play nicely with your sister, or would you rather take a nap?"
- Don't you just love to make your children laugh? Especially when the alternative is a preschool power struggle. "I don't want to wear that shirt!" she insists. "Fine, then I'll wear it,"

you concede while putting her size three shirt on your head and walking around bumping into things. "Here, now you try it. Hey, it fits you perfectly!" Or you can hop around on one foot that is wearing your son's little jeans that he refuses to wear. As often as possible, look for the humor in raising toddlers!

- In some ways, toddlers really can be easier to discipline than older kids. Try giving them this simple choice. Hold up two fingers and explain, "If you choose this finger and obey Mommy, you will receive the blessing in heaven. But if you pick this finger and disobey, you will be choosing the consequences here on earth." Most of the time you don't even have to have a punishment in mind; they love to choose the obedient finger. As they run off to obey, call after them with this encouragement: "I see God smiling at you from heaven while He's preparing your reward!"

- Use your child's desire for independence to your advantage. "I can do it by myself!" seems to be the battle cry of toddlers everywhere. That's why, if you offer them the choice of putting the toys away all by themselves or allowing you to help, they will usually go for the heady feeling of self-sufficiency. If they don't, however, "help" them by placing your hand over theirs while they pick up all their toys. That isn't quite as much fun as watching you clean up for them, and it makes the choice of allowing you to help a little less appealing next time.

Chapter 11

That's a Great Ideal!

$\mathcal{E}$ arlier this year, a television crew from NBC's *Extra* came to my house to shoot a segment on me and my choice to leave show business to concentrate on being a wife and mother. This was a novel concept to them. Throw in the fact that I homeschool my children, and it was downright controversial—perfect for their show!

Before the film crew arrived, I informed my children that they would also be filmed and that this was *not* the time to goof off and try to get a laugh. I even promised them that if they behaved, we would all go out for ice cream when Daddy got home. I should have promised ice cream for life, because they were hyenas.

There's something about a camera that makes my children go nuts. The first camera setup was of me homeschooling the kids at the kitchen table while having our "Bible Time." We had been studying about Moses. When I came to the part where God told Moses to take off his sandals, I explained that in Old Testament culture, people took off their shoes as a sign of respect. I jokingly looked under the table and said, "Uh-oh, I see some shoes on!"

"That's because we don't respect you!" giggled Clancy.

Then she and her siblings proceeded to put their feet up on the kitchen table and take off their shoes.

I scrambled to close in prayer. The cameras widened to get a good shot of Tucker looking at his watch during the benediction.

Next, the crew interviewed me. After they filmed my answers, they had to turn the camera around to get a shot of the reporter asking me the questions. I was not being recorded at this time so I had fun with the woman, giving phony answers to her questions. I went on and on about how much my children loved school—especially math—and how I had to force them to go outside and play because all they wanted to do was study.

This jesting would come back to bite me later.

After that, it was time to interview the kids. They were lined up on the couch, their hands neatly folded, looking adorable. They didn't fool me, however, and I began praying feverishly in the corner for them to behave.

The reporter fired away the first question: "Do any of your friends know your mommy is famous? If so, what do you say to them?"

Smiling, Tucker jumped in. "I say, 'Ha, ha! My mother's famous and yours isn't!'"

I cringed and stepped up the intensity of my prayers. He might as well have thrown in a "neener, neener, neener!" and been done with it.

The reporter then asked the kids if I'm a good cook.

"Oh, yes!" my darlings affirmed. "She's a great cook."

My relief was short-lived.

"She makes delicious toaster waffles and cold cereal every morning," Haven started.

"And we love her chicken nuggets and fish sticks for lunch!" added Clancy, giggling.

Then Tucker delivered the coup de grâce. "The best thing she cooks are peanut-butter-and-jelly sandwiches!"

I wanted to crawl under the table.

Unfortunately, the lady asked yet another question: "Would you like to say anything else to our audience?"

"I'd like to say something!" Tucker told her eagerly.

By this time, I was frantically looking for the cable to unplug the camera.

As the camera panned toward him, Tucker said, "My mother has *not* been telling the truth. We don't love school. We don't love math. And we would much rather play outside than do schoolwork any day!"

I promised the Lord that if He would make the woman wrap up the interview, I would tithe 20 percent.

Mercifully, the reporter asked the final question: "What do each of you want to be when you grow up?"

Tucker said that he was going to be an FBI agent, and Haven admitted she couldn't decide whether to be an actress or an architect. Clancy, however, saved the day with the only answer they ultimately used from the kids' interview.

"I want to be a mom, just like my mommy," she said sincerely.

I smiled at my youngest. God really *does* answer trench prayers.

THE TRUTH OF THE MATTER

It just goes to show you: We can instruct, correct, reward, and pray, but kids are still going to be kids. That's why I would like you to view everything you've read in this book as great *ideals* as opposed to great *ideas*. I've tried 80 percent of the ideas recorded in this book, but my creative parenting methods haven't produced perfect children. As you can see, my kids still act up and disobey.

The following quote perfectly captures my feelings about different methods of parenting: "An idea reveals what it does and no more. When you read a book about life, life looks simple; but when you actually face the facts of life, you find they do not come into the simple lines laid down in the book. An idea is like a searchlight: It lights up what it does and no more, while daylight reveals a hundred and one facts the searchlight had not taken into account."[1] It's easy to see the flaws in an idea when you're trying it out on your kids. On some days, the "light of day" is so bright that I wonder if they're learning *anything*. It is then that I'm reminded that parenting is a lifetime commitment, requiring long hours and hard work.

Be careful not to expect too much from a few new ideas. They are like a new pair of shoes: They're fun to try on, even more fun when they fit, but you won't know whether they're truly right for you until you walk in them for a while. And eventually they wear out, forcing you to find new ones again. The last thing I want to do is discourage you, but I also don't want to set you up for perceived failure and unnecessary guilt. I believe wholeheartedly in every idea I've shared in this book, but those ideas will not produce ideal children. Fortunately, God can continue to mold our kids even after we've tried everything. He can use us in our weaknesses, whether or not we feel we're being effective parents. But that still doesn't make the process easy.

Let me offer you my own reality check. Three weeks ago, I circled a date on the calendar to record a typical day at my house. I decided to share everything, good and bad, that happened on that day. My intention was to demonstrate that as much as we try to do all the right things, parenting is still a process. (And I had full confidence my children would prove this to be true!) Throughout the day, I carried a little pocket recorder around with me. When the kids asked what I was doing, I replied, "I'm just making some notes so I don't forget them later."

Seeing another parent's struggles is like walking into a friend's house and finding unfolded laundry on the couch, dirty dishes in the sink, and cereal on the floor. I hope you will find comfort in my failures and in my children's foibles. Here's what I recorded:

6:00 A.M.—My internal alarm clock goes off. It is overcast outside but cozy in bed. I push my "Snooze" button. Steve and I snuggle up like spoons for a stolen 10 minutes.

6:10—I start to feel guilty for staying in bed; there's so much to do and I dare not attempt it all without prayer.

6:15—I put a pot of coffee on, check my e-mail, and lay out the day's chore charts on the kitchen table, with little vitamin tablets as paperweights on top.

6:20—I notice that it rained during the night. This does not bode well for Tucker's mood today. We had our first rain of the season last week, and he has been in rare form ever since, constantly moving, talking, arguing, and bickering. I lay out his allergy tablet in an attempt to circumvent the drainage leading to chronic bronchitis.

6:25—I sit back in my recliner, with my coffee and my Bible. I'm reading in the Psalms and am struck at how much King David had to suffer, through no fault of his own. Yet, when I reflect upon his life, I usually only remember how blessed David's life was. That must be because even when pouring out his anguish to God, he always ended up praising Him.

6:45—Steve joins me in prayer before he leaves for work. Sadly, he will be gone before the kids awake, and because he plays the piano for choir rehearsal tonight, he won't be home until after they go to bed.

7:00—Tucker, Haven, and Clancy come downstairs to begin their day. (They are not allowed to leave their rooms in the morning before 7:00, even if they wake up earlier. But they often sneak downstairs for a quick kiss and then scurry back up again.)

7:05—I decide to make French toast for breakfast because the loaf of bread has only one good day left before it goes stale. I know the kids will be excited with this treat.

7:15—They've been up only 15 minutes, and already they're bickering. Tucker accuses Haven of breaking her daddy's foot. In actuality, Steve sprained his foot last night while running a relay with Haven during the local church's AWANA Club parents' night. Tucker is sent to the bathroom for five minutes to think of three things to say to build Haven up instead of tearing her down.

7:20—Tucker asks me if he has already, during a previous correction, told Haven that she is a good baseball player. I tell him that I don't think so. He says, "Good, because the only other nice thing I could think of would have been too embarrassing to say."

7:25—While in the other room, I hear fussing going on in the kitchen. Haven loses the privilege of talking for the rest of breakfast because she continued to bicker when I told her to drop it.

7:30—We clear the breakfast dishes and begin chores. The kids' everyday routine includes making their beds, cleaning their rooms, brushing their teeth, getting dressed, picking up their belongings around the house, reading a chapter of Proverbs, and practicing the piano. In addition, they have two assigned chores. Today Clancy must unload the dishwasher and clean the kids' bathroom. Haven must rewind and put away the videotapes and sweep the kitchen. Tucker must wash a load of towels and make my bed. (Hey, I'm no fool!)

7:40—While loading the dishwasher, I find a note on the table that reads, "Mom said it was only as far as from here to the door." I know immediately what this cryptic message means. Even though Haven had lost the privilege of talking for not dropping a squabble, she was determined to get in the last word and was able to continue arguing by writing down her comeback.

7:45—I find Haven and tell her to meet me in her room. Once we're both sitting on her bed, I begin my lecture: "Haven, I found this note on the table. It really makes me sad because I told you, in confidence, that Clancy got scared when the horse trotted from as far as my chair to the door. I shared that with you because I wanted you to be sympathetic toward her whenever we go horseback riding, understanding that she gets frightened more easily than you do."

"I'm sorry, Mommy," replies Haven.

I continue. "Haven, why are you a good horseback rider?"

"Because I practice?"

"No," I tell her. "You were good the first time you ever tried. God made you that way; it is a gift from Him that you are good at so many sports. God gave Clancy other strengths. Belittling her for not being a good rider would be like making fun of a poor child for not having a home as beautiful as yours. You would never think of doing that; it would make that child feel bad about something she couldn't help. Besides, you live in a nice home because your daddy pays for it, and it is a gift that he allows you to live in it. You've done nothing to deserve it."

Haven's eyes are downcast, and she offers: "Mommy, why don't you point out one of my weaknesses in front of Clancy so I'll know what it feels like?"

I am touched by her sincerity, but I've never been a fan of using humiliation for correction. I tell her that I will pray about whether I should do that; in the meantime, she could point out one of Clancy's strengths in front of everybody.

As I'm leaving her room, I stumble over a pair of tennis shoes. This is something we've really been working on with Haven. She is forever taking off her clothes, shoes, even candy wrappers, and leaving them where they fall. Because this clutters the house and creates more work for me, she is given an extra chore every time I find something of hers on the floor. On my way out, I tell her to put her shoes on the shoe shelf and to mop the kitchen floor after she sweeps it.

Passing by Clancy's room, I notice a pair of jeans on the floor. I begin to assign her an extra chore when she informs me that Haven tossed them there 10 minutes ago. Haven admits it and gains yet another chore.

"That's okay, Haven," Clancy tells her. "I'll fold them up and put them away for you."

8:15—I don my sweats and Walkman and unfold my treadmill. Theoretically, this is supposed to be my 30 minutes of uninterrupted time to do something for myself. I'm not able to pull this off much more than about half the time, but my intentions are there; that should count for a few calories. I play upbeat praise music and sort out my day and pray while the kids finish their morning routine.

Although I don't pay them for doing their chores, I do give them a bonus for diligence. They receive a dollar if they are finished with their whole list by 8:30. This helps ensure that school begins on time. This has also saved Steve and me money. We're no longer the bad guys if they see something they want in a store. I just reply, "Sure you can have it. Do you have enough money saved?"

8:20—I've been on the treadmill for five minutes and already have had one interruption. Haven wants to use the old mop instead of the new one to wash the floor. I tell her no. She argues with me and earns the job of cleaning up the backyard when she is finished mopping the floor—with the *new* mop.

She replies, "Come on, Mommy. Anything but another chore! Make me write a report or anything, just no more chores."

Bingo! It got through. I have a feeling that will be her last extra chore for the morning.

8:30—Tucker interrupts and pleads for five minutes of grace to finish his chores because he has only one left. He really wants that dollar and has been working hard, so I consent.

8:33—Tucker enters in a panic and asks, "Do I have to add softener to the towels? If I do, I won't get finished in time."

I tell him, "Yes, put the softener in. I'll grant you the extra minute."

8:36—Tucker approaches once again. "I can't find the little ball to put the softener in," he despairs.

I reply, short of breath and shorter of temper, "Forget the softener —we'll have hard towels. Just leave me alone!"

8:37—Tucker returns and asks, "Do you want me to go ahead and start the washing machine?"

I silently recite my mantra: *The anger of Mom does not produce the righteousness of God.* "Yes, Tucker, start the machine," I say with forced calmness.

8:40—Haven passes by my bedroom door, and I blow her a kiss. She's had so much correction this morning, I want her to know that I still thinks she's grand. She ventures in to see how much that tossed kiss is worth.

"Mommy," she says sweetly, "do I get a buck if I finish my chores before you finish your exercise?"

The girl has got guts, but I reply, "No, Haven."

She turns to walk away and then looks over her shoulder to tell me, "Thanks, Mom, for all the extra chores. It gave me a chance to serve the family, and I think it will help me remember to pick up my clothes."

I guess I got a kiss blown my way, too.

8:45—It's past time to begin school, so I consolidate 30 minutes of prayer into five minutes, fold up the treadmill, and hop into the shower. At least I'll get a few minutes of peace in there.

8:50—Clancy approaches the shower door and knocks. I got a total of five minutes alone; that should carry me through the day. She announces that she's finished with her list. I congratulate her and tell her that she can play until school starts.

8:51—Clancy returns to ask a question for Tucker. He wants to know if he can get on the computer until schooltime. I answer, "Yes!" a little too loudly. I convince myself that I'm merely trying to talk over the flow of water.

8:52—Clancy reports that she and Tucker have decided to remake his bed instead because he did it sloppily the first time. I say, "Fine."

8:53—Clancy knocks again and wants to know if they are

allowed to listen to a Carman tape while making Tucker's bed. I try to reply, "Sure," as sweetly as possible. (Carman is a handsome Christian singer who, Haven informed us, is not married because he is waiting for her to grow up.)

8:55—I give up and step out of my "relaxing" shower only to be greeted by Haven. She is upset because Tucker and Clancy won't let her play with them. I remind her that they are making up his bed and why would she want to join them for that?

She says, "Good point, Mom. I guess I'll go work on my memory verses."

I'm a bit stunned by this choice, but I'm sure not going to argue.

9:10—Heading downstairs, I pass my sewing table and notice a Brownie Scout beanie cap that needs to be sewn. I stitch it up quickly, though I don't know why. Haven has informed me that none of the other Girl Scouts wear them and that she would be too embarrassed to wear it to troop meetings.

9:15—I yell, "Five minutes to schooltime!" I hear a voice from Tucker's room: "Oh, crud!"

I yell back, "I sure hope that's 'Yes, ma'am!' in some foreign language."

9:17—I ask Haven if she brushed her teeth for two full minutes. She replies, "I think so."

"How about you go and brush them again, just in case?" I suggest.

She says, "Oh, I remember now—I did."

I respond, "Okay, I believe you, because we have trust."

"Yep, we have trust," she says, nodding.

9:18—Haven asks Tucker if she can sew up his Batman Beanie Baby, which is on my sewing table.

"No. I want a professional to do it," he answers gruffly, "not you."

Clancy interjects. "Haven, my Rainbow Bear is torn. You can sew him up for me."

I pull Tucker over to the side and caution him that he has been rejecting Haven all morning and he needs to be more careful of her feelings. I suggest that he invite her to play with him and Clancy later.

He replies in his most unenthusiastic voice: "Fine. Haven, wanna play later?"

9:30—We are finally ready to begin school (only an hour behind schedule). I go into the office to get my box of supplies for "Bible Time." Tucker's words echo from the kitchen: "Haven, just shut your mouth!"

"Tucker," I shout, my arms laden with school supplies, "meet me upstairs for hot sauce on the tongue."

This is a big offense in our house. No one is allowed to say "Shut up!" or use any other derisive language. But before heading upstairs, I ask Haven what she was doing before Tucker said that.

"Nothing," she insists. "I was just singing a little song."

That usually means "aggravating my brother." I can read through the lines. Sighing, I join Tucker in the bathroom, sit on the edge of the bathtub, and confess, "Tucker, I think I understand why you told Haven to shut her mouth. There have been times when I've also woken up irritable and grumpy. In fact, there have been times when you've frustrated me so much that I've said the same thing to you. Even though it might have been understandable, it didn't make it acceptable. I had to ask you and God to forgive me. So right now I'm going to have mercy on you just as the Lord had mercy on me and forgave my words."

There is a glint in Tucker's eyes. "Does that mean I'm redeemed?"

Just the night before he had learned that *redemption* means "freed from punishment forever."

I reply, "Sort of, except it's not forever. If you say it again, it's hot sauce for you."

We pray, and he heads downstairs to ask Haven to forgive him.

9:45—Now maybe we can get school started. After our prayer and praise time, we begin going over memory verses. It's now that the "I'll work on my memory verses" mystery is solved. Haven lets it slip that there is a little girl in her AWANA group that is further along in her book and that she wants to get back in the lead next week. "I want to beat everybody at Bible!" seems like a godly motivation for Scripture memory, don't you think?

10:25—At this time, while the children color or draw, I usually read a missionary adventure or inspirational story with a message. I believe it's also important that we remember to tell our own "stories." It can be from our childhood or even about our ancestors. Today I decide to share a more recent story.

"Kids, I want to tell you about what God is doing in my life these days. As you know, I'm in the middle of writing a book, and it's been very hard on all of us. There have been times when I wanted my old life back, just being Daddy's wife and your mom and teacher. The most difficult point came a few weeks ago when Daddy and I were in Dallas. I brought my computer so I could write in our hotel room while Daddy was working.

"As I sat alone in the room and stared at the blank computer screen, I cried out loud, 'I want to give up!' Then I prayed, 'Dear God, You created the heavens and the earth out of nothing, and You are going to have to do the same thing with this book, because I have nothing to offer.' I sat back in my chair and cried some more.

"Then this scripture came to my mind: 'I lift up my eyes to the hills—where does my help come from?' I couldn't remember the rest of the verse, so I searched for it using my Bible software. You'll never believe what the rest of that scripture [Psalm 121:1–2] says: 'My help comes from the LORD, the Maker of heaven and earth.' I almost burst into tears again, this time from joy and relief. God heard me, and He promised to help!

"When I got home the next day, there was a letter waiting for me from a friend in Maryland whom I hadn't heard from in more than five years. She wrote: 'Lisa, I was spending time meditating on the Lord and He brought you to my mind. I don't know exactly what this means, but He impressed upon my heart to write you a letter and tell you this: 'Don't give up.'"

When I finish my story, Haven says, "Wow! That is so cool, Mom."

"Yeah," Clancy agrees, nodding. "I heard you tell that story on the phone to someone."

Tucker isn't so impressed. "That's neat. What's for snack time today?"

I look at my watch.

10:30—He's right. It's snack time. I make some "slice and bake" cookies I find stuffed in the back of the freezer, while the kids play with our dog, Checkers, in the backyard.

10:45—Tucker takes his cookies and math into the office to work. Haven grabs her cookies and her history report to proofread in the dining room. I teach Clancy while she snacks at the kitchen table.

12:45 P.M.—We've switched workstations three times in the last two hours, and it's time for lunch, so I pop some fish sticks into the oven.

1:00—My neighbor Lynn calls while we're eating lunch and asks if I can keep her son later in the afternoon. This is Tucker's best friend, Daniel, so he's thrilled.

2:00—Yea! School is finally over! Haven and Clancy don their Brownie uniforms so we can deliver the nuts they've sold as a fundraiser. There's only one catch. We've lost the list and have no idea which neighbors bought what, if anything. We decide to take Checkers along with us to get some exercise. We get him leashed and go door-to-door, asking our friends if they bought nuts.

As we pass one neighbor's house, their dog begins to bark wildly at Checkers, which sends Checkers running, dragging me behind him. (Did I mention he weighs about 75 pounds?) I finally get him under control, and Haven admonishes him: "Checkers, remember we don't overcome evil with evil. We overcome evil with good." I guess I'll let Haven write the next book: *Doggie Creative Correction*.

3:00—Daniel comes over, and he and Tucker jump on the trampoline while Clancy plays on the computer and Haven watches cartoons. I head to the dining room to work on my in-laws' anniversary scrapbook.

4:00—Steve surprises us and walks through the front door. He explains that his foot is killing him, and he needs to prop it up for a while before he heads back to church tonight.

5:00—I make tuna fish pockets for the kids and place a tuna fish sandwich, chips, and a soda pop on a bed tray to take up to Steve. It may not be gourmet, but it's delivered with love.

5:15—I hear screaming outside and rush downstairs. Tucker is tormenting Clancy, pretending that he's going to grab her heels and make her fall on the trampoline. It's time to take Daniel home anyway, and this settles it. When I tell Daniel to get his shoes on,

Tucker angrily loses self-control and begins blaming Clancy for ruining the afternoon. I send him to his room to calm down. Then I ask Steve to make sure Tucker gets a shower and then stays in his room until I get back from taking Daniel home.

5:30—I talk to Tucker and try to remind him that the reason he was sent to his room was because of his response when I told him that it was time for Daniel to go home. He's too busy making excuses to listen. It's obvious that he needs a little more time to adjust his attitude, so I leave the room and tell him that he may read in his bed, but that is all.

6:00—Steve heads back to work, and the girls ask if they can take a bath together. I know I'll regret this, but I tell them yes.

6:30—I hear lots of laughter, screaming, and splashing coming from my bathroom. I figure they'd better quit while I'm ahead, so I yell for them to get out.

6:45—Once again I try to talk with Tucker, but his heart is not teachable. Resigned, I tell him that he must stay in bed and read until bedtime. I pick out a new book and read the first two chapters to him. Then I hand him the book and tell him to read two more chapters. I'll read a third one to him when I come back upstairs.

He tries to negotiate: "How about I read one chapter and you read two more?"

This is something we've been cracking down on Tucker about, so I remind him: "You know the new rule. If you argue, you not only do not get what you are negotiating for, but you also lose what you had in the first place. I'm sorry, son, but you'll have to read the rest of the book by yourself."

7:00—Haven and Clancy read beside me at the dining room table while I continue sorting my in-laws' pictures.

7:30—I put Clancy to bed and head for Haven's room. I trip over her damp towel in the middle of the floor. I inform her that I will be washing a load of towels overnight, and she will be required to fold them in the morning. I pray with her and put her tape on before heading for Tucker's room. I can tell just by looking at him that he's had an uncomfortable allergy day. His eyes are so puffy they're almost shut. I realize we never resolved the temper-tantrum issue, but I'm too tired tonight. I try to encourage him by telling him that he fought the good fight today; then I tuck him into bed with a kiss and a prayer.

8:00—Peace, sweet peace! They're all in bed, but now I'm too tired to do anything for myself.

8:15—Haven comes downstairs, complaining of having "cranky legs." I tell her she's going to have a "cranky bottom" if she doesn't stay in bed.

9:00—I try desperately to stay up until Steve comes home, but I can't make it.

THE PARENTING PROCESS

Here my family is, in all its glory . . . or lack thereof. As my day revealed, you can try as hard as you can—use the most creative, effective methods—and *still* wonder if you're getting through to your kids. If I were trying to sell you something, I wouldn't be doing a very good job, would I? Ironically, I recorded the chronicle above to encourage you.

Remember it's a process. We're instructing our children to "do and do, do and do, rule on rule, rule on rule; a little here, a little there" (Isaiah 28:10). We'll teach them to respect their parents, the Lord, and His Word. We'll tell them a story to reach their hearts.

We'll focus their eyes toward heaven, our real home. We'll keep them guessing about what creative correction we'll come up with next. We'll train them to form an upside-down point of view. We'll remind them that loving their neighbor starts with the kid in the top bunk. And we'll pray and pray, and pray some more.

Take courage. Your instruction *will* sink in. But it's not going to fall into place like an anchor to the bottom of the sea. Bit by bit, our children will be shaped into the people God intended them to be. But remember, it's God who ultimately does the molding. He uses *our* hands, but *He* touches their hearts.

Afterword

I sincerely hope that you have found at least one or two ideas in this book that you'll be able to use. I hope you have gained confidence in your own instincts and ability to hear some of God's creative suggestions for raising your child.

As you come up with creative correction ideas, stories, or object lessons, would you consider submitting them to me at my Web site, www.LisaWhelchel.com? I'll continue to collect these ideas to offer in further revisions of this book. You will not only be helping me, but more importantly, other parents who are also struggling to find fresh and effective ways to train their children.

If you're interested in continuing to build a "virtual" friendship—one that I hope has already begun with this book—you're welcome to join me online once a week for "Coffee Talk." Every Monday morning, I post a journal entry, along with personal family photos, recounting some of the things I'm experiencing and learning as my children continue to grow through new seasons of life. Or you can simply sign up for my e-letter and I'll send you a monthly e-mail with a personal story, a parenting tip, and a list of cities where I'll be speaking.

I would love a chance to meet you in person someday. But until then, may God bless you richly as you raise your children.

Study Guide

LESSON 1 (CHAPTER 1):

1. In the opening story, Lisa, the author, describes feeling harried and provides a lengthy list of what she feels she lets "slide" in her life. Think about your own list. What, if anything, do you let slide?

2. What are your priorities as a parent? Does your list reflect those priorities? If not, what things or people are getting in the way?

3. Read Matthew 11:28–30, then answer the following questions:
   a. Are you weary and burdened, like the crowd Jesus is addressing?
   b. What constitutes your daily load as a parent?
   c. What is the "yoke" Jesus is speaking of? Why does He tell those who are heavy laden to learn from Him (v. 29)?
   d. If you lack peace, what practical steps can you take to let God lighten your load?

4. If parenting resembles a highway (p. 10), where are you on that journey?

5. What roadblocks have you hit along the way? What did you do?

6. When facing a crossroads or detour, where—or to whom—do you usually turn for help or direction?

7. What are your expectations in reading *Creative Correction*? What parenting goals do you have? Take a moment to write them down—and be sure to refer to them as you work through this book.

LESSON 2 (CHAPTER 2):

1. Lisa states that children learn to relate to God through the example of their parents. With that in mind, how do you think your own kids see God? (If you're not sure, ask them!)

2. To project a healthy image of God, we must first be committed to having a vibrant relationship with Him. What is your relationship with God like?

3. How can you get to know Him better?

4. Besides spending time with God, how can we as parents represent Him to our children in a healthy way?

5. Read Hebrews 12:5–11, then answer these questions:
   a. Why does God discipline His children?
   b. What are the benefits of His correction?
   c. When and how has God disciplined you? What were the results?

6. What motivates you when disciplining your children? Are those motives pure?

7. Lisa also states that when our children trust us, they will obey (pp. 22–23). Do you find that to be true with your family? Explain, using examples.

8. What biblical characters obeyed their heavenly Father out of faith? What was God's response?

9. Respect and love are also essential in teaching our children obedience, but if we are to convey these principles to our kids,

we must first model them in our own marriages (p. 25). Does your marriage reflect love and respect?

10. Where can you and your spouse improve? What steps can you take to better love and respect each other?

11. What practical things can you encourage your children to do that will demonstrate respect to their elders? To one another?

From the Toolbox:

12. Do your children understand and respect your rules? God's rules?

13. Practically speaking, how can you teach your kids to love God's commands?

LESSON 3 (CHAPTER 3):

1. Think of a family where the parents have set strict rules, without explaining the principles behind them. What effect has this had on the children?

2. Now recall a family you know that is lax in establishing boundaries. What is that household like?

3. Describe a time in which, after correcting your child, you explained the importance of obedience to him. Now think of a time when you did not. Did he respond differently? Why or why not?

4. What is the point of obedience (p. 61)?

5. Read Matthew 19:16–22, then answer the following questions:

   a. The rich young ruler had kept all of God's commandments, so why did Jesus ask even more of him?

   b. What was motivating the man to follow God's rules?

   c. What, in effect, did Jesus say to him? What point was Jesus trying to make?

   d. How does this scripture change your perspective on keeping God's laws?

   e. Is your heart, like the rich young ruler's, in the wrong place? If so, how?

6. Do your children truly understand the heart of obedience (p. 61)?

7. What motivates them to obey? Love or fear—or something else?

8. Near the end of the chapter, Lisa explains that she often tells her children stories from her own life to illustrate principles of obedience. What stories from your life can you use as teaching lessons?

9. In what areas do your children continually disobey? Might they, as Lisa suggests, not truly "get" the heart, or importance, of obedience?

From the Toolbox:

10. Pick a few topics from the Toolbox and then, using the stories and object lessons, teach your children the principles behind God's rules. What is the result?

LESSON 4 (CHAPTER 4):

1. Describe a time in which you put your child's gifts, character, and actions into perspective. How did doing so affect the situation or your view of it?

2. On a scale from 1 (never) to 5 (always), how often do you consider the big picture when parenting?

       1   2   3   4   5

3. Why is this often so hard to do?

4. What are the benefits of maintaining a big-picture perspective?

5. Based on your children's current actions and character, think about the kind of people they might be in 10 or 20 years. Is this a positive or a negative picture? Why?

6. If it's a positive picture, how can you continue to affirm their character and choices?

7. If the image is negative, what steps can you take to help change your kids' bad habits?

8. For a list of important "big-picture" traits, read Galatians 5:22–23. Do you see any of this fruit in your kids' lives? What other godly habits can you work to instill in your children at an early age?

9. What figures in the Bible were noted for having an eternal perspective, even when life was difficult?

10. How were they able to maintain that eternal picture?

11. Make a list of all the activities each of your children is involved in. Are any of these activities distracting your kids from the big-picture priorities you're trying to instill? If so, discuss with your spouse and children the possibility of cutting out a few items that may be "cluttering" their eternal perspective and growth.

12. Lisa includes money as an issue that must be looked at with eternal eyes (pp. 104–06). What kind of example are you setting with your finances?

13. Do your kids understand God's economy? Do you? Explain.

14. How can you instill in your children a spirit of generosity and good stewardship?

From the Toolbox:

15. Do you use incentives to help develop important habits in your kids? Why or why not?

16. How does God utilize a reward system with us, His children? Does it work?

LESSON 5 (CHAPTER 5):

1. Of the four moms Lisa described at the beginning of the chapter, which one do you most identify with? Why?

2. Whose parenting style is most different from yours? How?

3. Each of the four friends described have children with different temperaments and needs, and at various stages of development. What special needs or qualities do each of your children possess? What stages of life are they in?

4. How can you adjust your parenting style in order to discipline your children most effectively?

5. When do your children need the most correction?

6. What "tools" of correction (p. 133) work best for them? If you have more than one child, describe how each one responds to various methods or tools.

7. What discipline dilemmas have you faced? Describe a time in which you experienced God's divine leading while correcting your children.

8. Who in your family usually doles out the punishment?

9. If the administration of discipline is unbalanced, how does that affect your kids? How can you and your spouse better share this responsibility?

10. On a scale from 1 (ineffective) to 5 (very effective), how successful is your discipline? Your spouse's discipline?

    1   2   3   4   5

11. How did you decide on that rating?

12. If your score was low, why do you think your kids continually push the limits? What keeps you from "laying down the law"?

13. Lisa notes that in order to administer effective correction, we have to know what's important to our children (pp. 136–37). What privileges are essential to your kids? How do they react when those privileges are taken away?

From the Toolbox:

14. Which of these ideas is most likely to give you immediate help in disciplining your child?

15. Pick one area you'd most like to see your child improve in, and then, using some of the toolbox ideas, focus on creative forms of discipline each time the opportunity comes up. Keep a journal, record what works—and then evaluate his or her progress in a month.

Lesson 6 (Chapter 6):

1. What are some good reasons for spanking? Not spanking?
2. Do you spank your kids? Why or why not?
3. What feelings do you have about administering corporal punishment?
4. How did your parents handle the issue of spanking with you?
5. How does your upbringing—or your spouse's family history—affect your philosophy of spanking?
6. If you have more than one child and use spanking as a form of correction, which one responds best to corporal punishment? Why?
7. Do you approach spanking differently among your children? If so, how?

8. When do you find spanking to be most effective? Least effective?

9. When should spanking *not* be administered?

From the Toolbox:

10. What principles or procedures do you follow when spanking your kids? How do they differ from the guidelines that Lisa outlined?

LESSON 7 (CHAPTER 7):

1. On a scale from 1 (combative) to 5 (blissful), what is the level of sibling rivalry in your home?

    1   2   3   4   5

2. How does that sibling rivalry (or lack thereof) affect the entire family?

3. In the beginning of the chapter, Lisa describes the jealousy that often occurs between her two daughters. Is jealousy a big problem among your children, too? Why or why not?

4. If envy is an issue in your family, how does it manifest itself?

5. What happens when jealousy between siblings is not addressed?

6. Describe each of your children's strongest qualities and/or strengths. How can you build on those strengths to help your kids develop their own identity and minimize some of the unfriendly competition?

7. Read Genesis 27:1–28:5, then answer the following questions:
    a. Why did Jacob cheat his brother out of his rightful blessing?
    b. What was the nature of Jacob's relationship with Esau before the deception? After?

   c. How did Isaac and Rebekah contribute to their sons' sibling rivalry?

   d. How did the brothers' rivalry and deception influence the course of their lives?

8. In the example from the book of Genesis, Rebekah favored her son Jacob—and that favoritism led to harmful consequences for Esau. Do you sometimes struggle with playing favorites or with giving more attention to one child? If so, how can you change that?

9. Which one of your children most often instigates the fighting? Why might she be such a bully? (Consider whether she is struggling with any unresolved issues or hurt feelings.)

10. When are your kids most susceptible to fighting?

11. What steps can you take to minimize the rivalry or even stop the battles before they occur?

12. What are the long-term consequences of unchecked sibling rivalry?

13. Do your kids understand the value of having a sibling? How, practically speaking, can you encourage them to become better friends (pp. 201-2)?

From the Toolbox:

14. Which one of these strategies for diffusing sibling rivalry will work best with your children? Why?

LESSON 8 (CHAPTER 8):

1. Describe in your own words what it means to live according to God's "upside-down" principles.

2. Besides those listed in the book, what are some other upside-down principles from the Bible?

3. How do these "topsy-turvy truths," such as turning the other cheek, play out in your household?

4. What are the benefits of living by God's upside-down rules?

5. What are some of the inherent struggles in following those rules and teaching them to our kids?

6. In the beginning of the chapter, Lisa discusses the three ways, good and bad, of dealing with conflict (p. 225): (1) Sinning back. (2) Talking to Mom and Dad about the problem. (3) Doing what Jesus did and following God's topsy-turvy truths. Which do your children most often choose?

7. Lisa lists separation from the world as one of God's upside-down principles. What are you doing to help protect your children from the world's negative influence?

8. Where can you make further changes?

9. Do your kids know that as Christians they are different? If so, are they comfortable with being different?

10. Evaluate each of your children's most significant relationships. Who is most often the influencer, your kids or their friends? What effect do those friends have on your children?

11. What kind of track record do your kids have in choosing friends? Do they exercise discernment? Why or why not?

12. Read Matthew 12:36–37. If your children had to give an account today for every careless word they'd spoken (p. 229), what would be the result? Would you be applauding or cringing?

13. Identify one person, a friend or sibling, whom your child can focus on building up with his words.

14. How well do your kids share with one another or with their friends? What things are most difficult for them to give up?

15. Read Matthew 6:19–21, and then answer the questions below:
    a. What treasures or material items are you storing up on earth?
    b. What about your children? What things do they prize?
    c. If your family struggles with materialism, how can you shift the focus from God's material gifts to His spiritual blessings?

From the Toolbox:

16. Of all God's upside-down principles listed in the toolbox section, which do your kids understand best? Which do they most need help with?

Lesson 9 (Chapter 9):

1. On a scale from 1 (never) to 5 (always), how often do you let your kids fail?

        1   2   3   4   5

2. Is this difficult for you to do? Why or why not?
3. Describe in your own words why it's important to sometimes let your children fail.
4. What can happen when a parent steps in all the time? Or not enough?
5. How do you decide when to intervene?
6. When in your own life have you experienced the most failure? What did you learn from it?
7. Describe a time in which one of your kids failed miserably but matured emotionally or spiritually. What lessons did she learn? How did God work through the situation?
8. How do your children respond to defeat or trials? How do they react when others fail them?

9. Right now, what is God teaching your children about failure? About His mercy?
10. Why are the concepts of forgiveness and mercy so important when confronting failure?
11. How do you balance showing mercy with administering discipline? Describe, using examples.

From the Toolbox:

12. How well do your children understand God's grace and forgiveness? If they struggle to grasp this, what keeps them from realizing His unconditional love?

LESSON 10 (CHAPTER 10):

1. Take a moment to assess your state of fatigue, as Lisa did in her journal. How are you doing physically, emotionally, and spiritually? What can you do to alleviate some of that day-to-day exhaustion and stress that come with raising a toddler?
2. Lisa alludes to several issues that often confront parents of young children: teaching toddlers self-control, dealing with their newfound desire for independence, and potty training and/or bed-wetting. Of these issues, which are you most struggling with? Which has been easiest for you? Why?
3. Reread Lisa's prayer and journal entry about spiritual warfare (p. 284). Do you, too, recognize that your child-rearing battles may be spiritual? Explain.
4. Read Ephesians 6:10–18, then answer the following questions:
    a. How, specifically, can you as a parent "stand your ground" (v. 13)?
    b. What does it mean to take up "the shield of faith" when raising a young child (v. 16)? To "pray in the Spirit" (v. 18)?

    c. Describe a time in which you prayed passionately for your toddler. How did God answer that prayer?

5. Do you agree with Lisa that spanking is an effective way to instill respect for authority (p. 286)? Why or why not? What other methods do you use to give your child a healthy "fear" of you?

6. Do you tend to be more flexible or rigid about following a routine? How might that affect your toddler?

7. What is your child's ideal daily routine? Write it down. Now write what usually happens over the course of an average day. How do those schedules match up?

8. What can you do to create the best routine for your child?

9. Think of several choices you can offer your toddler this week to help her safely exercise her need for independence. Now identify several consequences you might implement if she does not opt for either choice. How does she react when presented with choices?

10. Lisa writes that although she does not advocate "redirection" (creating diversions to avoid conflict with our children), she does believe parents should remove temptation from their homes (p. 290). Does your home need to be "temptation-proofed"? What things in your house might be better put out of sight?

11. When was the last time you used "tickle torture" instead of a well-deserved time-out? How did your toddler react?

From the Toolbox:

12. Does your young child cling to certain "security objects"? Read the list of suggestions outlined in the toolbox, and then identify which idea might work best to help him let go.

LESSON 11 (CHAPTER 11):

1. Lisa opens the chapter with a humorous story about how, despite her best efforts to control them, her children were acting like hyenas. Describe a time when, despite your best efforts, your kids went nuts. How do you react when all the best principles and methods of correction seem to fail?

2. What things do you often *not* take into account when trying out a new parenting idea?

3. Think of one new creative correction that, after trying with your children, seemed more like a ridiculous ideal than a great idea. Why didn't it work?

4. What method seemed like a long shot but actually worked perfectly? Describe the situation.

5. Read over the list of expectations and/or parenting goals you developed after finishing Lesson 1. Now that you've tried many of the ideas in this book, evaluate how those expectations line up with what actually happened.

6. What do those results say about your general expectations as a parent? Are they too high, too low, or just right? Explain.

7. What struck you about Lisa's reality check, in which she describes in detail a typical day? What would your own typical day, if recorded, reveal about your family?

8. What do you find most encouraging about Lisa's journal? Why?

9. As you continue to sort ideals from ideas, what will be your next step in molding your kids?

Notes

Chapter Two
1. Pam Forster, *For Instruction in Righteousness*, p. 2, copyright © 1993 by Doorposts, 5905 SW Lookinglass Drive, Gaston, OR 97119, www.doorposts.net. Used by permission.

Chapter Three
1. Corrie Ten Boom, with John and Elizabeth Sherrill, *The Hiding Place* (Grand Rapids: Chosen Books, 1984), p. 31.
2. For parents who are homeschooling their children, Todd and Renee Ellison offer practical materials. Contact Cross-Over on the Internet: Crossover.Ellison.net; by e-mail: Crossover@Ellison.net; by phone: (970) 385-1809; by mail: Cross-Over FLC 7028, 1000 Rim Dr., Durango, CO 81301-3999.

Chapter Ten
1. J. P. Knapp, *Studies in the Sermon on the Mount*, (Basingstoke, Hants, UK: Marshall Morgan and Scott Publications Ltd., 1960)

Topical Index

(Italic numerals identify pages with Lisa's personal stories.)

Other Faith and Family Strengtheners
From Focus on the Family®

Raising a Modern-Day Knight

How does a father teach his son to be a man? Author and pastor Robert Lewis explores the biblical perspective of manhood, plus gives insight on how to celebrate a boy's progress and accomplishments with ceremonies and traditions. Hardcover.

Parents' Guide to the Spiritual Growth of Children

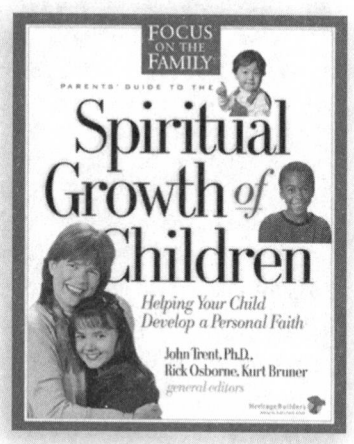

Building a foundation of faith in your children can be easy–and fun!–with help from the *Parents' Guide to the Spiritual Growth of Children.* Through simple and practical advice, this comprehensive guide shows you how to build a spiritual training plan for your family and explains what to teach your children at different ages. Hardcover.

Complete Book of Baby and Child Care

This is a comprehensive medical reference book that addresses the physical, mental, emotional and spiritual needs of children from infancy to the teen years. Each contributor to the book is a Christian doctor who is a member of the Focus on the Family Physicians Resource Council. Available in hardcover and paperback.

Look for these special books in your Christian bookstore or request a copy by calling 1-800-A-FAMILY (1-800-232-6459). Friends in Canada may write Focus on the Family, P.O. Box 9800, Stn. Terminal, Vancouver, B.C. V6B 4G3 or call 1-800-661-9800.

Visit our Web site (www.family.org) to learn more about the ministry or find out if there is a Focus on the Family office in your country.

FOCUS ON THE FAMILY®
Welcome to the Family!

Whether you received this book as a gift, borrowed it from a friend, or purchased it yourself, we're glad you read it! It's just one of the many helpful, insightful and encouraging resources produced by Focus on the Family.

In fact, that's what Focus on the Family is all about—providing inspiration, information and biblically based advice to people in all stages of life.

It began in 1977 with the vision of one man, Dr. James Dobson, a licensed psychologist and author of 16 best-selling books on marriage, parenting, and family. Alarmed by the societal, political, and economic pressures that were threatening the existence of the American family, Dr. Dobson founded Focus on the Family with one employee—an assistant—and a once-a-week radio broadcast, aired on only 36 stations.

Now an international organization, Focus on the Family is dedicated to preserving Judeo-Christian values and strengthening the family through more than 70 different ministries, including eight separate daily radio broadcasts; television public service announcements; 11 publications; and a steady series of award-winning books, films, and videos for people of all ages and interests.

Recognizing the needs of, as well as the sacrifices and important contribution made by, such diverse groups as educators, physicians, attorneys, crisis pregnancy center staff and single parents, Focus on the Family offers specific outreaches to uphold and minister to these individuals, too. And it's all done for one purpose, and one purpose only: to encourage and strengthen individuals and families through the life-changing message of Jesus Christ.

For more information about the ministry, or if we can be of help to your family, simpy write to Focus on the Family, Colorado Springs, CO 80995 or call 1-800-A-FAMILY (1-800-232-6459). Friends in Canada may write Focus on the Family, P.O. Box 9800, Stn. Terminal, Vancouver, B.C. V6B 4G3 or call 1-800-661-9800. Visit our Web site—www.family.org—to learn more about the ministry or find out if there is a Focus on the Family office in your country.

We'd love to hear from you!